Beyond New Labour

The future of social democracy in Britain

Beyond New Labour

The future of social democracy in Britain

edited by
Patrick Diamond
and
Roger Liddle

POLITICO'S

First published in Great Britain 2009 by
Politico's Publishing, an imprint of
Methuen Publishing Ltd
8 Artillery Row
London
SW1P 1RZ

10 9 8 7 6 5 4 3 2 1

Copyright © Patrick Diamond and Roger Liddle 2009

Patrick Diamond and Roger Liddle have asserted their right under the
Copyright, Designs and Patents Act 1988 to be identified as the editors of
this work.

A CIP catalogue record for this book is available from the British Library.

ISBN 978-1-84275-231-9

Set in Bembo and Zapf Humanist by Methuen Publishing Ltd
Printed and bound in Great Britain by Cromwell Press Group

Contents

Acknowledgements

The idea for this book of essays was conceived shortly after the 2005 election, when it was clear that Labour needed a substantial exercise in intellectual renewal if it was to govern successfully over the long term. The onset of the global financial crisis in 2008 was simply a confirmation of this.

We would like to thank each of the authors who agreed to contribute to this volume. We deliberately chose individuals who are not directly involved in elected politics but who have expertise in their own field. We only hope that our corralling of them for this project has not lost us too much goodwill or friendship.

Our next debt is to those who gave us practical help in putting this book together. Alan Gordon Walker was a terrific support as publisher, as was Jonathan Wadman as the editor at Politico's. We want to thank the fantastic team at Policy Network, in particular Michael McTernan, Olaf Cramme, Suzanne Verberne Brennan and Annie Bruzzone. Hannah Jameson and Simon Latham helped a great deal with the editing, as well as making substantive contributions of their own.

Finally, we would like to thank all those who over the years have helped and supported us in developing our ideas about the future of social democracy.

Patrick Diamond
Roger Liddle
April 2009

About the contributors

Melvyn Bragg is an award-winning writer and broadcaster. He has written, edited and produced LWT's *The South Bank Show* since 1978. His most recent novels are *Crossing the Lines* (2003) and *Remember Me. . .* (2008). A member of the House of Lords since 1998, he is a fellow of the Royal Society of Literature, as well as the Royal Television Society, and president of the National Campaign for the Arts.

Mary Daly is professor of sociology at Queen's University, Belfast. She was the chairperson of the Council of Europe's High Level Task Force on Social Cohesion in Europe and is a former chair of the Royal Irish Academy's National Committee for the Social Sciences. Her previous publications include *Parenting in Europe: A Positive Approach* (2007).

Patrick Diamond is senior visiting fellow at the London School of Economics and Political Science and transatlantic fellow of the German Marshall Fund of the United States. A former special adviser at 10 Downing Street and to Peter Mandelson, he sits on the board of the international centre-left think tank Policy Network. His previous publications include *New Labour's Old Roots* (2004), *Public Matters: The Renewal of the Public Realm* (2007), *Shifting Alliances: Europe, America and the Future of Britain's Global Strategy* (2008) and *Global Europe, Social Europe* (with Anthony Giddens and Roger Liddle, 2006).

Will Hutton is chief executive of the Work Foundation. A former editor in chief of the *Observer*, he is the author of *The State We're In* (1995), *The World We're In* (2002) and *The Writing on the Wall: China and the West in the 21st Century* (2007).

Hannah Jameson is head of research at the Involvement and Participation Association. She previously worked for the Fabian Society, contributing to their work on Britishness, citizenship and integration. She completed her master's in cultural history at the University of Manchester, where her research focused on the relationship between space and identity in the late nineteenth-century city.

John Kay is a distinguished economist and academic. A former director of the Institute for Fiscal Studies, he is a *Financial Times* columnist and has also held chairs at the University of Oxford and London Business School. He is currently a visiting professor at the London School of Economics and Political Science. His most important publication is *The Truth about Markets: Their Genius, Their Limits, Their Follies* (2003).

Simon Latham is a policy researcher at the international centre-left think tank Policy Network, where he is coordinating the research programmes 'The Politics of Climate Change' and 'An EU "Fit for Purpose" in the Global Age'. He is a graduate of the University of Oxford, where he chaired and was secretary to the university's Labour Club.

Roger Liddle is vice-chair of the international centre-left think tank Policy Network. He is a former economic adviser to the president of the European Commission, José Manuel Barroso, and a former European adviser to Tony Blair. His previous publications include *The Blair Revolution: Can New Labour Deliver?* (with Peter Mandelson, 1996) and *Global Europe, Social Europe* (with Anthony Giddens and Patrick Diamond, 2006). He is also a visiting fellow at the European Institute, London School of Economics and Political Science.

Donald Macintyre has been the *Independent*'s Jerusalem correspondent since 2004. Previously he spent eight years as the paper's chief political commentator and before that he was political editor of the *Independent* and the *Independent on Sunday*. He published a well-received biography of Peter Mandelson in 1999.

About the contributors xi

David Marquand is an academic, former Labour MP and former principal of Mansfield College, Oxford. His publications include *The Progressive Dilemma: From Lloyd George to Blair* (1999) and *Britain since 1918: The Strange Career of British Democracy* (2008). He is a fellow of the British Academy.

Iain McLean is professor of politics at the University of Oxford, an official fellow in politics at Nuffield College and director of the UK Public Policy Unit in the university's Department of Politics and International Relations. Recent publications include *Adam Smith, Radical and Egalitarian: An Interpretation for the Twenty-First Century* (2006). He is a fellow of the British Academy.

Peter Riddell has been a leading political commentator for the *Times* since 1991 and an assistant editor for the paper since 1993. He is also chair of the Hansard Society. He has written widely on both Margaret Thatcher and Tony Blair, his books including *The Thatcher Decade: How Britain Has Changed during the 1980s* (1989), *Hug Them Close: Blair, Clinton, Bush and the 'Special Relationship'* (2003) and *The Unfulfilled Prime Minister: Tony Blair's Quest for a Legacy* (2005, revised 2006).

Introduction

Why social democracy needs new thinking

Patrick Diamond and Roger Liddle

This book aims to stimulate a debate about the next-generation social democratic programme for Britain. We decided to compile it long before the magnification of the global financial crisis in autumn 2008. The scale of the crisis, however, underlines the validity of our central overarching argument.

Social democratic thinking has still to come to terms with the dramatic economic and social transformations sweeping the world. On the one hand the importance of the state has been reaffirmed and the social democratic critique of the market needs to be revisited and strengthened. On the other, it would be a profound mistake to think that the future can lie solely in a return to 1960s or 1970s 'statism' and a revival of post-war Keynesian social democracy. There is no doubt that this crisis represents an ideological turning point: in the British context it is for the neo-liberal orthodoxy that has dominated political thinking on both the right and, to an extent, the left since 1979 what the Winter of Discontent proved to be for post-war social democracy. There is no going back to the neo-liberal world of the 1980s and 1990s. Greater economic intervention may be wholly necessary; indeed, what is needed is a new confidence in the essential role an active state should play in regulating and managing capitalism. However, it is not sufficient. Equally, just as in the economy, there can be no return to the 'normality' that prevailed before the global crisis. Something new is needed. In reaction to the crisis, new questions and debates will emerge about what is meant by the 'active state', whether it possesses the capacity to exercise the responsibilities unexpectedly thrust upon it and in what ways the state should exercise them. The return of the economy to the forefront of political debate can only temporarily conceal serious tensions and unresolved dilemmas in the social democratic coalition between what we term 'cosmopolitan' and 'communitarian' world-views, essentially a gulf between those who welcome globalisation and those who resist it. Before a 'new' social democracy can be constructed that both masters the new economic conjuncture and reintegrates these underlying conflicts, a significant period of profound debate and rethinking is both necessary and unavoidable.

This statement of purpose raises several issues that need wider explanation. First, why do we choose to talk about a 'social democratic' programme rather than the looser, more inclusive language of centre-left or progressive politics? Second, why the focus on issues of structure, not agency, leadership and political direction? Third, when we speak of 'weakening', what is it that we think has weakened in social democracy and why?

Why talk about social democracy, not progressive politics?

We deliberately label our mission as about social democracy, rather than use the term 'progressive'. In British political discourse, the vogue for the word 'progressive' became more fashionable after the publication of David Marquand's landmark analysis of British political history, *The Progressive Dilemma*.[1] In this book Marquand argued that the twentieth century had been dominated by the Conservatives because of the historic split among 'progressives' created by the collapse of the Liberal–Labour coalition that had sustained the 'social liberalism' of Asquith and Lloyd George in the run-up to the First World War. In its place Labour became the only credible alternative government to the Conservatives, but its governing capacity and electoral appeal were limited in the Marquand analysis by the ideological baggage of its socialist origins. This continued to inspire Labour's party activists but deterred middle-ground opinion; the trade union interests gave it a solid base but came across to outsiders as uninspiring and at times highly sectional. These tensions were evident from the earliest days of British social democracy, as shown in Peter Clarke's fascinating study of liberals and social democrats in the early decades of the last century.[2] On Marquand's and Clarke's analyses Labour's potential to construct a broad-based progressive coalition was limited for most of the last century, for all the efforts that the party's leaders made to correct this profound electoral weakness.

Tony Blair skilfully seized on the Marquand–Clarke argument to advertise New Labour's distinctive credentials as a 'new party', no longer similarly constrained by ideology or dominated by sectional interests, that could resolve Britain's long-standing 'progressive dilemma'. He built a formidable 'progressive alliance' in terms of electoral support, but his 'big tent' failed to translate that support into the long-term principled partnership with the Liberal Democrats for which he, Roy Jenkins and Paddy Ashdown had originally hoped. Nevertheless the discourse of progressivism became favoured as an all-inclusive identity for many different stripes of opinion on the modern centre-left, even by those suspicious of Blair's talk of 'New' Labour as a party of the 'radical centre' and the 'Third Way' philosophising that became its intellectual trademark. 'Progressive' indeed became so much in vogue that after 2005 David Cameron's Conservative Party was desperate to seize the mantle for itself as part of its rebranding.

For this reason alone, the notion of 'progressive' has degenerated into a certain woolly generality. Marquand makes fun of this in Chapter 1 of this volume, in a revisionist *tour de force* of his own. On the left the idea of ineluctable 'progress' towards the fixed goal of a good society (the proposition behind Sidney Webb's famous definition of Fabianism as the 'inevitability of gradualness') is open to challenge. In his view, it has led to much imprecise, and arguably dangerous, thinking about an increasing role for the state in achieving human betterment. So now it is best avoided, at least on the domestic scene.[3]

This warrants a return to the language of social democracy. Social democracy is fundamentally about liberty and extending the boundaries of individual freedom through greater equality, while acknowledging that self-fulfilment for the greatest possible number can be attained only by recognising the collective obligations we owe each other in the context of a strong society. This British social democratic tradition traces its roots to the philosophical idea of 'positive freedom', which argues that every individual should have an equal chance to realise the human potential that is unique to them[4] but also believes that this goal can be realised only in a more equal and classless society. Among the proponents of this tradition we would include T. H. Green, J. A. Hobson, L. T. Hobhouse and A. J. Ayer: all with their distinct views but drawing from a common philosophical wellspring.

Our view is most eloquently expressed by R. H. Tawney:

> If rights are to be an effective guarantee of freedom, they must not be merely formal, like the right of all who can afford it to dine at the Ritz . . . A society in which some groups can do much what they please, while others can do little of what they ought, may have virtues of its own: but freedom is not one of them. It is free in so far, and only in so far, as all the elements composing it are able in fact, not merely in theory, to make the most of their powers, to grow to their full stature, to do what they conceive to be their duty, and – since liberty should not be too austere – to have their fling when they feel like it. In so far as the opportunity to lead a life worthy of human beings is confined to a minority, what is commonly called freedom would more properly be described as privilege.[5]

In the twentieth century British society made significant but incomplete progress towards that Tawney ideal. But for Tawney social democracy is also about a transformation of society's values that goes alongside these broader positive freedoms. Tawney sums these up with all his natural eloquence:

> Even if the way of co-operation did not yield all the economic advantages expected from it, we should continue to choose it. Both the type of individual character and the style of social existence fostered by it are those we prefer . . . Civilisation is a matter not of quantity of possessions, but of quality of life. It is to be judged not by the output of goods and services per head, but by the use which is made of them. A society which values public welfare above private display; which makes the first charge on its resources the establish-

ment for all of the conditions of a vigorous and self-respecting existence; which gives a high place to the activities of the spirit and the services that promote them; which holds that the most important aspect of human beings is not the external differences of income and circumstance that divide them, but the common humanity that unites them, and which strives therefore to reduce such differences to the position of insignificance that rightly belongs to them, such a society may be far from what it should be, but it has at least set its face towards the light.[6]

Here we have modern concerns for well-being, not just GDP; the elimination of poverty but the avoidance of a paternalistic culture; the view that there is such a thing as the good life which values 'activities of the spirit'. A social democratic society is one of responsibility and mutual obligation, not just individual opportunity for self-fulfilment, whatever the chance of birth or natural endowment. It seeks not only to guarantee a decent minimum standard of life and care for all, but to live by an ethic of personal responsibility to present and future generations of humanity. This is broader than, but not inconsistent with, the more limited meritocratic goal of a society genuinely open to all the talents where success is based on merit, not on chance or the accident of birth.

To fulfil these goals, social democrats have sought to develop the idea of an 'active state', which has been variously described as enabling, empowering, ensuring and developmental according to the size of state and form of political intervention envisaged. Mainstream social democrats have always emphasised their commitment to democracy. But for some this has primarily meant winning the power to direct the state through democratic means. For others, such as Tawney, democracy is more than competent management of the levers of power: it is about leading and not just following opinion, changing the values of society and promoting the idea of, and capacity for, democratic citizenship. Tawney's famous letter to the *New Statesman* protesting at the Labour chief whip's acceptance of a knighthood summed up his distinctive view of the role of politics. How can Labour, Tawney argued, 'suppose that it will convert the public to a belief in Equality if it does not in its heart believe in it itself? And does it expect to persuade them of the genuineness of its convictions if prominent members of the party sit up, like poodles in a drawing room, wag their tails when patted, and lick their lips at the social sugar plums tossed at them by their masters?'[7] His goal was social equality, his emphasis on the need to take a 'moral' stand if a more egalitarian society was ever to be brought into being.

Social democracy has always been a rich and diverse intellectual tradition. As David Marquand vividly points out, there could not be two more different proponents of British social democratic thinking in the first half of the twentieth century than R. H. Tawney and the Webbs, even though today they are often referred to in the same sentence in eulogies of the founding fathers.[8] The first he categorises as a 'democratic republican' in the lineage of the Levellers, Tom Paine and the Chartists. The Webbs, on the other hand, are the apogee of the 'democratic collectivists' with their ambition 'to "constrain" the individual through a better social environment, to become "a healthier, nobler and more efficient being"'.[9] Evan Durbin became in the 1930s a passionate believer in the capacity of an organised democracy to defeat the twin evils of fascism and communism (unlike the Webbs, who became blind to communism's failings), but even so, his commitment to build a better society through democratic means today sounds somewhat chilling: 'To the centralised control of a democratic Community our livelihood and our security must be submitted. It is the business of society to secure the welfare of all. To do so it must be able to set limits to the welfare of each of us.'[10]

These tensions between bottom-up moral renewal and top-down mechanical social change live strongly in the present. It is not that social democrats can easily be categorised into two opposing camps: the tensions are present in each of us and which is uppermost tends to vary from issue to issue and time to time. The 'democratic republican' strain needs, however, to be better recognised and respected.

It is legitimate to ask what is meant by the goal of social equality in an increasingly diverse and more atomistic society. It is essential at the same time to reconsider how 'politics', as opposed to the assumption of central state action that some interpret politics as meaning, can help bring achievement of this goal nearer. Marquand's dividing line between democratic collectivists and democratic republicans goes to the heart of the dilemmas for modern social democracy.

The theme animating this volume is how these basic ideas need to be recast and revitalised for the twenty-first century in the light of modern structural conditions. Governing as a social democrat in Britain has always involved complex trade-offs and dilemmas, and today's world is no different. Understanding and analysing the structural factors shaping present economic and social realities is therefore an essential first step in social democratic renewal.

To rethink and revise is not to urge a call for further retreat. New Labour attempted to make this process more comfortable with reassuring rhetoric about 'unchanging values in a changing world'. Analysis of today's structural realities may indeed suggest that the 'problems' social democracy needs to address have changed in nature – perhaps profoundly, but there is no need to question either fundamental goals or the basic means. However, if the analysis suggests more than that, social democrats should not be afraid. Keynes once quipped: 'When the facts change, I change my mind. What do you do, sir?'[11] We need a rigorous open-mindedness towards rethinking both ends and means.

Why focus on structure, not leadership or political direction?

The social democratic dilemma is not in our view primarily a question of leadership. Success in political leadership, as Peter Clarke reminded us, is always a combination of agency and structure.[12] Individual flair and talent matter, but the structural conditions need to be in place for that individual talent to catch a political tide. It is not just a question of personality: there has to be a programmatic dimension, in tune with and responding to the underlying structural conditions that enable a political leader to convey an overall sense of mission and purpose. This was as true of Tony Blair in the run-up to 1997 as it was of Margaret Thatcher in 1979 and has been of Gordon Brown in the global economic crisis of 2008–9.

In similar vein Andrew Gamble has commented that to be successful, social democratic parties need a governing strategy, an electoral strategy and distinctive policies.[13] It is our contention that all of these need revision in the light of economic and social change.

Social democracy has struggled to accommodate the economic and social realities of the post-industrial age. These changes are often attributed to globalisation but a multiplicity of factors are at work.[14] Crucial is an ever more rapid pace of economic change as a result of what Will Hutton describes as the discovery of new 'general purpose technologies'.[15] Such discoveries as steam power in the eighteenth century and electricity in the late nineteenth had profound effects. However, the creation of the internet in the late twentieth is but one of a number of technologically driven breakthroughs that will lead to fundamental upheavals in the way economic activity is organised, creating new patterns of 'winners' and 'losers' in their wake.

In our age, greatly expanded education plays a central role in shaping individual life chances, but the majority of the public think that whether a young person succeeds at school, college and university is largely a question of their own talent and hard work, not a question of privilege or embedded social disadvantage, despite objective evidence to the contrary.[16] Changing consumer demands and social values continue to transform not just structures of class and occupation, but also individual aspirations and expectations of life at every level of class and income. Progress towards gender equality, the rise in life expectancy and the growth of individualism, as well as increased migration, diversity and complexity, are changing the nature of family life and have been accompanied by rising concerns about well-being, social breakdown and identity. At the same time the nation state's power to put into effect lasting political change has weakened as a result of globalisation and the rise of interdependence, but the sovereignty pooling implied by deeper European integration at present lacks democratic legitimacy with the public.[17] One of the largest political 'unknowns' is whether more courageous leadership could reverse this.

In addition to these ongoing structural shifts, social democrats are struggling to be flexible and adaptive in the face of more recent upheavals that will be long-lasting in their effects: the 2008 economic crisis and recession that began with the 'sub-prime' crisis in the US mortgage markets in the summer of 2007; the rapid rebalancing of the world economy, particularly towards Asia; and public awareness of the new existential threat of climate change to add to existing ones like nuclear proliferation.[18] All of these have the potential to be hugely disruptive of present jobs and living standards.

For a complex series of reasons, the public's faith in politics has been in sharp decline: it is too early to tell whether the 'return of economics' with the global financial crisis will reverse the trend, though there is clearly an element of that in the US presidential election victory of Barack Obama in November 2008. This declining trust in the electoral process seriously damages social democratic parties that believe in the potential of political action to achieve profound economic and social change. 'Soft' Conservatives face nothing like the same problem as long as they can avoid the taint of neo-liberal dogmatism: hence the success of Continental leaders such as Angela Merkel in Germany and Nicolas Sarkozy in France. The impact of these structural factors is apparent on social democracy across Europe: in the late 1990s social democrats headed governments in eleven of the then fifteen EU member states; by 2008 this figure had fallen to three. On the Continent social democracy is squeezed by the rise of anti-immigrant populism on the right and anti-globalisation populism on the left. Its core constituency is 'broken', as René Cuperus describes it.[19] On the one hand, in Cuperus's view, educated social liberals favour economic openness and are comfortable with the knowledge economy, European integration, a multicultural society and the personal freedoms that recent decades have brought. On the other Cuperus argues that swathes of what remains of the traditional working class fear globalisation, favour a return to welfare states as they once were and are suspicious of 'modernising' reforms. They support traditional values, feel that due to immigration their country is no longer their own, and think that European integration has gone too far. The analysis may be too class determinist but it is evident that this clash of values exists in the New Labour coalition today. It is the basis of our contention that a fundamental 'cosmopolitan'/'communitarian' tension in social democracy is emerging.

These key questions are obscured in the current British debate about Labour and its future. The issues are commonly framed in terms of abandonment or some form of renewal; going further down the path of modernisation or retreating to a more left traditionalism.

Among academics debate rages between those on the one hand who believe that 'New' Labour is or was an electorally opportunistic set of positions designed to win and hold power, with few or no links to Labour's past,[20] and those on the other who have traced 'New Labour's Old Roots'.[21] Many people in the Labour Party think that since 1997 Labour could have been more successful in office with a genuinely radical social democratic programme and debate whether a bolder project may have contemplated some mix of higher taxes on the wealthy and a sharper critique of privilege. Others believe that New Labour reflected the ideological and electoral limits of the possible in the 1990s. In our view, these debates are too backward-looking and limiting.

Essentially the issue for Labour is how to construct a positive modernisation of social democratic doctrine on the basis of present and future structural realities. It is illusory to believe that there is some inherent compatibility or 'fit' between Labour's values and the challenges facing modern societies: the public may retain 'progressive' instincts, but there is widespread pessimism about trends in society. The new Conservatives have sought to develop a language of empathy with the concerns of voters, and have replaced the Thatcherite emphasis on individualism with the rhetoric at least of a belief that there is such a thing as society. They will try their hardest not to lose out in a game of 'catch-up' on the role of the state.

Labour has to convey a new optimism about the possibilities of democratic politics, but it can do this only if the public trust it and believe it is credible and competent enough to wisely use governing instruments such as the state.

What has weakened and why?

Our critique is that New Labour tried to sidestep too many of the dilemmas and contradictions of social democracy, which have grown more acute with Britain's economic and social transformation. Instead, New Labour ought to have engaged directly with the need to modernise social democracy, coming to terms with new pressures and demands. The risk of the dramatic 'return of economics' to the centre of the political stage is that it leads to neglect of the wider need for 'renewal', which was already apparent before the global financial crisis broke.

Labour's previous reluctance to genuinely renew itself reflects to a large extent the unresolved strategic dilemmas at the heart of modern social democracy. On the one hand, New Labour sought to build an election-winning machine through which it could emerge as the natural party of government. On the other, the party recognised the need to make far-reaching changes that would disrupt settled interests and coalitions of support, compromising its vote-gathering strategy. The 'big tent' approach was necessary in opposition as New Labour sought to build support among non-traditional Labour voters, particularly professionals in social class AB and aspirant C1 and C2 families on modest incomes.

But in government Labour displayed a lack of clarity and a peculiar reluctance to acknowledge obstacles or barriers to its programme, particularly where it offended powerful vested interests in the City and the private sector. The Blair government apparently lacked a coherent conception of the public interest – that is an account of the basic principles that ought to underpin the relationship between the state and the citizen as well as protecting democratic rights and obligations – leading to a great deal of confusion in the civil service about how to enact and implement 'new' Labour institutions and policy initiatives. As a consequence, four notable tensions were evident throughout Labour's period of unconfident hegemony, as set out below.[22]

1. **Competition versus market regulation.** New Labour wanted to embrace the City and the financial markets, strengthening Britain's competitive advantage in the global economy. But the reluctance to regulate markets in the public interest often put the government at odds with the needs of consumers, who sought controls on fuel prices, wanted reassurance about food safety and rightly demanded secure pensions and savings. Market dominance, particularly in the media, the creative industries and the defence sector, was often left unchallenged for fear of offending business interests. It was also becoming clear, well before the 2008 crisis removed any doubt, that markets left to themselves could not be guaranteed to serve the public interest, that competition was not in itself going to secure the

private investment urgently needed to renew Britain's ageing energy infrastructure or bring about a low-carbon economy. Abandoning housing to the market also exposed huge problems of unmet social need well before the sub-prime mortgage crisis.

2. **Greater equality versus 'Middle England'.** New Labour wanted to narrow the gap between the 'bottom' and the 'middle' of the income distribution by targeting resources at the least well off. However, it quickly recognised that securing middle-class support for universal services would require a step-change in public invest-ment combined with targeted tax rises in 2001/2 to pay for NHS modernisation. The government struggled to square the circle of alleviating the plight of the excluded minority and raising standards for all, especially in health and education. Progress on child and pensioner poverty was initially impressive, but slowed after the 2001 election. It was not clear whether further gains could be delivered without additional tax rises, although a recent report from the OECD shows that income inequality has declined faster in Britain than any other industrialised country in the last decade.[23]

Meanwhile, the lowest earners continued to pay far too much tax, as the 'tax take' as a proportion of GDP remained broadly static, a reflection of the need to protect the interests of 'Middle England'. The proportion of households that were categorised as 'working poor' barely changed over the decade. Labour succeeded in 'making work pay', but in-work poverty rates increased dramatically over this period.

3. **Tolerance verses the moral majority.** New Labour presided over the most far-reaching liberalisation of social attitudes since the Second World War, with notable reforms including civil partner-ships, equalising the age of consent, and new initiatives on race and disability equality. Nonetheless, the government sought to vigorously defend the 'traditional' family and to reassert basic moral values such as civility and decency. It attempted to define a world-view that combined private tolerance with public virtue, in which people could do as they liked in their private lives but were required to uphold social norms in their communities.

This rationale often looked fragile, however, and the government struggled to develop robust principles that could inform credible policies for dealing with social problems such as drug abuse and alcoholism. Labour was caught in the wider conflict alluded to earlier between 'cosmopolitans', who emphasised personal freedom and wanted Britain to be outward-looking, and 'communitarians', who sought to defend traditional ways of life, particularly in working-class communities.

4. New settlement versus incremental change. It was never entirely clear whether the purpose of New Labour was to initiate incremental reforms after the upheavals of the Thatcher era, as symbolised by the five pledges in the 1997 manifesto, or whether what Britain in fact needed was a radical shake-up in order to seize the opportunities of the twenty-first century. How modest or radical really were Labour's ambitions: did it intend to define a settlement that would permanently reorientate the centre ground of British politics in a progressive direction? Or, alternatively, was the purpose to take the sharp edges off the insecurities imposed by globalisation? The party wrestled with an enduring dilemma: voters demanded that government shield them from uncertainty and instability, yet they wanted greater choice and control within a reformed centralised state. This was perhaps the most profound conundrum of all, what some polling experts describe as 'cognitive dissonance', in which voters hold apparently contradictory views.

The refusal to address these tensions has inhibited the necessary process of political 'renewal' and has held Labour back from moving up a gear to develop a compelling argument about the future condition of Britain. The management theorist Charles Handy has powerfully argued that organisations must reinvent themselves while they are still successful, instead of waiting for a crisis or collapse of confidence before they move forward. Instead, Labour was still haunted by fear of the 1980s, scarred by four successive defeats that meant it struggled to display greater confidence about how the party wanted to change the country.

Establishing a new social democratic project will mean recognising the changing social, economic and cultural landscape of Britain, and the pace of that change. But it will also require a willingness to confront the tensions within social democratic thinking in Britain that have so often thwarted the success of the social democratic project in the past.

The next social democratic project for Britain

The authors of this volume each address how current social democratic doctrines are often weak or inadequate for understanding new social and economic challenges.

Part I presents an overview of the state of Britain and the British social democratic debate. These chapters discuss the changing structural and electoral dynamics facing a future social democratic project, including the empirical realities confronting Britain such as technology, changes in occupational structure, globalisation, labour markets, demography, gender equality, the changing nature of the family, long-term trends to post-materialism and the new emphasis on well-being. They also consider the challenges for politics and public opinion deriving from these changes, including declining concerns about public services reflecting the re-emergence of economic insecurities. In Chapter 1 David Marquand highlights the weaknesses of the traditional social democratic mindset as a vision of the just society, challenges the continuing validity of the term 'progressive' and calls for a renewal of social democratic thinking for the twenty-first century. In Chapter 2 Roger Liddle and Simon Latham provide an overview of the economic and social condition of Britain, in the light of the topical debate about 'Broken Britain'. In Chapter 3 Peter Riddell explores the contours of Britain's electoral map and the current disposition of public opinion.

Part II of this volume considers key issues in developing a progressive political economy, such as framing a role for the nation state in the global economy; the challenges of the service-driven knowledge economy and the power of intangibles in driving economic activity; the role of the cultural industries; new principles for governing markets in the public interest; progressive taxation and enterprise; whether social democrats should make growth or well-being their central goal; and why the left must understand, not eulogise, markets. In Chapter 4, Will Hutton shows how a new role for the state is needed to underpin the service-based knowledge economy, very different to the dirigisme of the 1960s and 1970s, but no less activist. In Chapter 5, John Kay demonstrates that traditional nostrums of market failure are unhelpful in resolving how best to govern and regulate both private sector markets and public services. In Chapter 6, Melvyn Bragg debates the new economics of culture.

Part III considers issues of equality, society and the family. Is individualism on the rise and what does it mean? What are the consequences of changing family formation and demography, migration and diversity as well as new forms of identity, fluidity and pluralism? In Chapter 7, Mary Daly shows the difficulties traditional social democracy has had in articulating a politics and implementing a policy that values family life while at the same time undoing the inequalities that have historically been manifest within and between families. In Chapter 8, Patrick Diamond shows how the traditional social democratic recipe for tackling the growth of inequality in incomes and purchasing power is running out of steam, and that a very different approach will be needed for the future. In Chapter 9, Hannah Jameson explores the challenges to social democratic thinking posed by increasing diversity and transience in modern Britain, changing forms of identity, and their relative importance in political life.

Part IV of the book debates the UK constitutional framework and Britain's relationship with the European Union. In Chapter 10, Iain McLean examines Labour's conflicting approaches to remaking the state and the unstable constitutional settlement that has resulted. In Chapter 11, Donald Macintyre considers why Britain's relationship with the European Union remains a central strategic issue in British politics and whether the EU offers a transnational space for coordinated action to fulfil progressive goals such as tackling climate change and promoting economic security.

Part I

Overview

1

After progress

David Marquand

Over time, political terms are apt to lose their meaning, sometimes with strange results. 'Socialism' is perhaps the most conspicuous example in recent times. The early socialists were a tiny and quarrelsome band, but there was no doubt about the fundamentals of their creed. They looked forward to a world remade, in which poverty, exploitation and injustice would be no more. They knew that their path to the new world would be hard, but they had no doubt of their destination. The expropriators would be expropriated, and the exploited would inherit the earth. The earth they inherited would be incomparably richer than the existing one. Social ownership was bound to be more efficient than private, and a rationally planned economy more efficient than the wasteful chaos of the marketplace. Once production for use replaced production for profit, a promethean upsurge of wealth creation, far outstripping anything experienced in previous phases of history, would infallibly take place. Socialists also took it for granted that they had discovered society's laws of motion, and that their prescriptions for the future were uniquely compelling because they had done so. Last, but by no means least, they saw their creed as the instrument, inspiration and mentor of the labour movement, and allotted a unique redemptive role to the working class.

By the early 1970s, at the latest, it was clear to all but the *enragés* of the far left that the god had failed. The socialised economies of the communist bloc were grotesquely inefficient and unproductive. The nomenklaturas that ran them were corrupt and incompetent. The system was kept going only by dumb resignation at the best, and by heresy hunting, police surveillance and bouts of more or less brutal repression at the worst. The fate of western democratic socialism was kinder, but equally remote from the certitudes of the pioneers. It was most successful in Scandinavia, but the nominally social democratic regimes of the Nordic countries presided over a form of collaborative capitalism that had little or nothing to do with socialism as originally understood. In Britain, the post-war Labour government failed dismally to make a reality of the 'democratic planning' on which it had based its claim to power, and staggered from economic crisis to economic crisis. Its greatest achievement was to realise the non-socialist visions of a welfare state and managed economy, proposed by two great Liberals, William Beveridge and John Maynard Keynes. The Labour government of the 1960s was a sad failure, and that of the 1970s a catastrophic one. In France, Italy and, above all, West Germany, a promethean upsurge of wealth creation did take place, but the credit did not belong to socialists or socialism. It was the product of a rich stew of influences, including Catholic social teaching, a long-standing French tradition of apolitical techno-cratic rationalism and the German theorists of the social market economy.

Yet, though the god failed, the religion survived. The British Labour Party did not jettison its commitment to public ownership until the 1990s. The French socialists turned their backs on socialism after François Mitterrand won the presidency in 1981, but they never openly acknowledged their apostasy. The Italian socialists were mired in corruption, but they too still called themselves socialists. The social democrats of central Europe and Scandinavia abandoned the Marxism of their founders fairly early, and as the world-wide capitalist renaissance of the 1980s and 1990s roared ahead they sloughed off what remained of their social democratic skin, but they were reluctant to admit that they had done so. Though the details differed from country to country, the broad outlines of the story were the same all over Europe. Socialist and social democratic parties fought elections; their leaders sometimes formed governments; their apparatchiks wrote manifestos and devised slogans; the intellectuals who circulated around them debated the future of their creed with solemnity and occasional passion. But the language in which they did so had a diminishing purchase on reality, and their relationship to socialism and social democracy as traditionally understood was about as distant as that of the Renaissance Popes from the Sermon on the Mount.

The bland lead the bland

In Britain, at least, something similar now seems to be happening to the insipid language of progress which has replaced the socialist language of old. Self-styled 'progressives' are everywhere. Under Tony Blair, there was talk of the twenty-first century becoming a 'progressive century' – an alarming prospect for those of us who believe in pluralist politics. Gordon Brown apparently wants a 'progressive consensus'. The Labour–Plaid Cymru coalition now in power in Wales claims that it has already achieved one. The Fabian Society has held a series of high-level lectures by assorted ministers on the theme of a 'progressive manifesto'. The left-Labour pressure group Compass appeals for support to undefined 'progressives'.

It is not difficult to see why. The old socialist certitudes have not just lost credibility; they have been stood on their head. There is no longer a working class in the old sense. There is a vast middle class, fringed by a tiny class of super-rich and a larger – but still minority – underclass, reminiscent of the 'roughs' that tormented the imaginations of *bien-pensant* Victorians, and that Marxists scorned as the *Lumpen-proletariat*. The promethean upsurge of wealth creation that changed the face of western Europe after the Second World War has been outdone in China and India, but under the aegis of a free-booting, environmentally destructive and grossly inegalitarian capitalism more reminiscent of Industrial Revolution Britain than of any socialist or social democratic vision of a good society. Everywhere, the historic struggle between socialists and capitalism has ended, and capitalism has prevailed.

An emotional, ideological and semantic vacuum has resulted. For a while Blair tried to fill it, first by insisting with brazen chutzpah that Labour stood for 'social-ism' rather than socialism, and then by repackaging the young Harold Macmillan's 'middle way' as a remarkably vacuous 'Third Way'. But 'social-ism' never caught on, and the 'Third Way' soon followed it into the oubliette reserved for slogans that outlive their time (or in some cases never had a time to outlive). Talk of 'progress', 'progressives' and even 'progressivism' is the latest attempt to find a substitute for the socialism and social democracy of the heroic past.

But there is a cruel irony in this endeavour. Like socialism, progressivism once meant something. Around the turn of the nineteenth and twentieth centuries, it signified the remarkable overlap between the gradualist democratic socialists of the Independent Labour Party and the Fabian Society on the one hand, and the 'new' or 'social' liberals who provided the ideological justification and rationale for the domestic policies of the Asquith government on the other. In the county of London (the biggest local authority in the country), Progressives with a capital 'P' contested elections under that name, and controlled the council for significant periods. Progressives with a small 'p' exchanged ideas in a surprisingly long-lived discussion group called the Rainbow Circle.

Ramsay MacDonald, the first secretary of the infant Labour Party and later the chairman of the Parliamentary Labour Party, was a notable member of the Rainbow Circle. He became a key figure in the so-called 'Progressive Alliance' between Labour and the Liberals, which had been foreshadowed in his secret electoral pact with the Liberal chief whip before the 1906 election, and which came fully into being after the Asquith government lost its overall Commons majority in 1910. MacDonald's close friend J. A. Hobson, the pioneer of underconsumptionist economics, a precursor of John Maynard Keynes and at that time a Liberal in politics, was another typical progressive (and a prolific paper giver at Rainbow Circle meetings). With some differences of emphasis Sidney and Beatrice Webb, the archetypal Fabian socialists, belonged in the same camp, as did the New Liberal apologist and theorist L. T. Hobhouse.

The upheavals brought by the First World War and the emergence of the Labour Party as the main anti-Conservative party in the state shattered the alliance of the pre-war years. The Liberal Party was hopelessly split; though it recovered a precarious unity a few years after the war, it had lost its élan and sense of purpose. As I tried to show some time ago, the 'progressives' who had belonged to it before 1914 and younger liberal-minded people who would have joined it if they had been politically active in its great days thus faced a painful dilemma.[1] Either they threw in their lot with a proletarianist, intolerant, often anti-intellectual and frequently illiberal Labour Party, which meant being untrue to themselves, or they remained faithful to their Liberal antecedents, which spelled political futility. This is not the place to examine the varied ways in which progressives responded to the dilemma. The important point is that the dilemma was real, and that it stemmed from an inescapable tension between the values and culture of liberal-minded 'progressives' and those of the Labour Party.

None of this is true of the self-styled 'progressives' of our day. Most of them are not and never have been Liberals with a capital 'L'. Many of them are not liberals with a small 'l' either, as they showed by supporting the stream of illiberal legislation passed by the Blair government under the rubric of the 'war on terror'. For all their talk of a progressive consensus, they show no sign of wishing to create a modern version of the Liberal–Labour 'Progressive Alliance', which sustained the Asquith government between 1910 and 1914 and helped to make it one of the most successful governments of the twentieth century. Naturally, they would like to win over Liberal Democrat voters, but they have shied away from the close, detailed inter-party give and take without which no alliance worthy of the name could come into being. For them, 'progressivism' is essentially a semantic comfort blanket, designed to conceal the fact that the social and economic changes of the last quarter of a century have shredded the socialist or social democratic clothes they once wore.

Progressives and history

Until recently, I saw no harm in this. Such comfort blankets have often played an important role in politics. (I sometimes used the language of 'progressivism' myself, though more out of intellectual laziness than anything else.) Now I am not so sure. The language of 'progress', 'progressive' and 'progressivism' may be intellectually vapid, but it carries a heavy emotional and ideological charge. Looming in the background is a set of questionable and even dangerous assumptions – about the nature and direction of political and social change, about the role of the state and its relationship with civil society and, on a very deep level, about the feasibility of economic and political prediction and the prerequisites of human flourishing.

At first sight, the word 'progress' is pure comfort blanket. It has no obvious meaning, and it is warm, cuddly and unthreatening. It is manifestly a Good Thing, advocated by Good People. Who but the most curmudgeonly reactionaries can possibly object to it or cavil about the use that is made of it? But, on closer inspection, there is a lot more to it than that. Whatever its users' motives may be, it has a logic about it which carries them along, sometimes without their realising it. As John Gray has brilliantly argued, progressivism is nothing more or less than a secular version of Christianity.[2] It promises salvation in this world rather than in the next, but the promise itself belongs to the same essentially eschatological category as Christ's promise that those who believed in him would enter the Kingdom of Heaven. The word 'progress' implies not just change, but desirable *and unavoidable* change. To talk of progress is to say that the future will be better than the present, which is itself better than the past. When people call themselves 'progressives', they are not just saying that they have worthy aims which they would like to realise at some stage in the future. They are saying that their aims run with the grain of history; that they stand for the future, buried in the womb of the present. For the language of progress also implies determinacy. In progressives' eyes, history moves in a knowable direction towards a knowable goal – characteristically towards peace, justice and harmony. Their claim to power is based on the assumption that they have discovered where history is going; and that, by virtue of that discovery, they are entitled to guide the rest of us in the desired direction.

How anyone can believe all this after one of the bloodiest, cruellest and most destructive centuries in human history, and at the start of a new century threatened by an unprecedented planetary environmental catastrophe, which no government seems willing to avert, is a mystery I cannot pretend to solve. Progress? Really? After the Holocaust, the gulag, Pol Pot, Mao Zedong, Nagasaki, Rwanda, the bombing of Hamburg and Dresden and the degradation of the Aral Sea? Determinacy? After the sudden, unpredicted collapse of the Soviet Union, America's astonishing defeat at the hands of the Viet Cong, the revolution in genetics that followed the discovery of the double helix, the micro-electronic revolution and the explosive growth of the internet, to say nothing about the failure of innumerable attempts to procure complex social and cultural changes through progressive social engineering?

The fact is that confident progressive predictions have been falsified on repeated occasions in the last 200 years, sometimes spectacularly. In the early nineteenth century, progressives believed, with Richard Cobden, that universal free trade would usher in universal peace. But the rising powers of imperial Germany and the United States soon saw that universal free trade entrenched Britain's industrial hegemony; they refused to accept that hegemony as a fact of life and adopted protectionist policies on the lines advocated by the German economic nationalist Friedrich List, to safeguard their own political and economic autonomy. Defying progressive predictions, in short, Britain's 'free-trade empire' became a force for protectionism elsewhere. In the early twentieth century, most progressives agreed with Norman Angell that, thanks to rising prosperity and spreading enlightenment, war had become a 'great illusion'. Five years after the publication of his book with that title,[3] the (unpredicted and unpredictable) assassination of the Archduke Franz Ferdinand in Sarajevo sparked off the most destructive war in history up to that time. In the later stages of the war and the early stages of the peace, most progressives shared Woodrow Wilson's belief in the inherent right of ethnically homogeneous nations to self-determination and rejoiced when the ramshackle but comparatively stable multi-ethnic Habsburg empire was replaced by a series of small nation states, determined to assert their right to a place in the sun.

But Wilson and his progressive followers did not foresee that the small successor states of the Habsburg empire would be unstable, quarrelsome and increasingly chauvinistic. Still less did they foresee that the demise of the Habsburgs would let loose a wave of ethnic nationalism that eventually culminated in Adolf Hitler's Nazi revolution and the subsequent Holocaust. In the 1930s, many British progressives were adamantly opposed to rearmament, and thought careful and deliberate appeasement of Hitler's Germany would remove her grievances and make a second European war unthinkable. Unfortunately, Hobbes, Nietzsche and Bismarck turned out to be better guides to the 1930s than Cobden or Angell or Wilson. To their horror, bemused progressives discovered that the eirenic, tolerant, supremely rational values that lay at the heart of their dream were not universally shared. Men and women of 'blood and iron' refused to play the parts allotted to them in the progressive script, and the script writers were intellectually and morally becalmed.

As Albert Hirschman showed in a characteristically elegant study,[4] a favourite trope of progressive rhetoric ever since the French Revolution has been the claim that irrevocable laws of motion are carrying mankind willy-nilly in the direction which progressives in any case wish to take. Karl Marx was perhaps the greatest master of this trope in the history of social thought, but he was by no means alone in employing it. The interwar pioneers of the post-war mixed economy did so too. According to them, history inevitably progressed from the disorganised to the organised, from the dispersed to the concentrated, from the individual to the collective. In that spirit, the maverick Conservative, but undeniably progressive, Harold Macmillan saw existing forms of economic organisation as a temporary phase which would sooner or later give way to a planned economy. For his part, the Labour and equally progressive economist Evan Durbin dismissed the liberal economics of Ludwig von Mises, Friedrich Hayek and Lionel Robbins with what he evidently assumed was the unanswerable objection that 'social systems have rarely developed backwards'.[5]

Twenty years later, another progressive, Anthony Crosland, argued in his great book, *The Future of Socialism*, that the contradictions of capitalism once anatomised by Marx had been resolved – and not just for a while, but for ever. Thanks to John Maynard Keynes, mass unemployment had been banished and would never return. The business class had lost power to the state, again irrevocably. The high rates of growth which had brought unprecedented prosperity to North America and western Europe would continue indefinitely – or, at least, until the beneficiaries were so sated that increases in leisure would seem preferable to yet more goods. The fact that Britain's rate of growth was lower than those of most of her Continental competitors was no cause for concern. Nor was her loss of market share. Indeed, anguishing over comparative growth rates would soon be hopelessly outdated. Before long, the time would come for democratic socialists to switch their attention away from economics and towards 'culture, beauty, leisure, and even frivolity'.[6]

Twenty years after *The Future of Socialism* (and forty years after Durbin), the Cabinet of which Crosland was one of the most distinguished members was racked by a crisis of 'stagflation', which eluded the categories of Keynesian economics and which Keynesian methods were powerless to overcome. The government had to seek a massive loan from the International Monetary Fund and abandon the programme on which it had been returned to power. After a short interval, the neo-liberal government of Margaret Thatcher proceeded to show that social systems could easily 'develop backwards', that the business class could regain power from the state if the state so wished, and that in the interdependent global economy then coming into being, it was not only possible but necessary to abandon the whole Keynesian paradigm.

But the real charge against the long line of mistaken progressives of the last century is not that their predictions turned out to be inaccurate. It is that they assumed that accurate long-term social and political prediction was feasible in the first place; they forgot (or perhaps never realised) that, as G. K. Chesterton once put it, mankind's favourite game is 'Cheat the Prophet', that the only thing we know about the future is that it will be different from the present, in ways we cannot predict. Above all, they forgot that, simply because human ambitions are infinitely various and subject to unforeseeable shifts of fashion or belief, history is necessarily the realm of the contingent. In one form or another, futurism – the assumption that the future is knowable, that those who know what it will be have no choice but to embrace it and that those who embrace it are entitled to lead the rest of us towards it – is part of the progressive mindset. But that assumption has no empirical foundation. It is what Isaiah Berlin once called a 'theodicy': a way of justifying inherently contestable choices by appealing to a higher power – no longer God but History.

It offers a route out of the realm of argument and debate, and into the realm of faith. Like Christians, sustained by the knowledge that, however painful their tribulations in this vale of tears, they will one day be saved by a transcendent redeemer, progressives have consoled themselves for their failures with the belief that they are, by definition, the outriders of history, and that no one can argue with history. They did not realise – or, more accurately, they could not bear to realise – that Clio is a fickle muse, even less trustworthy than the Holy Trinity or Mother Church.

Progressives and the state

The characteristic progressive approach to agency has been equally misguided. For most progressives, the vehicle of history has been the enlightened, rational central state. There were distinguished exceptions, of course. John Stuart Mill, a slightly ambivalent progressive, feared that an over-mighty state would choke the springs of personal growth and public spirit. If the state did too much there would be no space for the public to acquire the habits of active citizenship, without which they would be governed like 'sheep by their shepherd'. But his near contemporary Edwin Chadwick, the utilitarian radical who pioneered public health legislation and was partly responsible for the notorious 1834 New Poor Law, was a thorough-going statist; and by the early twentieth century most progressives were closer to Chadwick than to Mill. J. A. Hobson thought the 'general will and wisdom' of society were 'embodied in the State'.[7] Ramsay MacDonald saw the state as society's 'organised political personality', which 'thinks and feels for the whole'.[8] Before the First World War, progressives of all stripes welcomed the growth in the size and role of the state ushered in by the Asquith government's social reforms. After the war, the embryo welfare state of pre-war days developed incrementally under all governments (including Conservative ones); and progressives in both the Labour and the Liberal parties advocated greater state intervention in the economy to promote employment and national development.

The experience of total war and post-war reconstruction gave progressive statism a mighty boost. The wartime British state was a far more impressive creature than the US, Soviet or Nazi states. It procured an extraordinary concentration of effort on military purposes. By 1943 public expenditure accounted for 54 per cent of GDP as against 24 per cent in 1938. (The comparable figure for 1917, the third full year of the First World War, was 37 per cent.) By June

1944 the armed forces and munitions industries absorbed 55 per cent of the labour force, compared to the US figure of 40 per cent. The means of production were still privately owned, but in the key sections of the economy the government, not the owners, decided what should be produced and what to charge for it. Ministers and officials in Whitehall could and did allocate raw materials, ration most items of consumer expenditure, control prices, fix profit margins, subsidise food, conscript women and evacuate children. For the talented young, and even for the staid middle-aged, the moral seemed clear: given the right mixture of rationality, intelligence and public spirit in its managers, there was hardly anything the state could not do.

And once the war was over, it did a great deal: universal and compulsory social insurance; a comprehensive health service, free at the point of use; the nationalisation of the Bank of England, civil aviation, electricity and gas supply, coal mining, the railways, long-distance road haulage and, after a fierce Cabinet battle, iron and steel. More than two million workers were transferred from the private to the public sector. The poorest in the land became entitled to the best medical care available. Despite the succession of economic crises I mentioned earlier, Labour progressives were entitled to feel that their faith in the beneficence and competence of the central state had been vindicated. (Liberal ones were not so sure.)

But the Attlee government marked the high point of triumphant statism. The statist experiments of the Wilson government of the 1960s, and still more of the Wilson–Callaghan government of the 1970s, fared very differently. Attempts to change the behaviour of wage bargainers through a complex mixture of moral suasion, technocratic institution building and legal penalties failed miserably, and the government's modest attempt to tame the jungle of industrial relations suffered a humiliating collapse. The net effect was to enhance trade union power and encourage strikes. By the same token, the wholesale introduction of comprehensive schools, the ark of the progressive covenant, backfired badly. Instead of mitigating class differences, they strengthened them. Middle-class parents who could afford school fees deserted the state sector; a range of previously free grammar schools turned themselves into private schools, dependent on fee income; and it became more difficult for bright working-class children to win places at elite universities. In both domains, the Law of Unintended Consequences foiled progressive hopes.

Blairite statism fared no better. It was, of course, an odd kind of statism. Tony Blair and his colleagues had no intention of returning to the mixed economy or indicative planning of the post-war period. They were Thatcher's children, not Attlee's, Wilson's or Callaghan's. Whereas the progressives of the post-war period had sought to tame capitalism in the interests of national unity, democratic inclusion and social justice, Blairite progressives sought to soften the rough edges of the newly untamed capitalism they had inherited from Margaret Thatcher and John Major in order to entrench it more firmly in the political and moral economies. But (like Thatcher and Major before them) they discovered that the 'taming' of capitalism depended as heavily on minute and continuous state intervention as its untaming had done. Against their original expectations, privatisation and marketisation were as fundamental to the Blairites' project as they had been to its Thatcherite predecessor; and they soon discovered that only the central state could privatise and marketise on the necessary scale.

Here too the Law of Unintended Consequences loomed in the background. In most of western Europe, the great achievement of the second half of the nineteenth century and the first half of the twentieth was the creation of a public domain, ring fenced from the exchange relations of the marketplace. In the public domain, citizenship rights rather than market power governed the allocation of social goods, and the ethic of public service trumped the profit motive; market rationality was transcended by a civic rationality. It was a social space, where strangers encountered each other as equal partners in the common life of the society – a space for forms of human flourishing which could not be bought in the marketplace or found in the tight-knit community of the clan or family or group of intimates. In the public domain, individuals were not producers or consumers, clients or kinsfolk. They were *citizens*.

Almost by definition, progressives were for the public domain. They believed in the ethic of citizenship and service, and they wanted to implant it in the public culture. As the size and role of the state grew during the twentieth century, however, a fatal misunderstanding seeped into the progressive mentality. Progressives increasingly came to believe that citizenship rights and the civic ideal could be realised only by and through the state; and they drew the fatal conclusion that the growth of the state would translate, almost automatically, into a wider public domain with a more deeply entrenched civic ideal. But over the last quarter of a century we have learned that the public domain is quite separate from the state. It is protected and sustained by a wide range of civil society institutions, which do not depend on state power and can easily be damaged by it. In Britain, at least, the public domain was a child of the last third of the nineteenth century, when the state was very small. State enactments – such as the creation of county and parish councils; the Ballot Act, which freed voters from the threat of intimidation by landlords or employers; and (crucially) the Northcote–Trevelyan reforms, which created a professional civil service recruited on merit instead of by patronage – all furthered the growth of the public domain, but they did not affect the size or functions of the state itself. The state did not start to grow significantly until the First World War, and its growth was given a further boost during and after the Second.

But, by a cruel paradox, the expansion of the state which took place under the 1945–51 Labour government narrowed the scope for civic engagement, and in doing so narrowed the public domain as well. Before 1945, local authorities owned and ran a wide range of public utilities, as well as much of the hospital service. The government's much-vaunted nationalisation programme took locally controlled public utilities out of the hands of local government and handed them over to remote and impersonal national bodies. The same thing happened to locally controlled hospitals. The well-intentioned progressives who passed the necessary legislation believed that these changes would make public services more efficient. Even if they were right (and, to put it at its lowest, that cannot be taken for granted), the price of efficiency was less local democracy and an attenuated public domain. And that has been a leitmotiv of progressive governance ever since. In sphere after sphere, progressive ministers have strengthened the central state at the expense of the localities – often, it must be said in fairness, following the lead of conservative predecessors who had forgotten their conservatism. On both sides of the once-familiar, but increasingly meaningless, left–right divide the State has turned out to be as untrustworthy an ally as History.

Where next?

Is there an alternative? The answer, I'm afraid, is summed up in Denis Healey's Law of Holes: 'If you're in one, stop digging'. It is time for self-styled progressives to throw their comfort blanket away, to abandon the delusive certainties of teleological prediction, to accept that God and History are broken reeds and to view the central state with a healthy caution rather than wide-eyed admiration – in short, to grow up. There are plenty of evils to combat. The ancient enemies of mankind – poverty, indignity, cruelty, injustice – have not disappeared, and almost certainly never will. Sometimes the central state will have to play a role in combating them; often, supranational institutions will have to play a part as well. But it is one thing to use state power to combat particular known and visible evils, in a wary and cautious spirit, quite another to imagine that enlightened social engineers, guided by the pure light of reason, can remake society from the top down. In a famous essay, Isaiah Berlin wrote that his hero, Alexander Herzen,

> believed in reason, scientific methods, individual action, empirically discovered truths; but he tended to suspect that faith in general formulas, laws, prescription in human affairs was an attempt, some-times catastrophic, always irrational, to escape from the uncertainty and unpredictable variety of life into the false security of our own symmetrical fantasies.[9]

Self-styled progressives have put their faith in 'symmetrical fantasies' for too long. They would do well to make Berlin's Herzen their mascot.

2

'Broken Britain'?

The new economic and social realities facing British social democrats in the twenty-first century

Roger Liddle and Simon Latham

Introduction

This chapter examines the structural factors, both economic and social, shaping the politics of modern Britain. It argues that the concept of 'broken Britain' is tendentious and misleading, and that the best lens through which to examine the challenges facing our society is the new pattern of opportunities and risks being created by structural change and value shifts. It is only through a close understanding of these structural changes that social democrats will be able to discover their own response to the fears which the 'broken Britain' narrative resonates with. The broad conclusion holds that Britain, far from being 'broken' or, conversely, unique in its strengths, is comparable to other western European countries, subject to the same dominating trends in, for example, economic structure, gender equality, the nature of the family and the individualisation of values.

The chapter divides into three sections: the first will examine common trends and patterns across Britain and, where relevant, Europe too; the second will then consider their impact on the social risks that individuals' life courses face through the model currently favoured by leading social experts such as Gøsta Esping-Andersen and Anton Hemerijck;[1] and the third section, by way of conclusion, will explore whether they amount to serious challenges for revisionist social democracy.[2]

The media and popular culture have coalesced to sketch a bleak narrative of British society which now largely informs public opinion – one where binge drinking, teenage pregnancy, familial breakdown, gang culture, junk food, consumerism and celebrity culture are all cited as culprits of social decline.[3]

These popular representations of British society, and young people in particular, have resulted in a deep pessimism about the long-term prospects for individuals and society at large, even though self-reported life satisfaction and happiness have remained stable for a generation. This pessimism is both paradoxical and striking; we may be the first generation since the great advance of material progress initiated by the Industrial Revolution to believe that life will not be as good for our children and grandchildren as it has been for us. When asked whether citizens think that people's lives will be worse in the future, on average 56 per cent of Britons think they will be. In particular, 61 per cent of Britons believe that future earnings will fall in the wake of Chinese and Indian competition, while 83 per cent believe that inequalities will rise over the coming decades and 70 per cent believe that cost of medical treatment will become unaffordable.[4] However, what is striking about this data is the fact that this pessimism is not unique to the UK. Although the British are more pessimistic than the EU-wide average, on the majority of issues the French, Germans and Italians appear to be in a worse state of pessimism than Britons.[5]

Is this pessimism well founded? Our aim here is to paint a broad-brushed picture of British social trends and highlight the new social risks that these entail. In the next section we look at some of the key trends that are shaping Britain today: the shift to a knowledge and service economy; gender equality; life expectancy and the ageing society; the impact of globalisation; and the individualisation of values. Rather than indicating a 'broken Britain', they suggest a society undergoing rapid change, with new opportunities and risks which Britons are unequally equipped to take advantage of.

A reality check? Social and economic patterns in Britain

The shift to a knowledge and service economy
The last thirty years have seen a dramatic shift in the occupational structure of Britain. This shift has had a profound impact on social

relations in Britain and the constituencies from which social democrats have traditionally gained support. Although often attributed to globalisation, in truth the new occupational structure largely reflects technological advances and shifts in consumer demand as European societies have become richer. The number of jobs in the EU15's knowledge-based sectors has risen by a quarter since the mid-1990s, four times the rate of jobs growth for the economy as a whole. These changes in Europe's economic structure have engineered new occupational divisions. Most European countries are rapidly becoming post-industrial and predominantly knowledge-based economies; the UK is no exception and in fact is further down the road towards the knowledge economy than many of its European counterparts.

In 1978, more than six million jobs, or 29 per cent of the UK total, were in manufacturing; by 2007, that figure was three million out of a workforce of twenty-nine million, or 11 per cent. To highlight this decline is not to deny the continuing economic importance of manufacturing in terms of productivity growth, added value and exports.[6] But the social significance of the decline of traditional working-class jobs in core manufacturing is huge given that they were typically male, unionised and often seen in their communities as 'good' jobs.

Alongside this, there has been a large increase in jobs in the finance and business services sectors, where numbers doubled between 1978 and 2007 to 5.7 million. Meanwhile the number of jobs in the distribution, hotels and catering industries increased from 1.8 to 6.5 million; those in public administration, education and health increased from 2.2 to 7.3 million. This became the sector with the largest number of employees in 2007, although, overall, four-fifths of British workers are employed in the private sector.[7]

The story of the last thirty years is not simply a shift of similar jobs to different sectors. One of the most striking features of the modern British and European labour markets is the rising demand for skills, and not necessarily for so-called 'traditional' skills. At least a quarter of jobs are now thought to require IT skills in some shape or form. 'Personal' skills are often also important in the increasing number of service jobs that demand direct contact with customers and clients. There has been a concomitant growth in low-skilled service jobs in both the public and private sectors, alongside the rapid erosion of 'good working-class jobs' – principally for men. Maarten Goos and Alan Manning have argued that that the UK labour market has effectively hollowed out since 1975, assuming an hourglass shape as it displays a pattern of job polarisation with rises in the employment shares of the highest- and lowest-wage occupations.[8] Many traditionally highly skilled jobs such as compositing and graphic design in the printing trade and machine tool making in engineering have disappeared as a result of the information technology revolution and digitalisation. The same is now happening to once 'safe' clerical jobs in functions such as accounting and book keeping. This shift towards a labour market polarised by 'lovely' and 'lousy' jobs is mirrored across Europe. Although there is still a demand for 'traditional' skills, some of these skills are subject to low-cost competition and outsourcing.

The position of unskilled workers in the labour market is generally worsening, particularly for men in areas of manufacturing decline. Although there have been plenty of job vacancies over the last decade, the available jobs have not been evenly spread throughout the country, they have often required relocation and they have lacked the same long-term protections as before. The growth in insecure work and the steady decline of trade union presence have been powerful factors in the increasing vulnerability of unskilled workers. Many men, moreover, may feel demeaned by the 'McJobs' in the service sector that have replaced more traditional semi-skilled and unskilled positions in large, unionised, industrial firms because the new service jobs appear to them not only to offer little status or sense of self-worth, but also to require face-to-face social skills with people outside the immediate experience of traditional working-class communities. This could in part explain the growth in labour market inactivity among older ex-industrial workers, as well as the problems that low-skilled or unskilled young people experience in attempting to gain a foothold in the labour market. Those who feel excluded from today's labour market are more liable to problems of long-term sickness, mental illness or drug and alcohol abuse. As a result, the numbers of claimants of incapacity benefits can remain stubbornly high even in areas of labour demand.

The deteriorating situation of low-skilled and unskilled workers is compounded by the fact that trade union density has sharply fallen in the UK. Most of this occurred as a result of the decline of traditional industries and the labour shake-out in the utilities that followed privatisation in the last decade. Density fell from 32.6 per cent in 1995 to 28.4 per cent in 2006.[9] Union density in the public sector is still high enough to be influential, but private sector union membership has declined rapidly.

In spite of these rapid changes in occupational structure, the overall employment rate in the UK was over 71 per cent in 2006, meaning that the UK has already reached the target for 2010 of 70 per cent employment across the EU, which the Council of the EU set at Lisbon in March 2000.[10] However, UK youth unemployment was still at 13.7 per cent in spring 2008 – more than double the standard unemployment rate.[11] Employment rates also vary a great deal within the UK: in 2006 the highest regional working-age employment rate in England was in the South-East at 78 per cent, while London for all its riches had the lowest with 69 per cent. Scotland had the highest employment rate of Britain's constituent nations (76 per cent), while Northern Ireland had the lowest (71 per cent); save for West Somerset, London also contained all the local authority areas in the UK with employment rates lower than 60 per cent in the boroughs of Tower Hamlets, Newham and Hackney.[12] These figures pre-date the impact of the global financial crisis in 2008.

While the unemployment rate for the EU27 was on a downward trajectory until 2008,[13] it is notable that this did not necessarily lead to an increase in secure employment. Contractual insecurity takes many forms, among which are agency work and fixed-term contracts for periods too short to entitle a worker to statutory employment rights. In its support of the UK's prolonged resistance to EU legislation extending employment rights to agency workers, which the UK ended in 2008, the Confederation of British Industry estimated that there were 1.4 million agency workers in the UK, with half of agency placements lasting less than twelve weeks and therefore exempt from coverage of the new rights.

Across the EU and in the UK part-time work now accounts for around one-fifth of employment, having grown slightly over the last twenty years. However, as a form of flexible work it is heavily concentrated among women, often offering employment opportunity to those who at a particular stage in their lives do not wish to work full time. In the UK the introduction of the national minimum wage in 1998 introduced a floor for hourly wages (now the third highest in the EU) and prevented employer exploitation. Low-paid workers were also supported by the introduction of tax credits. As Richard Dickens and Abigail McKnight conclude: 'Overall the evidence suggests that WFTC [working families tax credit] benefited a larger number of low wage families with higher average awards [than the family credit system that preceded it] and improved employment retention among male recipients without a detrimental impact on wage growth.'[14] They found no evidence that employers had used WFTC to keep wage growth down, largely because of the simultaneous introduction of the national minimum wage.

Nevertheless, many people undeniably face marginalisation and insecurity in the British labour market. The worst of low-wage poverty and exploitation has been addressed but, again according to Dickens and McKnight, low-paid workers often find themselves stuck in dead-end jobs. 'Alternative policies are required to improve job progression: a job is a step in the right direction but not an automatic leg-up onto a jobs ladder.'[15]

Yet there is a curious paradox at play in European labour markets. Citizens not only claim to be largely satisfied with their jobs, but job quality appears to have risen. In the UK the proportion of people in employment working more than 45 hours per week has steadily decreased from 26 per cent at the start of 1997 to 20 per cent in summer 2008.[16] The 1,673 hours worked annually by Britons is on average 121 hours more than their fellow Europeans at 1,552 but 144 hours less than their US cousins at 1,817. Some of this differential is involuntary, but less in the UK than on the Continent, and some a matter of choice. Key workplace risks have also lessened. Safety has vastly improved with the decline of heavy manual and industrial work. Between 1994 and 2004 the incidence rate of accidents leading to more than three days off work fell by 29 per cent. However, Steve Tombs and David Whyte show that at least 1,300 people died as a result of fatal occupational injuries in 2005/6 in England and Wales. This evidence is significant, since the figure is almost double the equivalent number of homicide victims: an interesting insight into the media and the public's perception of social risks.[17]

There are further stresses and risks of polarisation despite this greater leisure time and largely safer working environment. Among European workers, 28 per cent feel that their health is at risk because of work, or declare themselves to be suffering from health problems caused by work or made worse by their current or past employment.[18] While accidents are in decline, work intensity may also be rising. High rates of sickness absence are a problem in many European societies. It has been estimated that in the UK on average seven days per employee are lost each year to sick days, amounting to a loss of 175 million working days and a cost of £13 billion to the British economy.[19] The public sector has the highest absence average: nine days per employee as against only 6.3 days in the private sector.

Trends to gender equality

Undoubtedly one of the biggest transformations in European society over the last thirty years has been in the position of women. Full gender equality remains unachieved – not only in terms of equal job opportunities but also in the equal sharing of responsibility for childcare between mothers and fathers. Yet the general picture is one of considerable advance. The EU's Lisbon agenda target of 60 per cent female workforce participation is now exceeded by more than 5 percentage points in the UK. Although across the EU the gender gap in employment rates is still more than 10 percentage points and there is a difference of more than 15 points in male to female employment rates for 55–64-year-olds, this has narrowed considerably.[20]

However, the World Economic Forum shows that the UK's gender gap lags behind that of the Nordic countries, Germany, New Zealand, the Philippines and Sri Lanka – especially in terms of wage equality.[21] Of the overall workforce, female part-time workers comprise 40 per cent, but male part-timers only 10 per cent. At the same time, the gender pay gap in the UK is still strikingly high at 20 per cent, though it is considerably down on what it once was.[22] Sectoral and occupational segregation by gender remains high, with female employment levels rising in sectors already dominated by women. Women are heavily represented in the expanding low-skilled sector – for instance, health and social care workers, as well as jobs in hotels, shops, cafés and supermarkets. Among top jobs, the presence of female managers in companies has remained at a third,

while only 20 per cent of MPs are women.[23] The Equality and
Human Rights Commission's 2008 report looking at women in the
highest positions of power and influence across the public and private
sectors suggests a worrying trend of reversal or stalled progress. Of
twenty-five professional categories, there was a year-on-year
decline in women holding posts in twelve, and in a further five
numbers were unchanged.[24] This data sits uneasily alongside increasing
female educational attainment. Women record higher levels of educational achievement than men across the EU; in the UK 80.3 per cent
of women aged 20–24 had reached at least upper secondary school
in 2006, while men could only muster 77.3 per cent.[25] Furthermore,
a majority of recent university graduates are women.

Declining fertility is the other side of the coin of greater gender
equality. In the UK the fertility rate in 2007 was 1.9 – its highest
level since 1980, but in an overall trend towards lower reproduction
rates since the turn of the 1970s. Improved access to contraception,
the participation of women in higher education, the delay of family
formation and increased childlessness over the last thirty years have
all played their part in the story of Britain's falling fertility. However,
the modest increase in the fertility rate since 2001 is worth noting,
if only to highlight the range of factors affecting women's reproduc-
tive choices. Analysis of census data indicates this change is not simply
due to immigration, as is commonly supposed. In 2006, one-fifth of
UK births were to non-UK-born mothers, whose average fertility
rate is 2.54. But the vast majority of women of child-bearing age are
UK born, and their specific fertility rate has risen to 1.79.[26] Nor is
teenage pregnancy the reason. Britain may have one of the highest
rates of teenage pregnancy in Europe, but this still affects only just
over two in every hundred 15–19-year-olds.[27]

In 2007, women in the 30–34 age band had the highest fertility
of any age group, while the mean age for first births rose to 29.3.
This suggests that the earlier fall in the birth rate had been due to
women postponing the birth of their first child. Whether women of
child-bearing age today will in the end have the same-sized family
as earlier cohorts of women is at this stage unknown. There is,
however, some survey evidence for Europe as a whole that the present
generation of women reaching the end of their child-bearing years
have had fewer children than they ideally would have wished: on this

measure average family size is at least 10 per cent smaller than it would otherwise have been.

The changing structure of the family is a significant factor here. The dual-earner household is increasingly the socio-economic norm. The relative prosperity of a family is no longer dependent on the salary and status of the 'male breadwinner'; instead, it is the earning power of both partners and the long-term stability of their relationship that are the crucial factors in determining relative prosperity and risk of poverty. In the EU15, it appears that it is those countries with the most easily accessible childcare where the birth rate has been maintained and female participation in the labour market is highest. In the Nordic region, the fertility rate has risen in Denmark and Finland, though it has fallen a little in Sweden. These member states offer, alongside accessible childcare provision, a variable mix of child benefits and flexible working time to facilitate the combination of part-time work with child bearing. From birth to the age of three in Belgium, Denmark, France, the Netherlands and Sweden, childcare provision covers more than 35 per cent of children. In 2005, the member states with the highest public expenditure on day care were Denmark, Sweden, Finland and France, ranging from 1.7 to 0.7 per cent of GDP, while Austria, Germany and Greece spend 0.4 per cent. In 2005, UK coverage was patchy and public expenditure low, though in recent years it has been rising fast. By 2007/8 the number of childcare places had doubled in a decade and nearly 3,000 children's centres, focused on deprived areas, were planned (building on the earlier success of SureStart) but government spending on early years and childcare, even at more than £5 billion, was still less than 0.4 per cent of GDP.

Increasing life expectancy and an 'ageing' society
European societies are now populated by fewer children and young people and far more retirees. People are living longer and fertility, whatever the short-term trend, has declined considerably from the baby-boomer years. There is little sign that the UK is bucking these trends. The number of people aged sixty-five and over is expected to exceed the number aged under sixteen by 2021. We should not forget the gains in human welfare. In Britain, the twentieth century saw the largest ever recorded advance in

human life expectancy. Life expectancy at birth is now 77.1 for men and 81.1 for women.

These demographic shifts represent profound social change. The increasingly cone-shaped distribution of European and British populations will have a substantial impact. It will increase pressures on public expenditure and taxation while at the same time reducing the potential for economic dynamism and productivity growth. It will have big consequences for consumer behaviour, social norms, infrastructure and structures of welfare provision. This is not to mention political priorities, because the over-sixties are, of all age groups, the most likely to exercise their vote.

The abolition of extreme levels of poverty and the wide availability of (comprehensive) healthcare have contributed to longer lives. Social insurance provisions and pensions have greatly reduced humiliating and undignified poverty for the elderly. Indeed, older people now have a greater share of national wealth and income than ever before and for many the experience of an 'ageing' society is one of a long and comfortable retirement. There are, however, three significant caveats.

First, within the EU there are still serious issues of poverty: one in six over-65s, chiefly women living alone, live in poverty – some twelve million people. In the UK, according to Help the Aged, one in five of the pensioner population is living in poverty, with many struggling to survive on less than £6,000 per year.[28] This amounts to approximately two million people, with the same number failing to claim all the benefits to which they are entitled.

Second, a far wider group of older people suffers from loneliness as well as the need for social and medical care. Help the Aged found that 77 per cent of people in the UK expect to be living independently in their own homes into very old age.[29] Indeed, more than a third of British elderly people now live alone, including half of women over the age of sixty-five, while nearly half a million pensioners leave their homes only once a week and a further 300,000 are completely housebound. The situation can be so bleak and lonely for elderly people that Help the Aged reported that the only daily human contact some of these pensioners have is with their postman[30] and almost half of older people say that television is their main form of company.[31]

Third, although the number varies from country to country, between one- and two-thirds of over-75s are dependent on some form of social and medical care, albeit mostly on an informal basis. Although rising life expectancy is an apposite measure of good health, healthy-life years are fewer. The number of years fully enjoyed without serious illness or disability is for men on average only 63.2, and for women 65.

The impact of globalisation

Globalisation is often seen as the overarching force driving social and economic change in our society. Anton Hemerijck argues that international competition is challenging the redistributive scope of the national welfare state; the increase in cross-border competition in the market for goods and services has reduced the leeway of nation states as the increased openness of the European economies exposes states to trade competition and permits free transnational flows of capital.[32] Moreover, as Maurizio Ferrara notes, we have now also entered into an era of 'semi-sovereign welfare states' thanks to the enmeshment triggered by successive waves of European integration.[33]

For all the focus on globalisation, it is important not to gloss over the impact of regionalisation within the EU itself for the upheaval in social realities that is occurring. Europe has been transformed over the past twenty years through massive structural reforms. Of importance here are the single market, capital mobility and economic and monetary union, as well as successive waves of enlargement and its implications for the free movement of labour. This market has eased the rationalisation of traditional manufacturing by multinational firms and has impacted heavily upon traditional working-class employment. Enlargement, meanwhile, has facilitated a further round of supply chain reorganisation in Europe as most manufacturing can be undertaken more efficiently in the eastern bloc of newer EU member states – and of course migration within the EU has dramatically changed the composition of the labour market.

Nevertheless, the effects of globalisation are evident elsewhere. The bubble of bloated bonuses in the financial services sector may now have burst as the effects of the global financial crisis bite, yet neo-liberalism and the culture of deregulation have not only incentivised unacceptably high-risk investments which now need to be regulated, but also created vast polarising inequalities within European societies. However, it is worth noting that in Britain much of this growth in inequality has been driven by the pulling away of the top 0.5 per cent of society – the so-called 'super-rich'. Income inequality among the remaining 99.5 per cent of the population has fallen since 2000.

Nonetheless, the prospect of increasing socio-economic polarisation is a serious one, given the bleak prospects for unskilled and uneducated British workers in a global age. If the supply of low-skilled and unskilled labour continues to exceed demand in Britain and the wider EU, this is likely to drive down wages for this group in real terms. This would accentuate inequalities, as demonstrated by the declining real wages of the low skilled in the United States for most of the past three decades, apart from during the Clinton boom in the late 1990s, when strong demand for labour, plus more generous earned income tax credits, strengthened their relative position. Some argue that the decline of the low skilled could be entrenched if the flow of migrants into Britain and the EU remains unstemmed, but the evidence on this point is so far mixed.

Migration, external and internal, is, however, changing the face of our cities. The likelihood that cities such as Birmingham and Leicester will soon have non-white majorities is well known. What is less well understood are the complex and differing patterns of internal and external migration. During the twentieth century there was a movement of population from the north of England, Scotland and Wales to the Midlands and the south-east as workers were forced by the decline in the coal, shipbuilding and steel industries to seek work in light industry and the service sector. So far the twenty-first century has seen a reversal of this trend in internal migration, with a net gain to the north every year since 2001 and the south recording a loss of as many as 35,000 people in 2003. (The north–south divide for this purpose was defined as a straight line running roughly between Gloucester and Grimsby.) London has seen the greatest net reduction through internal migration every year for at least three decades, losing an average of 60,000 people annually. However, there was a net inflow of around 191,000 people to the UK in 2006, which is the equivalent of adding a little over 500 people to the population each day. London remained the most popular destination and its population loss was more than offset by the inflow of around 170,000 international migrants settling there. The south-east was the next most popular destination with more than 80,000 new arrivals. Between 1998 and 2003, total net immigration to the UK remained fairly steady at around 150,000 a year; this increased sharply to 244,000 in 2004 but then eased off to an estimated 191,000 in 2006, as mentioned above.[34]

More individualist values
British society is becoming more secular, heterogeneous and post-materialist. This is a consequence of a whole complex of factors. Some are structural: changes in the world of work, the decline of old class divisions, the spread of higher education and greater socio-economic mobility and transience. Others reflect value shifts, such as the idea that life is an autobiography one writes for oneself, concepts of gender equality that challenge traditional gender roles, new sexual freedoms and the decline in religious practice.

Britons live in an increasingly post-materialist society, where the basic needs of consumption are satisfied. This is reflective of Abraham Maslow's 'hierarchy of needs'[35] and has driven the demand side of the shift towards a knowledge economy. Today's citizens prioritise well-being; as consumers they now demand organic food, personal trainers and counselling. Business now seeks all kinds of consultancy, while politicians feel pressured to identify with 'green' concerns. The advent of mass affluence is crucial here. The availability of the internet and a mobile communications system, as well as the ability to travel freely and widely, has broken down the barriers of cultural isolation and insular industrial communities.

These shifts are reconfiguring the traditional notions of the family unit and weakening the hold of the extended family. Across Europe as a whole the divorce rate has virtually doubled in a single genera-tion. Approximately a quarter of families in the UK are headed by lone parents, the vast majority of whom are women. Divorce tends to be higher the more secular the society, with the UK having one of the highest divorce rates. More significant, though, is that today's couples are increasingly prepared to have children outside formal marriage; in the UK more than 40 per cent of children are born out of wedlock. Marriage is no longer necessarily a good indicator of relationship stability, if it ever was. More people now live with a partner without being married. Moreover, Britain is now also increasingly tolerant of diverse sexuality and lifestyles: 55 per cent of Britons believe that same-sex couples should be allowed to marry – though only 44 per cent believe that they should be able to adopt children; 60 per cent of British people believe the ages of consent for homosexual and heterosexual intercourse should be the same, though 24 per cent think gay sex should be made illegal.[36]

It is this evolution of values that in part fuels the notion of a 'broken Britain' and arouses intense controversy. Some argue that in response to these trends public policy should be redesigned to strengthen the institution of marriage. A report from the Centre for Social Justice, established by the former Conservative leader Iain Duncan Smith, argued that pre-nuptial agreements should become legally binding and cohabiting couples refused the same rights as those who wed.[37] Measures would also be taken to improve access to children for fathers and grandparents. An alternative view is that public policy should be designed to support stable relationships and promote the welfare of children, leaving to one side questions of marriage or sexual preference. This seems more realistic in terms of the realities and real behaviours of modern British life, though the ideal of successful marriage still has considerable emotional purchase.

The new social risks in the light of these trends

In this section we discuss the social risks that individuals face in the light of our preceding analysis of trends. In particular we focus on the 'new' risks that have emerged since the welfare state was introduced in the immediate post-war era. We look at this by analysing the course of an individual life. William Beveridge, the iconic British champion of universal welfare provision, argued that the purpose of a welfare state was to ensure the protection and support of citizens from the 'cradle to the grave'. But that mindset was not followed through in post-war welfare state policy making. Policy quickly became compartmentalised by function – social security, pensions, employment, health and education, for example – rather than by an integrated assessment of social risks and needs as they affect life at various critical stages – the needs of babies and young children; schooling and entry to the labour market; family formation; mid-life crises and transitions; and older age, retirement and the final years.

This analysis of new risks during the life course is consistent with the current emphasis on life chances in the design of social policy. The post-war welfare state was designed to cope with the major social risks of its time such as unemployment, sickness, industrial injury, widowhood and old age. The nature of these risks has changed: poverty has become more extensive among people in work; spells of temporary employment as a result of fluctuations in economic activity have for some become structural unemployment and long-term inactivity for working-age people; the incidence of industrial injury has declined, but mental stress and illness have become significant risks. The old welfare state's commitment to horizontal social transfers between the generations looks unsustainable in the light of demographic change and the need for 'active ageing'. The causes of variation in economic circumstance through the life course have become more complex, and include such issues as relationship breakdown and problems with maintenance payments and the wide differences between the asset rich and the asset poor as a result of increases in home ownership and large swings in the house price cycle.

Birth and early years

In the past, in the search for equal opportunity, social reformers tended to load expectations onto schools for transforming life chances, but these have proved impossible to fulfil. What determines life chances is often already set in stone by the time a child reaches school. Disadvantages have their roots in family breakdown, parenting skills (or the lack thereof), ethnic background and discrimination, chronic ill health and disability, unemployment and poverty, and the character of the neighbourhood where children are raised.

Poverty is still a powerful factor in determining life chances, even before birth. Across the EU, 10 per cent of all children live in jobless households; in the UK, the figure is rather higher at one-sixth. Indeed, poor children experience a disproportionate share of disadvantage, deprivation, ill health and poor levels of educational attainment. When these children reach adulthood, they are more likely to become unemployed, to get low-paid jobs requiring few or no skills, to live in social housing and to be the subject of a police investigation, and they are more at risk of alcohol and substance abuse problems. Moreover, in most countries they are likely to transfer their poverty of opportunities onto their own children, thereby entrenching generational inequalities.

Under New Labour, more than half a million children have been lifted out of poverty. This is a significant and laudable reduction, which has been achieved through a resourceful policy agenda. However, if child poverty is to be abolished by 2020, as Prime Minister Blair promised, anti-poverty measures need to be widened beyond tax credits. The Joseph Rowntree Foundation (JRF) has proposed a new, more comprehensive strategy that focuses on reducing worklessness (especially in two-parent families where only one partner is in low-paid work), raising child benefits (for non-working families in addition to the present reliance on in-work benefits) and labour market strategies to improve working parents' incomes. This can be achieved, the JRF argues, through measures that, for example, make childcare more affordable and comprehensive in a post-industrial labour market, facilitate job flexibility for parents, especially vis-à-vis working patterns, and ensure that government agencies provide support that genuinely responds to parents' needs. Ultimately, this policy agenda must repair any pre-existing mistrust between parents and the state; this will facilitate the creation of a reliable social security system that helps families escape poverty.[38] There is not only a social and moral incentive for this, but an economic one too: child poverty costs the UK at least £25 billion per year, including £17 billion that could accrue to the Exchequer if it were to be eradicated. Although the elimination of child poverty would not lead to these returns in the short term, huge sums would be saved through not having to remedy child poverty and its associated social ills in the long term.[39] But realising these social benefits depends on the government's willingness to make a down payment on increased public expenditure in order to ensure that a further two million children are hoisted above the relative poverty line.

Yet even as child poverty and embedded disadvantage blight life chances at the bottom, the children of better-off parents receive more attention, with sustained parental efforts made – unprecedented in previous generations – to ensure their educational success. There is more homogamy in modern relationships; clever educated men are more likely to partner with clever educated women than in previous generations. Along with other European countries, Britain has concomitantly entered the 'prized child' era. For the middle classes and those with higher education, having a child has now largely become an act of conscious choice, in which the promotion of the child's perceived welfare has become the central preoccupation of their parents' relationship. As a result we have seen the advent of 'helicopter parenting', in which parents intervene to an unprecedented degree in their child's educational activities. 'Pushy parenting', meanwhile, can also lead to distress and sentiments of feeling unloved in children affected by (perceived) parental pressures on their educational attainment and social success. Clearly, the 'prized child', 'helicopter parenting' and 'pushy parents' phenomena are principally ones of affluence; not all parents have the socio-economic means to subject their children to these pressures or provide them with such material pleasures.

Less advantaged families have fewer resources to manage the enormous pressures of the work–life balance, which they often put on themselves in order to meet their aspirations for a decent standard of living. But concern for child welfare is widespread across society, with an explosion of concerns for children's physical safety and the prevention of abuse. The tragic handful of cases of gross child neglect and abuse receive enormous media attention, but there is little publicly expressed concern for the significant number of parents who are struggling to do their best for their children according to their own (albeit perhaps limited) lights, against heavy odds.

Anton Hemerijck argues that access to 'affordable quality childcare is *sine qua non* for any future equilibrium' in European societies;[40] it enables mothers to go back to work and helps them to be better parents. Inaccessible childcare entrenches low fertility, low-quality childcare is harmful to childhood development, and low female employment raises child poverty levels. Moreover, it is in single-parent families that children are at the highest risk of poverty and social instability, as Anastasia de Waal has recently demonstrated.[41] A third of children in single-parent households are at risk of poverty.

Schooling and entry into the labour market

Social reformers have always imagined that widening educational opportunities was the route to a truly meritocratic society. But the challenge is much more complex than was once imagined. Public spending on education is a necessary, though not sufficient, condition for extending educational opportunity. Although, in 2006/7, the UK spent 5.5 per cent of GDP on education,[42] the OECD has been unable to demonstrate a clear relationship between relative spending levels and levels of educational achievement.

The argument is often made that in a knowledge society a significant section of the population is condemned to a diminishing supply of unskilled work because they lack the intelligence to acquire skills, but empirical evidence seems to discount this line of thought. The EU's total number of pupils without basic reading proficiency still languishes at an unacceptable average of 19.8 per cent, although Finland has reduced this number to 5.7 per cent (further reducing it to 2.4 per cent for girls). The Netherlands and Ireland have also reduced theirs to 11 per cent. These figures cannot only be explained by differences in intelligence levels; instead, they can be accounted for by the quality of teaching, the performance of national curricula and deeper social factors that determine pupil aspiration and engagement.

Education is widely perceived as the gateway to social mobility. To ask a majority of European citizens about what matters to get on in life is to discover that most people view hard work and educational attainment as the overwhelming factors in this respect, not the luck of birth or the perpetuation of widespread social injustices. The centrality of educational opportunity is reflected in rising university attendance numbers. Yet if we compare the proportion of students attending university from graduate homes as opposed to those from homes with no educational qualifications, we discern a massive gap that cannot be exclusively accounted for by differences in natural intelligence.[43] In Britain this failure in state education is often excused on the basis that better-off parents educate their children in the private school system and thereby remove the leavening of able pupils from the state system.

The hollowness of this explanation is highlighted by cross-European comparisons, where few parents go private but many manipulate public education systems to their children's advantage, as in the UK.

These facts raise serious questions about the persistence of inequality and embedded disadvantage in British society. Education outcomes matter far more today because education in the knowledge economy makes a huge difference to life prospects. Simply put, the better educated you are, the less risk you run of becoming unemployed. In 2007, 88 per cent of working-age people in the UK with a tertiary-level educational qualification were in employment, compared with 47 per cent of those with no qualifications. Indeed, people with a tertiary education earn 120 per cent of the national median wage. Only 7 per cent are at risk of poverty, compared to 20 per cent of those with only low-level qualifications. In the old economy, early school leavers could get by without higher qualifications; in the new economy, such people are almost certainly guaranteed to lose out. Yet, despite New Labour's commitment to 'education, education, education', more than one-fifth of 18–24-year-olds are still in no form of education or training, and have left school early. And in every one of the EU25, boys leave school earlier than girls. These are shocking figures for a country and a continent that aspire to retain their relative prosperity and living standards in a globalised world.

The expansion of higher education not only offers well-attested benefits in terms of increased earning power, it has also profoundly affected middle-class attitudes: women, for instance, are far more likely to pursue a career if they have a degree. There are, nonetheless, serious issues to do with feelings of failure and alienation from those who do not make it through the education system, which can often have a detrimental impact on wider society in the form of anti-social behaviour, crime and chronic unemployment. Educational opportunity is perceived as being pretty universally on offer. Yet, for all its meritocratic advantages, it is a source of optimism only for those who succeed; to a not insignificant minority, it is deeply alienating. This is an equally profound but much less discussed challenge. For those who fail in the education system, there is a loss of self-esteem accentuated by the decline of 'good working-class jobs' that once offered young men status and security. This makes it less likely that they will settle into stable long-term relationships. In many countries there are growing problems of alcoholism, drug abuse and mental illness as young people are unable to cope with the hand that society has dealt them. The large (and in some cases growing) numbers of young people not in education, employment or training bodes ill for their ability to settle satisfactorily in the longer term.

In the shift towards a knowledge economy, lifelong learning is vital. The Lisbon agenda proposes a threshold of 12.5 per cent of all European adults participating in such learning programmes by 2010. The EU27's average in 2006 was 10.4 per cent for women and 8.8 per cent for men; the UK's figures were much higher at 31.2 and 22 per cent respectively.[44]

However, the lifelong learning process is equally biased to those that have already succeeded in gaining qualifications: provision is inverse to need. This has a reinforcing effect on educational inequalities.[45] One issue is whether a more determined government could intervene directly in the labour market to introduce training provision and enable low-paid workers to raise their earning power in rapidly growing sectors where there is evidence of 'market failure' in skills and firms find themselves unable to break out of a low-pay, low-productivity economic model. This could well hold true for rapidly expanding sectors such as residential and home care for older people, as well as hotels and catering. The model of Ernest Bevin's wartime Catering Wages Act comes to mind.

Intergenerational social mobility may well be in gradual decline, though Jo Blanden and Stephen Machin argue that this decline 'may well have flattened out', since, in particular, there was no change in the relationship between test score performance around the age of five and family income from the mid-1980s to the turn of the millennium.[46] If corrective mechanisms are not created, the knowledge economy could polarise society. Moreover, the life chances of low-skilled workers seeking a 'second chance' in the European labour market are particularly poor, especially the difficulties that working-class men experience of transferring vocational training into the life skills demanded by the knowledge economy.

Family formation
Patterns of family formation in European societies are changing, often taking place later in life than was usual thirty years ago. This is

the consequence of a number of factors. Academically successful young people stay in education longer. They sometimes get into debt in order to complete their studies. A study of women at the age of forty in 2000 showed sharp differences in levels of childlessness according to educational attainment. Less than a fifth of women who had left school with low educational qualifications remained childless, whereas this was true for a quarter of graduate women and a third of the tiny minority who had a master's degree or higher.[47] In certain countries graduates have great difficulty finding an entry-level job that pays a salary that matches their skills and qualifications. The work of Louis Chauvel on the French labour market shows how generational inequalities have grown sharply in a society where income inequality on average has been more stable than in other parts of Europe.[48] But the same effect could be observed in the UK as a result of the impact of sharply rising house prices (up to 2007) on the ability of first-time buyers to set up their own home and the pressure on their stretched disposable income. This puts pressure on the young just at the time they are thinking of establishing a family. Rising house prices have led to a reliance of first-time buyers on parental sources for assistance in deposit and mortgage payments. A JRF report concluded that 'home ownership may increasingly become the preserve of the children of existing homeowners'.[49]

This is the so-called 'generation Y' phenomenon, contrasting with the 'baby-boomer' one. The JRF report shows that over the past thirty years the UK has witnessed the emergence of fractured and extended transitions to adulthood; a steady increase in the proportion of young people in the parental home – more commonly boys than girls; younger people adopting a 'live for today' attitude to financial planning; rising levels of student debt diminishing some of the financial advantages previously linked to graduate status; and a steady decrease in proportion of mortgage borrowers in their twenties.[50]

The salience of housing as a major social and 'quality of life' issue has re-emerged. Serious problems of accessibility to housing exist in certain European countries, especially in fast-growing regions where there have been high levels of inward migration. Of particularly grave concern are Greater London and the south-east of England in the UK. Indeed, the rapid rise in house prices in recent years has the potential to be a major social risk, posing problems of affordability

in good times and the risk of negative equity and repossessions in
bad times.

There are other serious issues that influence family formation.
While the gender employment gap continues to narrow and sexual
equality becomes an entrenched value in European society, pressure
on the work–life balance continues to increase. This pressure threatens
the sustainability of the 'dual earner' model that underscores modern
family life. In the UK, for instance, the debate about the family has
been sidetracked into a discussion about the status and benefits of
marriage, when instead it should be focused on the inadequacies of tax,
welfare and social support for the dual-earner couple regardless of
their marital status. However, 72 per cent of married and cohabiting
mothers were employed, as were 57 per cent of lone parents – up
4 points on the 2002 figure.[51]

Mid-life crisis?

Among 55–64-year-olds in European societies, 40 per cent of men
and nearly 60 per cent of women have dropped out of the labour
market. To compare employment levels for this age group in 1971
with those in 1999 is to discern a marked fall in its participation in
the labour market: from 83 to 59 per cent in the UK. Bringing these
inactive groups back into work is a major social challenge faced not
only by the UK but by her European partners, too: the risk is that
inactivity becomes embedded through the generations.

Indeed, while old forms of employment are dissipating, new jobs
are being created at a very rapid pace. And young people are now
very likely to job-hop. While 23 per cent of retired workers and 21 per
cent of the over-55s had never changed employer, the figure is only
16 per cent for younger age groups.[52]

Job changing is not in itself an intrinsically negative trend. For
example, Denmark has one of the highest rates in Europe. But
thanks to the social investment in 'flexicurity' Danish workers fear
job losses less than citizens from any other EU member state. 'Flexicurity' is a proactive labour market policy which combines greater
flexibility to hire and fire for employers with higher security for
employees, such as increased unemployment benefits, but which at
the same time insists on a binding moral commitment to accept
offers of new work and retraining. Some 81 per cent of Britons

agree with the concept of 'flexicurity', but our model is a lot less comprehensive and generous than the Danish one.[53] Yet, if combined with a comprehensive lifelong learning scheme, it would help older British workers to reintegrate into the labour market.

Retirement

Working longer and delaying final retirement is the only viable means of sustaining the welfare provisions of European countries in the face of demographic change and an 'ageing' society. Europeans are living longer and enjoying more 'healthy' years than ever before, not to mention benefiting from increased levels of education in each new generational cohort. An extended working life, as Anton Hemerijck highlights, would be both equitable and effective. 'It is efficient because it operates simultaneously on the nominator and denominator: more revenue intake and less spending at the same time. It is also inter-generationally equitable as retirees and workers both sacrifice in equal proportions.'[54]

That this is the only sensible way of alleviating the increasingly severe pensions burden is self-evident. But most people are resistant to the very principle of extending the age of retirement: only 27 per cent of Britons agree that people retire too early – a significantly lower figure than the 45 per cent average for the EU25.[55] The average age of labour market withdrawal for women and men over fifty was 61.9 and 64.6 respectively in the period April–June 2008.[56] Although there is evidence that is strongly suggestive of age discrimination against older workers who wish to prolong their employment lives, most workers nowadays look forward to a long and leisurely retirement in which, if they are lucky, they can enjoy the fruits of both their labour and their family for decades.

There are, however, dark clouds that overshadow the sustainability of this model. In the light of the cone-shaped demographic challenge now faced by Britain and other European societies, it is unclear whether existing welfare entitlements can be sustained with more retirees. The pension systems of most European countries are under considerable strain, owing to a lack of flexibility and the debilitating and shuddering effects of the 'credit crunch'. There is also a gaping absence of well-developed services and social care for elderly people, who are dependent – almost exclusively – on the state.

A challenge to revisionist social democracy?

Our broad-brushed painting of the socio-economic landscape of 21st-century Britain may illuminate cracks in the canvas of British society. But these blemishes often date back to the persistent long-term unemployment and chronic lack of investment in public services of previous decades, not to mention the new unforeseen and unpredictable impact of globalisation. Yet the notion of a 'broken Britain' seems, at best, nebulous and inconsistent: it is designed with populist appeal to nudge people towards an unclear concept of how society can be changed for the better, and it is conceived and applied in narrow conservative terms that perpetuate the myth that things were better in the 'good old days'. It is always worth remembering that the high point of the post-war myth – the 1950s – occurred in a class-ridden, male-dominated Britain, a country of censorship and repressive social values, tolerant of violence and wife-beating in the home while at the same time intolerant of divorce (except for the upper classes), racial diversity and what was then described as sexual deviance. While grammar schools did extend educational opportunity for clever working-class children who were good at passing the eleven-plus exam, those who failed were dumped in secondary moderns as fit only for a life of manual labour. This retrospective myth is now quite incompatible with the technological realities and moral ideals of today's Britain.

A. C. Grayling argues that to charge individualism as a social evil is to negate the fact that individual liberty 'promotes the widest variety of experiments living good and flourishing lives'. This is especially true given people's propensity to perceive Britain through rose-tinted spectacles. In this respect, Grayling's argument is instructive: 'Every generation thinks that the past was a better place and that its own time is one of crisis.' This is the case even though, by almost any rational standard, contemporary western liberal democratic societies afford better lives for the great majority of people than was the case in the Victorian era or even fifty years ago.[57]

Indeed, right-wing arguments pertaining to the absence or withdrawal of society seem to miss the central point in the 'broken Britain' debate: that society is an evolutionary entity, which shifts according to deep-rooted trends towards individual freedom, processes of technological innovation and collective prosperity. Ben Page shows that the British are mainly bothered about young people and social disorder[58] – but when you focus on why most Britons believe crime is rising, only 23 per cent say it is based on their own experience. Grayling argues that if 'public policy is determined by the attitudes of the more conservative and fretful members of society, who see bogeys under the bed when none such are there, the resulting distortions will be harmful. Arguably, this is indeed the case in our society, and it needs redress.'[59] To lament the decline of traditional concepts of community is not only to overlook the new forms of community created by the internet – ones which are international and multicultural in scope and opportunity – but also to obfuscate the fact that traditional community life was often stultifying and insufficient in terms of reliability, organisation and resourcefulness to shoulder the responsibilities that public institutions can now provide.

Nonetheless, these multiple societal challenges are both serious and potentially destabilising – and revisionist social democrats must keep abreast of them. Brian Brivati has noted that one of New Labour's chief successes was to provide an antidote to the Thatcherite 'no such thing as society' thesis through its focus on fiscal investment in public service provision, allowing Britain to be become a confident and modern nation state – one which no longer perceives itself as in decline.[60] But it is vital that this accomplishment does not result in British social democracy resting on its laurels. Although perceptions of a breakdown in civil intercourse and traditional concepts of society are hyperbolically inflamed, they do highlight an area in which government needs to reconcile increases in individual empowerment and freedom with new forms of state action. In 21st-century Britain, the state needs to overcome allegations of being both out of touch and ineffective. A social democratic governing strategy must not allow the compartmentalisation of its welfare functions to hinder the already notable problems in delivering public service provision – while it must be able to mitigate or prevent new polarities triggered by the seismic shifts of the global financial crisis and future economic challenges, such as the transition to a low-carbon existence, from disadvantaging the 'losers' and consolidating the power of the 'winners' in our society. With the presence of a 24-hour media that can, at its most malevolent, stoke citizens' prejudices and fuel their anxieties, the state must become more mobile, responsive and active to the needs of those it is designed to serve. This is the task of revisionist social democracy now.

3

The electoral map

Peter Riddell

The British electorate has changed substantially over the past sixty years: it is older, more middle class, more affluent, better educated; it is more tolerant and liberal about personal behaviour, but more worried and often authoritarian about threats to its security; it is increasingly impatient about the delivery of public services; but it has often contradictory and inconsistent views about poverty, public spending and taxation. In short, there is no easy or straightforward electoral strategy either for social democrats or for the centre-right.

The centre-left has been prone to alternate bouts of euphoria and depression about its long-term prospects, depending on its immediate electoral situation. But short-term cyclical pressures need to be separated from longer-term structural changes. The one lesson of the post-war period is that any statement of portentous certainty will turn out to be wrong within a few years. Of course, the electorate is changing, but this does not automatically prejudice voters against or for the centre-left. It merely alters the environment in which parties have to operate.

Go back nearly sixty years to Labour's third, and heavy, election defeat in a row in October 1959 by Harold Macmillan's Conservatives. This was the 'never had it so good' election of affluence, immortalised by the Vicky cartoon showing Supermac surrounded by, and thanking, a range of newly available mass consumer goods. Anthony Crosland, then at the peak of his fame and influence as the leading revisionist of his generation, was engaged in a fierce exchange with Richard Crossman. In a Fabian pamphlet of 1960, entitled *Can Labour Win?*, Crosland argued: 'If the necessary changes are not made, the Labour vote will probably decline, unless some sudden crisis supervenes, by about 2 per cent at each general election ... and the pendulum, when it swings against the Tories, will swing towards the Liberals.' On the same theme, Mark Abrams of Research Services Ltd carried out an extensive analysis of Labour's prospects. Originally published in September 1960 in the revisionist monthly *Socialist Commentary* – and then in a tellingly entitled paperback, *Must Labour Lose?* – Abrams 'produced striking evidence of the extent to which Labour had lost touch with the newer elements in the electorate. The party's image remained predominantly working-class, though the number of people regarding themselves as working class was steadily declining.'[1] This is when roughly two-thirds of the electorate were in working-class occupations, either skilled or unskilled manual. Of course, within four years of this pessimism, the Conservatives were defeated, and Harold Wilson and Labour were in, by a narrow margin – though Crosland was correct that the main gainers in share of the vote, though not seats, at the general election in 1964 were the Liberals.

Go forward twenty-eight years to the 1992 general election and Labour's fourth defeat in a row, albeit by a smaller margin than previously. Professor Anthony King was wondering whether Britain had adopted what political scientists call a predominant party system, such as Sweden and Japan then had (but soon relinquished). In 'The Implications of One Party Government', his chapter in a book about the election, King discussed the problems of making Labour more electable:

> The obstacles to be overcome are formidable, consisting as they do of the party's narrowing social base, of its ties to the declining and now largely discredited trade union movement, of an ideology and set of social attitudes that seem firmly anchored in the past, and, perhaps above all, of voters' accumulated suspicions of a party associated in their minds, fairly or unfairly, with high taxation, high inflation, numerous strikes, the endless disruption of public services, and hopelessly incompetent economic management.[2]

Similarly, David Butler and Dennis Kavanagh concluded that the election 'appears more clearly still as a rejection of what was offered by Labour and raised questions about the party's future as a party of government. Nineteen ninety-two echoed the earlier elections and confirmed the Conservatives' dominance over Labour and the imbalance in the British party system.'[3]

These views were widely shared at the time, not least in 1992 by Tony Blair and the Labour modernisers. They adopted a strategy designed both to reduce, if not eliminate, the negatives and to change the party's image in order to broaden its appeal to what were defined as aspirational voters: 'Mondeo man' and 'Worcester woman', of the new middle class. This reflected the influential analysis of Giles, now Lord, Radice, entitled 'Southern Discomfort', which highlighted the challenge for Labour of gaining the support of voters, notably in a swathe of marginal seats in the M25 belt and in the Midlands, who mistrusted the party on economic competence and tax. Blair sought to reinvent Labour to accommodate the social changes of the Thatcher era, to attract many of Thatcher's children to vote for New Labour. The double-edged nature of this repositioning is discussed later.

How different Britain has become was brought out in a presentation in 2006 by Ben Page, director of the Ipsos MORI Social Research Institute (available on its website). Between 1979, the year of Thatcher's first election victory, and 2005, Blair's third win, Page noted the following changes, with my comments in brackets:

- Population had risen by more than four million to over sixty million. [Increasing numbers aged over 65, and a rise in net migration, with 8.3 per cent of people at the 2001 census born abroad, up from 6.2 per cent in 1981.]
- The middle class (defined in conventional terms of professional, managerial and white-collar occupations) had risen from 33 to 54 per cent. Conversely, the number defined as working class on the same basis had declined from 67 to 46 per cent. [These are broad definitions since many service jobs, counted as non-manual, are little different in many essential characteristics from manual jobs in, say, manufacturing. Indeed, several surveys have shown that, despite the big shift in the balance of classes as measured by occupation, nearly three-fifths of people still identify themselves as working class, and fewer than two-fifths as middle class. Female participation, as a percentage of the

adult workforce, rose from 63 to 70 per cent between 1984 and 2005, while male participation rates fell.]

- Trade union membership fell from 30 per cent to 16 per cent of the workforce. [This reflected the contraction of the heavily unionised manufacturing and utilities sectors, the privatisation of most of the latter and the growth of the low-unionised service sector.]

- Self-employment nearly doubled to 16 per cent. [The rise of White Van Man.]

- Home ownership went up from 53 per cent to 72 per cent of the total. [This was partly thanks to the sale of council houses, but it also reflected a more general boom in home ownership, not without its problems with negative equity and repossessions in the early 1990s.]

- Share ownership went up from 7 to 27 per cent. [This was largely a reflection of privatisation and several large building societies becoming public quoted companies rather than remaining as mutuals. Unlike the spread of house ownership, much of the increase was thin with relatively small shareholdings in financial terms.]

- University attendance quadrupled to 43 per cent. [In part this reflected the expansion of former polytechnics, which became universities.]

- Households with a car rose from 57 to 74 per cent. [A sign of increased affluence and strengthening the lobby against green policies such as increased real fuel duties.]

- Mobile phone ownership went from zero to 85 per cent of the adult population. [This produced a big change in social habits and networking, especially among under-forties.]

- Internet access grew from zero to 55 per cent. [There are sharp age and social differences in degrees of internet use, with a vast impact on means of communication and public debate. There is evidence from the report of the twenty-third annual British Social Attitudes (BSA) survey in January 2007 that the internet has not meant a reduction in the amount of time people spend socialising. If anything, internet users are more likely to be socially connected, not less: for instance, by belonging to clubs and organisations, and spending time with friends.]

- Married couples fell from 64 per cent to 52 per cent of house-holds. [This reflected a combination of factors, notably a sharp increase in the number of cohabiting couples as well as a rise in the number of single-person households, both among those in their twenties and among those over seventy.]

Page went on to draw some implications: more couples with both spouses or partners working; better-educated consumers; more pensioners putting more strain and demands on younger workers; longer working hours linked to more holidays for many; more mobility leading to more traffic; more diversity and migration resulting in less cohesion. Overall, this meant more anxiety and a search for security.

These changes have had profound political implications, not least in challenging previous assumptions about the links between class and voting intention. The famous statement of Peter Pulzer in 1968 that class was totally dominant, and 'all else' was 'embellishment and detail', now looks very dated. Even then, between a quarter and a third of working-class people voted Conservative, otherwise the party could never have won a general election. Partisan attachments were never as strong as believed at the time and British politics was not as uniformly tribal as it has been seen in retrospect. By the early 1980s, this model looked inadequate, as fewer working-class people voted for their natural party, Labour, and fewer middle-class people backed their natural party, the Conservatives. There was both class dealignment as class loyalties weakened and the traditional working class shrank in size, and partisan dealignment as the number of people strongly identifying with a particular party declined.[4] According to the invaluable long-term data compiled by the British Election Study (BES), the number of people saying they very strongly identified with a party declined from 44 per cent in 1964 to around 20 per cent in the 1980s, before falling to 8 per cent by the time of the 2005 general election. Even taking very strong and fairly strong identifiers together, the decline was from 84 per cent in 1964 to around 63 per cent in the 1980s, and to just 45 per cent in 2005. By contrast, the number expressing no partisan identification was just 5 per cent in 1964, rising to 14 per cent in the 1980s and 18 per cent in 2005. According to the BES, reinforced by the annual BSA surveys, there has been a marked decline in the strength of the relationship between social class and party identification, from roughly two-thirds in the mid-1960s to a third by 2001. Some critics have sought to reformulate traditional class-based analyses in terms, for example, of private versus public sector status. But these reformulations only modify, rather than negate, the weakening of the link between class and voting.

Parties have not been able to count on traditional or habitual ties. They have to campaign harder to attract support from the less committed, rather than just rely on mobilising the shrinking band of the committed: the floating-versus-core vote dilemma. One result is the falling share of the total vote taken by the Conservatives and Labour together, from a peak of more than 96 per cent in the 1950s down to 75 per cent in 1974 and no more than 81 per cent since then, with a low of 69.5 per cent in 2005.

None of this, however, means that voters lack interest in politics or current affairs. The BES and BSA data have shown a pretty consistent level of around 65 to 70 per cent of the public saying they take an interest in politics. This ranges from 7 to 8 per cent saying 'a great deal', to between 20 and 25 per cent saying 'quite a lot', and 35 to 40 per cent 'some'. That leaves about 25 per cent saying 'not much', and 6 to 9 per cent 'none at all'. Interest, not surprisingly, tends to be higher in general election years than at other times. But the most striking point is the stability of the public's interest in politics over three decades.

This is borne out by the annual surveys carried out by Ipsos MORI for the Hansard Society's Audit of Political Engagement. Those saying they are 'very' or 'fairly' interested in politics have fluctuated in a narrow band of 51 to 56 per cent, with those in the 'not' or 'not at all' interested category in an even narrower 44 to 47 per cent range. A consistent group of 13 per cent very interested has been balanced by 19 per cent not at all interested. The audit shows sharp gender, age and social class divisions, with men very or fairly interested by a 58 to 45 per cent margin compared with women, according to the late 2007 survey (published in 2008 as *Audit of Political Engagement 5*). On the same basis, 18–24-year-olds are only about 50 to 60 per cent as likely to say they are interested as over-55s. And there is roughly a two to one margin of interest between professionals and managers (ABs) and unskilled workers (DEs). These contrasts are matched in questions about perceived knowledge of politics, where a small majority say they do not feel they know very much or anything at all about politics. Contrary to the claims of some advocates of direct democracy, there is no evidence in this or other surveys of a high level of activism: just one in eight people are politically active in the sense of having done two or three things from a list of eight over the past two or three years (signing a petition, boycotting certain products, urging someone to get in touch with a local councillor or MP, presenting their views to a representative, going to a political meeting, taking part in a demonstration, donating money or paying a membership fee to a political party or taking an active part in a political campaign). Nearly half the public has done none of these things.

So there is no evidence for a sudden decline in interest in politics. The British public has always taken a detached view, with few taking an active part, or wishing to do so. Not many people are now, or have ever been, very interested in politics. Satisfaction with the workings of democracy is closely correlated to attitudes towards the performance of political leaders and the government of the day.

In face of the social changes noted above, and the decline of class loyalties, what does motivate voters? Political scientists are not agreed, and there are two main views, which are not incompatible as explanations. The first – reflecting work based on the BES – is that a mixture of issues and party leader images are crucial. This turns on what Professor Donald Stokes called valence issues. These are ones on which there is general agreement about the desirability of the goal, such as low inflation and low unemployment, but where debate centres on which party and which party leader is most likely to achieve that goal.[5] Other examples include healthcare, crime prevention and education. The debate is essentially about delivery and competence. This model of politics also stresses the role of party leader images. It is essentially managerial and consumerist. On this view, the Tories' image of incompetence over Black Wednesday and the subsequent tax increases doomed them, while New Labour won in 1997, and then won re-election in 2001 and, to a lesser extent, in 2005 by conveying an image of competence on the issues of greatest concern to voters. The danger in this analysis is that it can become circular: governing parties lose elections because they fail. But it is not just a matter of competence, or rather incompetence, important though that is. Perceptions of where parties and leaders stand also matter.

Consequently, the second view focuses on positioning – by parties and leaders in relation to the perceived views of voters. This derives from the rational choice approach pioneered by Anthony Downs, with a lively debate about whether being close to a party matters more or less than having the same ideological views. The Downs argument, that successful vote-seeking parties shift their general stance and position on issues in response to voters' policy preferences, can be turned on its head. Shifts in position by parties can, in turn, influence voter attitudes. Neither parties nor voters are passive and unchanging. These two interpretations can exist alongside each other. Voters can both take a view on so-called 'position issues', such as redistribution, and on valence issues, where the key is managerial competence.

Professor John Curtice of Strathclyde University has offered a fascinating analysis of the interaction of these influences. Using the BES data, he shows how Tony Blair succeeded in transforming the image of Labour from its origins as a party promoting the interests of labour and the unions. In 1987, 46 per cent thought that Labour looked after the interests of working-class people 'very closely', while just 6 per cent reckoned it did the same for middle-class people. By 1997, only 33 per cent thought Labour looked after working-class interests 'very closely'. There had been little change in the middle class proportion, but the number thinking Labour looked after middle-class interests 'not very closely' or 'not at all' had declined from 38 to 14 per cent. After four years in power, slightly more people thought that Labour looked 'very closely' after the interests of middle-class than working-class people (14 per cent against 11 per cent). Curtice noted: 'This transformation of the class image of the Labour Party was one of the major achievements of the New Labour project instigated by Blair. Labour was truly "rebranded" under his leadership.'[6]

However, much of the change in the party's image occurred after it came to power rather than beforehand; it was as much a consequence of the style and policies of the Blair government as it was a

result of the pre-1997 election-winning strategy. The same trend was
seen on specific policy positions: again much of the change occurred
after, rather than before, Labour won in 1997. This appears to vindi-
cate Blair's repeated phrase about the importance of governing as
New Labour. For instance, by 2005 voters were as likely to put
Labour to the right of centre on nationalisation as to the left of
centre. The same shift was apparent on attitudes towards more
spending and taxation, getting people back to work versus keeping
prices down, and equalising people's incomes. This rebranding and
repositioning succeeded in ensuring that Labour did relatively better
among middle-class voters and those living in southern England,
even though, in absolute terms, the party continued to draw more
support from working-class voters and from northern England.
There was some evidence of a polarisation of support, with the
Conservatives unable to achieve any local council representation in
big cities such as Newcastle, Sheffield, Liverpool and Manchester
even after their revival in 2006–8 – despite having had MPs in
these cities in the past. This largely reflected social changes within
the cities, with middle-class voters moving to the suburbs. So the
Conservatives were able to make gains in the rural and suburban
areas around these old industrial cities. Consequently, a simple
north/south divide is misleading. A more accurate contrast is
between big city and metropolitan areas and small town and rural
areas, wherever they are in Britain. The electoral battleground lies
between the extremes of inner cities and entirely rural constituencies.

Curtice qualifies this focus on the perceived ideological position
of a leader and his party. 'So long as a party is not beyond the pale
ideologically (as indeed Labour may well have been in the 1980s but
not necessarily by 1994), what matters most in determining whether
its fortunes wax or wane are not perceptions of its ideology but its
competence.'[7] Hence Labour lost votes at the 2005 general election
not because of any shift in its positioning but because of voters'
disillusionment with the Blair government, particularly, but not
exclusively, over the Iraq War. Similarly, following Blair's replacement
by Gordon Brown, Labour suffered because of an impression of
incompetence – over the credit crunch, the 10p tax row and so on
– rather than because of any ideological repositioning.

However, the most intriguing question raised by Curtice's analysis is how far the New Labour rebranding has itself changed the terms of the political debate. In other words, if Labour has moved to the centre under the Blair/Brown team, have many of its supporters and the electorate? If a party moves towards the centre, the centre itself may shift. The BSA data shows that on two key indicators – a belief that unemployment benefits are too low, and that government should redistribute from the better off to the less well off – there was a sharp drop in support from the mid-1990s onwards. Moreover, the decline accelerated after the Blair government took office in 1997. For instance, the number saying that unemployment benefits were too low fell from a peak of 58 per cent in 1993 to 46 per cent by 1997, and continued down to 26 per cent by 2005. On an aggregate of five questions about equality and attitudes to business, support for a left-of-centre position dropped from a peak of 64 per cent in the mid-1990s to 44 per cent by 2005. Curtice argues that 'during Blair's tenure in office Britain changed from being a predominantly left-of-centre country to a majority right-of-centre one'.[8] Moreover, the decline in support for redistribution and for broadly left-of-centre positions was considerably greater among Labour supporters than Conservative ones. The number of Labour identifiers backing redistribution fell from 68 per cent to 39 per cent between 1994 and 2005. By the time Blair left office, only a bare majority of Labour identifiers could be classified as left of centre. This is the nightmare of the Labour left: that a decade of Blairism had discouraged people from supporting the values with which the party had traditionally been associated.

The centrist strategy of Blairism not only produced electoral success but may also have limited the achievements of his government. Professor Pippa Norris has argued that Blair tied his hands in terms of visionary policy change: 'Cautious moderation, located in the centre of Westminster politics, has proved both a blessing and a curse for Blair. It has been the bedrock of his political success and yet the limit of what he can do with his popularity.'[9] Moreover, given the steady decline in the proportion of the electorate who identify with Labour, and other parties, the Blairite electoral success remains contingent rather than relying on lifelong loyalties. It depends on circumstance, perceptions of competence and the positioning of other parties.

The key questions are about attitudes to public expenditure and taxation. The Curtice analysis implies growing resistance to paying higher taxes in order to fund better public services. An analysis in *British Social Attitudes: The 23rd Report*, published at the end of 2006, showed that support for increasing taxes and spending more on health, education and social benefits had declined from a peak of 62/63 per cent in 1997/8 to 46 per cent by 2005. This was the lowest since the high point of Thatcherism in the mid-1980s. Moreover, fewer than two-fifths of 18–34-year-olds favoured increased taxes and spending, compared with a half of those aged fifty-five and over (the latter expecting to use state services more as they age). Over the same period, the number saying they wanted taxes and spending on these services to be kept at the same level as at the time of the survey rose from 31 or 32 per cent to 43 per cent. However, the number saying they wanted reduced taxes and less spending on health, education and social benefits remained in single figures, as it has ever since the question was first asked in 1983. The figure of 7 per cent for tax/spending cuts is double the level of the late 1990s, but that is hardly enough to encourage those who want to roll back the state.

Alternatively, what we may have been seeing is more of a cyclical phenomenon, rather than a longer-term underlying change in attitudes. On this view, support for higher taxes and increased spending on public services peaked at the end of the long Conservative period in government when there were complaints about under-funding of health and education. These charges became a centrepiece of New Labour's campaign before the 1997 general election. At first, the Blair/Brown team was very cautious and stuck tightly to its public pledges of not raising the basic and higher rates of income tax or widening the base of VAT – though indirect means of raising revenue via what became known as stealth taxes caused increasing resentment. However, there seemed to be support for extra taxes provided they went specifically to ends of which voters approved. Consequently, in the 2002 Budget, Brown announced an increase in national insurance contributions paid by both employers and employees. For workers, these had the same effect as an increase in the basic rate of income tax. This was put forward as a means of increasing the NHS budget following a report by Sir Derek Wanless, a former chief executive of NatWest, which pointed to a large funding gap. The initial public reaction was positive because people supported the stated goal of the tax rise, an increase in spending on the NHS.

However, voters became increasingly sceptical about whether the rapid increase in public spending, and the associated rise in the tax burden, was being well managed. By the time of the 2005 election, and afterwards, the Blair and then Brown governments were losing the tax/spending argument – even though voters were still unsure of the Conservative approach until 2007. This shift in attitudes was because of doubts over the effectiveness of the extra spending and complaints about waste, as well as opposition to higher taxes. Spending and taxation cannot be viewed in isolation. They are crucially linked in public attitudes towards spending programmes and their value for money. That has become the key argument for social democrats, just as it was in the late 1970s when similar doubts were expressed.

Professor Peter Taylor-Gooby has highlighted a disconnect between tax and spending in British attitudes: 'While most people endorse adequate provision for everyone across a range of services, particularly the big spending areas of healthcare, education and training, and basic pensions, they don't support the taxes necessary to finance this.'[10] According to BSA data, there has been an increasing proportion saying they want more social spending, but who, at the same time, do not also support higher taxes for the better off. Even fewer support higher taxes on middle- or lower-income groups. This scepticism also affects attitudes towards green taxes. Several polls have shown that, while in principle voters back taxes on pollution, they are highly sceptical about specific higher taxes since they think that the money will just go to the Treasury and be wasted. That is why, for example, the Conservatives have adopted a form of semi-hypothecation, arguing that any money raised by additional green taxes should go into a family fund to finance direct tax cuts.

Taylor-Gooby has highlighted two further disconnects which challenge traditional social democratic thinking. The first is on poverty and inequality. The BSA data shows that popular concern about poverty and inequality has remained high throughout the past twenty years, despite fluctuations linked to economic cycles. However, support for government intervention to address these issues has been on the decline, as noted earlier in the Curtice analysis. While inequality is recognised as a problem by between 50 and 60 per cent, the proportion of people thinking that the government should take action to redistribute income from the better off to the less well off fell from about a half to roughly a third between the mid-1990s and 2006.

Second, shifts away from universal state provision appear to be increasingly accepted. The percentage of those finding it acceptable for the better off to buy health and education was the same as that of those disagreeing in 1999. Since then the balance has shifted towards the market and towards the belief that government should have less responsibility for meeting the needs that most people recognise. Moreover, these shifts are uniform across social groups.

These trends suggest that the Labour left's alternative of a return to redistribution and government intervention on behalf of 'our' people, a core vote, class-based strategy, has few electoral attractions. There is just not sufficient support for such a shift, even among those who have voted Labour in recent general elections. The risk, rather, would be a revival of doubts about Labour's suitability as a party of government, which Neil Kinnock, John Smith, Tony Blair and Gordon Brown worked so hard to remove.

A subtler shift may be equally significant: within the context of largely taxpayer-financed core public services, towards a more diverse and personalised structure of provision. This has been linked with a broader shift towards greater individualism rather than a collective approach. For instance, the baby-boomers, those born between 1945 and 1955, are more likely than those aged over sixty-five to question the notion that 'people in charge know best' (by 14 per cent to 26 per cent), as well as wanting a greater say in medical treatments. According to research by the Henley Centre, 56 per cent of people regard providing a choice of services as among the 'most important areas the government should focus on', and 58 per cent say shorter waiting lists. In a report in February 2008 entitled *Realising Britain's Potential: Future Strategic Challenges for Britain*, the Cabinet Office's Strategy Unit noted how 'higher real incomes mean higher expectations of standards and people increasingly want services to adopt private sector customer service policies, with over 50 per cent saying that the NHS and state education should adopt more of the customer service policies of the private sector'. Apart from increased choice,

more than four-fifths of the public, according to a 2004 survey by
Ipsos MORI, believe that public services need to change to fit their
lifestyles.

These findings suggest that the policy debate has to be seen as
much more complicated than the traditional left–right spectrum,
useful though that can often be as a shorthand for placing parties
and their leaders. Populus has conducted annual questionnaires for
the *Times* asking voters to place themselves, the parties and their
leaders on the left–right spectrum. This has consistently shown that
voters put themselves slightly to the right of centre with the Conservatives considerably to the right, and the Liberal Democrats
generally the most left-of-centre party. Blair was seen as being exactly
where the average voter placed themselves, underlining the success
of his centrist strategy. Brown has, however, been seen as further to
the left, not only of his predecessor but also of the average voter. The
regular BSA surveys have shown that the gulf between left- and
right-wing values among the British public has declined, reflecting
the convergence in the policy positions of the main parties on
welfare, the role of the government and the market economy. As
suggested above, on left–right issues, the values of Labour supporters
have moved away from the left towards the centre. However, the
values of Conservative supporters have changed little. Dr Robert
Johns, co-author of this study in the twenty-fourth report of the
BSA, published in January 2008, concluded: 'Citizens with weak
attachments to values and a "pick and mix" view of policy options
become increasingly difficult to satisfy, and parties have to pay more
attention to designing mixed policy packages.'[11] Moreover, a person's
views on left–right issues are now a much less powerful predictor of
whether or not they will vote Conservative or Labour.

Some analysts argue that it is necessary to examine views in
terms of a quadrant – not just collectivist versus market (in effect
left versus right), but also libertarian versus authoritarian. There is
something in such a breakdown, particularly as old ideological ties
weaken. An analysis by MORI and the Institute of Economic
Affairs in 1997 showed that well over half those classed as authoritarian were Labour voters, while a quarter of libertarians were
Conservative voters. However, there is increasing evidence that
voters are libertarian on some issues and authoritarian on others.

British Social Attitudes: The 24th Report, published in January 2008, showed, for example, that:

- 70 per cent of people think there is nothing wrong with sex before marriage, up from 48 per cent in 1984;
- 66 per cent think there is little difference socially between being married and living together;
- in 1987, three-quarters thought that homosexuality was always or mostly wrong, now just a third think so;
- people are more traditional where children are concerned, being equally divided about whether one parent can bring up a child as well as two parents;
- more people, 42 per cent, disagree with the view that a gay male couple are as capable of being as good parents as a man and a woman, with just 31 per cent agreeing.

Several polls have shown that race relations and immigration have become much more important to the public, as has crime, according to regular Ipsos MORI surveys. More than a third rank crime as the most important issue facing Britain today. Voters are sceptical about official statistics showing a steady decline in recorded crime and claims of an increase in police numbers. There has been clearcut, and consistent, support for the introduction of ID cards and for the detention without charge of suspected terrorists for forty-two days, despite the opposition of both the Conservatives and the Liberal Democrats. The more people are worried about the threat from terrorism, the more willing they are to downgrade civil liberties and to back draconian measures for scrutiny and detention as a 'price worth paying' to prevent attacks. But the primary reason for the change in public attitudes has been a toughening in the attitudes of political leaders rather than any attacks themselves. Moreover, since the 9/11 terrorist attacks, there has been an increase from 25 to 30 per cent in the number of people describing themselves as 'very or a little' prejudiced against people of other races. However, this is still less than the 34 per cent recorded in 1985 (according to BSA figures). The increase has been entirely among those saying they are a 'little' prejudiced. Furthermore, a substantial minority, a third, think that equal opportunity measures for black and Asian people have 'gone too far'.

The social and political changes described above have led to a debate about the blurring of national identities. Does Britain's membership of the European Union make people feel less British? Or is devolution more important? Europe generates much heat among a minority of voters, notably on the sceptic side, but it is of very low salience. It consistently comes very low on voters' list of priorities, and matters, if at all, as evidence of a party's unity or disunity or extremism. Nonetheless, the BSA data suggests a distinct, though not large, decline in the proportion of people saying that 'British' is the best or only way to describe them, from 52 per cent to 44 per cent between 1996 and 2006. In 1992, 63 per cent of people living in England said that 'British' was the best or only way of describing their national identity, but just 48 per cent did so in 2005. This is partly explained by an increase from 31 per cent to 40 per cent in the number choosing 'English' as their best or only identity. In this England is partly catching up with Scotland and Wales, where a big majority have always thought of themselves as Scottish or Welsh rather than British, but it may be less to do with devolution than generational changes as younger people have not acquired the same strength of attachment to Britain as older generations did in their youth. Moreover, there is no evidence of an English backlash against devolution for Scotland and Wales. Views about devolution are similar throughout Britain, and there are also few variations in underlying social and political values, or on policy issues (apart from a slightly greater support in Scotland and Wales for variations within the UK on domestic policies).

The central conclusion is that a narrow class-based view of the electorate is wrong. Values and attitudes matter and change, often more as a result of shifts by political leaders influencing voters than by the more commonly asserted adaptation by parties to the views of voters themselves. Circumstances can matter enormously. For instance, the banking crisis of autumn 2008 saw the Brown government taking large share stakes in several leading British banks in a £37 billion rescue package. This produced jokes about Labour returning to public ownership and fulfilling one of the pledges of its disastrous 1983 election manifesto, or about the principles of the old Clause IV, abandoned by Labour under Tony Blair in 1995. But this huge extension of state involvement was not only backed by the

Conservatives, and the Liberal Democrats, as a means of saving, rather than replacing, free market capitalism, but was also adopted by strongly centre-right governments throughout the world, notably the then Republican administration in the United States. The ideological battleground is uncertain. There are many ambiguities. Voters generally want taxpayer-financed welfare, health and schooling, but they want them to be delivered in a different way, offering more choice and more attuned to their personal needs. And voters are reluctant to accept the tax consequences for themselves of such state provision. British voters want north-west European standards of public services but are reluctant to pay north-west European levels of taxation. That presents problems not just for New Labour but also for the Conservatives.

More important in determining votes have been questions of competence, and therefore leadership. The analysis in this chapter explains why, and how, David Cameron has tried to rebrand the Conservative Party since 2005. In ideological terms, he has positioned the Tories as accepting taxpayer-financed core public services, while offering to respond to voters' concerns about greater choice and personalised services. For instance, he has advocated a Swedish model of a quasi-market system of secondary schooling, presented a new tolerant face on issues of sexuality and lifestyle, but taken a tough line on immigration and law and order. At the same time, the Conservatives hope to exploit voter disillusionment with the competence of Labour on the economy. There are not exact parallels between the post-1992 period and post-2005 one. Immigration and worries over personal security have become more important. But just as the Blair team sought to position itself as offering a better and more caring form of Thatcherism, so the Cameron team has sought to build on the public service reforms of the Blair era. In electoral terms, the key battle will be over competence, especially the management of the economy. That is the precondition for future Labour victories. Everything else is secondary.

Part II

Economy and culture

4

Progressive economics

Will Hutton

British finance, once the self-proclaimed titan of the British economy that used to insist that it needed as little regulation and government as possible to prosper, is now neither a titan nor capable of survival without massive taxpayer insurance, investment and regulation to restore confidence and trust and government strategic leadership about what business model will be viable in future. By the end of 2008 British banks had received £37 billion of taxpayers' direct support, more than £250 billion of Bank of England lending and £250 billion of guarantees in the interbank market. No sector in the British economy has ever needed such intervention, but still there are complaints that the financial system is so stricken by losses from former excess that credit is simply unavailable even for good risks – threatening to plunge the UK into the worst recession since the early 1980s and possibly the 1930s. More support may yet be needed before the crisis is over. The assumption that has ruled without challenge for thirty years – that the man from the ministry can never do as well as the private sector – is no longer plausible. No official or minister could lend the billions that British banks did to the disgraced fraudster Bernie Madoff without engaging in any due diligence whatsoever.

Rarely have the once mighty fallen further or faster with such dramatically adverse affects on others. Nobody believes that Britain can sustain a financial services sector on the current scale; indeed, managing its relative decline while the economy finds other industries to fill the gap has become a major economic policy challenge. But on top of this, one of the fictions of the 1980s, 1990s and 2000s – the market fundamentalist argument that in economic affairs the only mistakes that matter are made by governments rather than firms and markets – has been exploded. Banks have proven that the private sector can make mistakes on an epic scale, and that government intervention in the economy is a necessity. This does not mean that we should swing from one universe in which the private sector was seen as inherently superior to another in which it is seen as inherently flawed. But it does mean that thinking and policy has to recognise the interdependence and coequality of both. Viable business models and sustained wealth generation are co-produced by the private and the public sectors.

In retrospect it seems amazing that anybody could ever have believed that the financial markets alone could pioneer a new economic future or believed for a nanosecond in the efficient market doctrine – that markets as free as finance could not make systemic mistakes. But individual rationality did and does not mean collectively rational outcomes. What might have seemed rational for one bank was not rational for all when they all lent too much simultaneously. House prices went too high; mortgage debt ballooned too far. It is now obvious that the regulatory agencies should have been more actively countering what was happening, but at the time, any regulator trying to rein in the markets would have created a storm of protest for being 'anti-wealth generating'.

Finance has not broken old truths that the state is inextricably involved in the economy, however little it might have seemed to need support. Rather it has proved that the combination of innovatory speed and cost of mistakes if things go wrong makes the need for state watchfulness even more urgent. The relationship between government and market may be subtler – it should not get in the way, for example, of financial innovation – but a readiness to intervene remains, something that needs to be widely understood as both legitimate and necessary. The bubble and subsequent bust would have been a lot less acute had these lessons been heeded.

So what is new? States have always had to follow the precepts of both Adam Smith, allowing markets to do their work, and John Maynard Keynes, necessarily intervening pre-emptively to prevent them going wrong. Equally it is hardly news that technology and innovation are disruptive and bring new challenges: after all, Joseph

Schumpeter invented the notion of creative destruction before the First World War. But just as the financial markets move ever faster and mutate more quickly, needing close monitoring and sometimes intervention, so do other components of the upstream, higher-value-added parts of the economy – the new economic ecology which the concept of the 'knowledge economy' tries to capture. It will be Britain's capacity to exploit the opportunities that will be a key determinant of how quickly we can recover from the recession of 2009.

Knowledge builds on knowledge exponentially – highlighted by Moore's law, which predicts that computing power doubles every eighteen months. The innovations that have transformed economies over the centuries have been 'general purpose technologies' – such as the wheel or three-masted sailing ship and now the internal combustion engine and the internet. If there were four in the nineteenth century and eight in the twentieth, exponentiality means that one could expect as many as sixteen in the next hundred years. The impact on our economy and society will be dramatic.

The internet has transformed the business models of postal services and music, newspaper and book publishing companies, to name but a few. Nokia, Yahoo!, Vodafone and Microsoft have emerged from nowhere in less than a generation. This disruptive change will become the norm in the decades ahead. No industry or process is immune. Already, for example, it takes a mere twenty-three months to take a car from design to manufacture compared with six years in 1990. At the same time better-educated, richer and more discerning consumers – graduates, for example, now constitute 31 per cent of the workforce – provide a mass consumer market for these high-value-added knowledge-based goods and services. As a result creative destruction is happening continuously and faster – for example the iPhone is already making the mobile and iPod obsolete. Successful firms are finding that speedily responding to ever more demanding consumers and continually innovating are pivotal to sustainable business success. The state can no more micromanage these complex processes than fly. But it can invest in increasing knowledge, the supply of educated people and the capacity to develop intellectual capital to help this economy. It can ensure there is a financial system that is fit for purpose and capable of nurturing new start-ups to scale. It can build wider infrastructures of transport, digital communication and sustainable energy. It must, as with the direction of the financial markets, be ready to shape, design and steer the new markets so they deliver what they promise. Economic intervention is still needed, but it has to be very much more sophisticated.

So what is this knowledge economy – and is it more than just another fashionable idea that won't survive an economic slowdown? One of the most remarkable proofs of the new economic dynamic is where firms are increasingly directing their investment. In 2004 firms invested £105 billion in traditional investment – machines, tools, computers and buildings. But that same year they invested much more – £130 billion - on so-called intangible investments which contribute to their responsiveness and innovativeness. They spent some £50 billion on their human capital, building up the skills of their workforce, quality of management and smartness of their organisational processes. They directed another £22 billion to computerising their information and communication flows. They invested some £12 billion in traditional research and development, but on top spent £27 billion on design and 'non-scientific research' – architecture, new design, copyright and licence fee costs and new product development in financial services. And lastly companies spent £19 billion on disseminating information about themselves and their products in their markets.

Nothing remarkable about any of that, you might think. But put the clock back to 1970 and firms were investing just £4 in intangibles for every £10 in tangibles, so that if the same relationship had held in 2004 (the latest year for which we have detailed figures) British firms would have spent a mere £40 billion on intangibles – £90 billion less than they actually did. It is that stunning build-up of investment in people, innovation, information and communication technology, organisational processes and knowledge dissemination that is at the heart of the knowledge economy. The trend may pause during any economic slowdown; but it is so deep seated that it is sure to reassert itself.

This is a generalised phenomenon, but it is more important in some sectors than others. Statisticians at the OECD and the European Union agree that pharmaceuticals, aerospace, computers, electronic communications, scientific instruments, chemicals, motors, post and telecommunications, finance and insurance, education and health are the chief knowledge economy sectors – and the EU adds the cultural and creative industries to the list. They invest more heavily in intangibles; they employ higher numbers of professionals and graduates; and they are growing faster than non-knowledge industries such as traditional low- and medium-tech manufacturing, utilities, mining, agriculture, transport, distribution and retailing. This does not mean that everybody who works in the knowledge industries has graduate-level education, is actively problem solving all day while deploying expert and cognitive skills. What it does mean is that those industries have more of such staff engaged in such activity and that the configuration of technology and demand is making them grow faster than others. In 1992 they constituted 36 per cent of all British value added; ten years later that had grown to 41 per cent. Today the proportion is estimated to be some 44 per cent.

In the 1930s it was new technologies and industries – cars, radios and white goods – that helped drag the economy from recession. In the 2010s it will be knowledge economy industries – ranging from new forms of car, power and food to generalised ways of living sustainably and healthily. Nor should the knowledge economy be seen as a substitute for manufacturing, heralding a London-based metrosexual world of finance and the creative industries; far from it. Rather, high-tech manufacturing in particular is a key part of the knowledge economy. In the United States the combination of strong knowledge economy sectors such as pharmaceuticals, chemicals, aerospace and semi-conductors together with a falling dollar led to a remarkable 28 per cent jump in industrial exports and a 10 per cent jump in capital goods exports during 2008, so that the country reclaimed its place as the world's number one exporter. Some 36 per cent of its manufacturing exports come from high-tech manufacturing.

One way of thinking about financial services is that it is a component of the knowledge economy that got too big for its boots. It may need to retrench but, along with business services, will remain an important, albeit more modest, part of the economy. The City has played a major role in Britain's knowledge services export success story, providing 40 per cent of its revenues, which have grown at 15 per cent a year over the last decade to top £75 billion and which have generated a trade surplus of some £35 billion – without which our international trading position would have been unsustainable. But 60 per cent of knowledge service exports came from beyond the City in areas such as education, advertising and culture. This is not to dismiss finance – banks used to contribute around a quarter of Britain's corporation tax. Finance is a plainly a useful part of the knowledge economy and created by the same drivers, but it is not so useful that it deserves special concessions. Indeed, what is now needed is for the financial system to be largely recast so that it does its proper job – supporting business – rather than imagining there is a future making money from money.

It is the interplay between discerning demand and the new 'general purpose' technologies that lies at the heart of the knowledge economy. Today's consumers are richer, better educated and more discriminating. In the 1950s the American social psychologist Abraham Maslow argued that as individuals became richer so they moved up a hierarchy of need, away from basic satisfaction of their wants towards more desire for different and rewarding experiences that provided empowerment and self-fulfilment. Today's consumers are proving him right.

One piece of evidence is the growth of Britain's creative and cultural industries – which should not be airily dismissed as fantasy sectors creating candyfloss jobs. They now employ a million people directly and another 800,000 indirectly and generate 7.3 per cent of the country's added value, only fractionally less than financial services. Part of the growth of the creative industries – design, software, advertising and architecture – has been stimulated by the boom in intangible investment, as it has in other advanced economies. But our cultural industries – film, television, books, music and art – have also done well. UNESCO says that on its measures British cultural exports exceed even the USA's. Britain has proportionally the largest cultural sector in the OECD. The 4,500 live concerts every night and record attendance at art fairs and literary festivals are tribute to consumers wanting self-fulfilment and aesthetic pleasure – and in a consumer boom, consumers have wanted more of it. Britain has a powerful network of cultural institutions – ranging from the BBC to our libraries, galleries and art schools – that both shapes demand and supports the public and private sector in responding successfully to it.

For consumers increasingly want 'experience' from what they buy. Although there is no doubt that the service sector became overblown and is now going to suffer a severe retrenchment, consumers will not suddenly drop their appetite for quality and the experiential. Recovery will be led by the companies who can provide it.

Knowledge economy production and employment has continued to grow at home in the west because success requires close proximity to western markets to interpret and respond to the new patterns of demand and offer 'experience' – whether an independent television production company such as Endemol or Shed, the goods in a high-value-added retail chain such as Zara, or business services in companies such as the fast-growing Serco or Compass. This is why some of the current concern that the rise of Asia means the inevitable decline of western economies is so wide of the mark. Two-thirds of China's exports are made by western multinationals who essentially assemble goods in the export zones on the Chinese coast – but the goods are basic staples. As the Chinese leadership well understand, China's inability to challenge the western hegemony of the knowledge economy constitutes a crisis. Essentially it remains a large sub-contractor to the west.

It is now estimated that 42 per cent of Britain's workforce are knowledge workers; if so, 58 per cent are not. What about them? The widespread fear is that the labour market is polarising into one world of well-paid knowledge workers with high job satisfaction and poorly paid non-knowledge worker drones. Research at the Work Foundation[1] (from which much of this chapter is drawn) suggests that the evidence for this is slight, and that the two sectors so far are sufficiently interdependent – after all knowledge workers shop, use utilities and travel – that both will benefit from the new trends. The inequality established in the 1980s certainly remains but it does not seem to have grown. There has been a small increase in male blue collar work at less than the median wage; but women have been doing better, claiming a larger share of the growing number of jobs paying twice the median wage. Overall the position has been one of high but stable inequality rather than yet more inequality.

Another fear is that the country is producing too many graduates burdened by student loans who are being forced into relatively low-paid non-graduate jobs. It is true that more graduates are taking jobs as low-paid clerks and in personal services, such as caring, health and beauty, fitness and interior and garden design; but so far the demand from the knowledge economy for graduates has more than compensated, so that the proportion of graduates in the knowledge and non-knowledge economies has hardly altered. The average financial return from achieving a degree remains stable.

The open question is for how much longer more polarisation and further inequality can be avoided. One storm warning is the way the knowledge economy has been the midwife to the extraordinary and largely unjustified increase in executive pay. The financial sector has become a pace setter for extravagant rewards, which have rapidly become the norm among the CEOs and directors of FTSE 100 companies. And while it may be true that average graduate pay is holding, the numbers dispersed around the average are growing. There are 110,000 more graduates working in personal services than a decade ago, 120,000 more working as clerks. There will be a tipping point when graduate employment will clearly bifurcate into the knowledge and non-knowledge sectors, making talk of average graduate pay nonsensical – and for a critical mass of graduates the returns from a degree will plummet.

But the most explicit warning of further inequality, unless pre-emptive action is taken, is the way the knowledge economy is developing geographically. Broadly speaking London and the south-east are winners, along with the Leeds–Harrogate corridor in Yorkshire, Manchester and north Cheshire, Bristol and Edinburgh. But swathes of Birmingham and the West Midlands have been less successful and some towns, not all in the north of England, such as Stoke, Burnley, Plymouth and Hastings, are stuck.[2] As low- and medium-technology industries weaken, so the life chances especially of young unskilled men in these parts of the country have diminished; now they are vanishing. While in London and the south-east there are still plentiful jobs in the non-knowledge industries and firms supplying the knowledge economy, those towns and cities with weak knowledge economies and little else to compensate are in a vicious downward spiral.

There is thus a series of problems dramatised by the onset of the credit crunch. Britain's knowledge economy is unbalanced; put bluntly, the financial sector has been too focused on unsustainable property lending, bids and deals and supporting the likes of Bernie Madoff while the high-tech manufacturing sector has been too neglected. British investment in knowledge – the share of GDP devoted to investment in research and development, software and higher education – runs at an alarmingly low 3.5 per cent. By comparison the United States spends 6.6 per cent of GDP, Sweden 6.4 per cent and Japan 4.3 per cent. Even France and Germany spend more. Although government spending on R&D, and higher education more generally, has increased over the last decade, it has not increased enough. The country has too few companies like Rolls-Royce; as its chief executive, Sir John Rose, has argued, it needs to nurture those that survive – and think much harder about the panoply of policies, from the anti-industrial priorities of the financial system to the cultural attitude towards engineering, that hold British high-tech manufacturing back. This is as much, if not more, the future as financial services. Britain's high-tech manufacturers represent 35 per cent of manufacturing exports already; we need them to grow even larger to match American high-tech industry's surprising – and unsung – performance.

If rebalancing the knowledge economy is one challenge, another is trying to limit spatial inequality. Place is beginning to loom larger and larger as a determinant of life chances. National policy needs to be much more conscious of the powerful virtuous and vicious circle effects that the knowledge economy generates. Everything – from education to transport policy – needs to be more carefully organised to set up countervailing forces, and regions, cities and towns need to have much more financial and political power to help themselves. Universities, as Leeds, Manchester, Bristol, Nottingham and Edinburgh demonstrate, are key assets in the knowledge economy; so, for example, as university investment is stepped up, disadvantaged towns and cities need to be targeted. Transport policy needs to be organised to connect the knowledge and non-knowledge economy cities and towns; there needs to be as much connectivity and movement as possible. Skills development – the Cinderella of British education policy, much talked about but still undelivered – needs to be organised with a greater eye on geography; for example a new wave of residential further education colleges needs to be built to give working-class students the same opportunity to escape stagnating towns and cities and acquire knowledge economy skills as their middle-class counterparts. Living away from home to build a career should not be the preserve of the middle class – and the curricula should accent so-called 'soft skills' (empathy, conversation, team working, problem solving) as much as 'hard' knowledge and certificates.

Above all the financial system needs to be rethought from its foundations. Britain cannot allow the fundamental importance of the routine transmission of money and the furnishing of credit to consumers, businesses and home buyers to be compromised again by vast losses in the second 'shadow' financial system – the world of securitisation, derivatives trading, proprietory trading desks, credit default swaps and all the rest. We need to seal off investment and commercial banking so that one does not pollute the other. Regulation of the shadow financial system needs to be tough, well resourced and uncompromising. And a network of specialist banks should be created to finance infrastructure spending, house building and the knowledge economy. We need to rethink the responsibilities and rights of share ownership so that ownership is understood to have responsibilities rather than be an entitlement to gamble.

None of this is easy, but it is made much harder by the mantra entrenched in government and opposition alike that the natural proclivity of markets is to work well – and that the only justification for government action is proven 'market failure'. Events since summer 2008 and the proven needs of the knowledge economy demonstrate otherwise. The government cannot dodge its responsibility. The kind of action it has taken on the credit crunch has to become more generalised and smarter, as, in fairness, Messrs Brown, Darling and Mandelson openly recognise. It has a massive role – investing in education and knowledge creation, designing markets so they work well, creating the infrastructure in which knowledge companies prosper, acting quickly to get markets and firms back on their feet when things go wrong – and above all making sure that this new emergent world is fair. This is natural territory for progressive politics and politicians. It is an opportunity that must be seized.

5

Market failure

John Kay

Does the modern centre-left have an economic theory? It has come, reluctantly, to acknowledge the primacy and ubiquity of the market but demands intervention to reduce inequality of outcomes and to improve equality of opportunity. The most articulate rationale for this economic philosophy is the doctrine of market failure. This notion was the centrepiece of Gordon Brown's most extended exposition of economic philosophy, a speech to the Social Market Foundation (SMF) in 2003. The argument was then amplified in a book published a year later, entitled *Microeconomic Reform in Britain*. (The status of this volume, part economic treatise, part political tract, is curious. The author is described as HM Treasury, and the editors are Ed Balls, then Brown's right-hand man and now in the Cabinet as children, schools and families secretary; Joe Grice, a career civil servant; and Gus O'Donnell, then permanent secretary at the Treasury and now Cabinet secretary. The work also contains a foreword by Brown himself.)

The market failure doctrine described in *Microeconomic Reform* has been the guiding principle of the Treasury since 1997. Sophisticated lobbyists have learned to frame arguments in terms of market failure. The thesis also wins wide acceptance among economists and is as influential in Brussels as in Whitehall. In this chapter I explain the content and origins of the market failure doctrine, why it is flawed, why it can never provide the economic philosophy which the moderate left is seeking and what the outline of an alternative might look like.

The traditional claim of the centre-left – that unaided, markets do not give acceptable outcomes to the provision of education and pensions, transport and health — remains valid. In these spheres choices are unavoidably political, in the sense that they are and should be based on collective decisions about the nature of society, not simply on the self-interested decisions of individuals. Nor is there in these areas, or in general, a dichotomy between the economic sphere and the political: far from being in opposition to the market, social and political dimensions of conduct are central to an understanding of how markets work.

The doctrine of market failure cannot accommodate these considerations. By conceding too much to market fundamentalists it loses both intellectual coherence and political resonance. The market failure doctrine is based on an imperfect understanding of why markets succeed, not just why they fail, and hence provides a misleading guide not only to when government intervention is necessary and appropriate but also to the ways in which market forces can improve the operation of the public sector.

A succinct summary of the market failure doctrine can be found on page 337 of *Microeconomic Reform*. Four conditions, it is said, assure the effectiveness of market outcomes. First, companies must operate in a competitive environment. Second, consumers must possess good information about their needs and the quality of service available from alternative suppliers. Third, there must be no 'externalities', so that production and use of a good or service affects no one other than the company that provides it and the individuals who directly choose to consume it. Fourth, the product must not be a 'public good', so companies can identify the individuals who use the service they provide, and are able to quantify the consumption of it and charge for it.

The market failure doctrine concludes that where these conditions are met, there is no efficiency justification for state intervention in markets. Conversely, violations of these assumptions — monopolies, asymmetries of information, externalities and public goods (in the economists' sense) — provide a rationale for such interference. But once you start looking, it is possible to find minor violations of these assumptions everywhere. So, the argument goes, market failure must be measured against 'regulatory failure' — the difficulty a government may encounter in its achieving its own objectives.

Of course, politics and policy making are too complex for any single doctrine – including the market failure doctrine – to encapsulate. And what politicians do is not always the same as what they say they do. But what they say they do frequently has substantial influence, direct and indirect, on what they do. And the redressing of market failure is what the Labour government says it does in economic policy.

The economic model that underpins this doctrine is based on a fundamental separation between economic and political spheres. Production and efficiency can be left to profit-maximising firms, while equity and allocation should be the responsibility of a government which oversees the distribution and redistribution of resources. Fairness is secured by the tax and benefit system, not by control of the means of production. Along with this notion of separation between production – a job for the private sector – and distribution – a job for government – comes a strong emphasis on incentives. Individuals and firms are assumed to have identifiable, self-interested objectives, and the objective of policy intervention is to devise structures which ensure that the pursuit of these self-interested objectives is consistent with broader social goals.

The common use of the term 'market failure' and this structure of argument, which I shall call 'the model', goes back to a 1958 article by Francis Bator, a mathematical economist who later worked as an aide to Lyndon Johnson. Bator emphasised monopoly, externalities and public goods as common violations of the assumptions of the fundamental theorems of welfare economics. Information asymmetry as market failure was added later as a consequence of a revolution in economic thinking in the 1970s, which emphasised the role of imperfect information.

The level of abstraction implicit in this model is high. There is nothing intrinsically wrong with this – scientific method relies on abstraction. But care is required, in economics as in science, in making correspondences between models and the external world. Ordinarily, a failure of correspondence between the assumptions of a model and the world is a problem for the model, not for the world. When it turned out that light did not in fact travel in straight lines, no one suggested that the solution was that those tiresome deviations from Newtonian mechanics should be straightened out. And in the real world, a variety of social and economic institutions – reputation, trust, cooperative relationships – have evolved to manage issues such as information asymmetry and externalities. Thus, these 'market failures' are not failures of the market itself but failures of a particular representation of the market.

The basic philosophical differences that divide left and right concern the priority that should be given to claims of individual rights and private property relative to those of solidarity and social justice. The left insists, and the right denies, that the public interest is more than an aggregation of private interests. The model that underpins the market failure doctrine answers these questions, and others, in the right's favour. A particular philosophy is inherent in the mathematics. The model takes individual preferences as given, along with personal resources and property rights, and sees social welfare as an aggregation of individual preferences. The primacy of material incentives as determinants of economic behaviour is not a prediction of the model, but an assumption.

These issues become quickly apparent in the application of the framework to the most pressing of policy issues – the management of health and education. Gordon Brown's commitment to a tax-financed NHS is well known. But the market failure doctrine requires this preference to be expressed in the language of market failure itself. This is precisely what was done in Brown's SMF speech and in *Microeconomic Reform*. The principal market failure identified is information asymmetry: 'people are unable to predict their future healthcare needs', 'consumers may lack sufficient information to make optimal choices', there are 'asymmetries of information between insurers and healthcare providers'.

While these statements about healthcare are largely true, they do not suggest any reason why such problems are better resolved in Britain's publicly funded, publicly provided NHS than in the mixed systems of most other European countries. More importantly, they have nothing to do with the real reasons why most people – including Brown – support a publicly funded NHS. These reasons begin from ethical concepts such as compassion and fairness rather than economic concepts such as information asymmetry.

If illness were truly an unpredictable event, then private medical insurance would work better than it does. The major informational problem in medical insurance is not that consumers do not know their future healthcare needs but that insurers know relatively well which categories are likely to prove expensive and which are not. Private insurance is fine for healthy employees but not for the old and the poor. And while information asymmetry is endemic in health provision – if we didn't think the doctor knew more than us, why would we visit the surgery? – medicine is a particularly clear case of an activity in which effective social institutions manage inequalities of information in the provision of complex products. Centuries of ritual and experience are designed to maintain, mostly justifiably, the faith of the patient in the doctor.

The rationale of public intervention is different. If individuals decide that they will not make provision for the emergency medical treatment of themselves and their families, we will not respect that decision and we will not let people die in the street. Staff and patients in the NHS seek a caring service in which they believe that the motives of providers are largely uninfluenced by commercial considerations.

Equality of provision matters far more in healthcare than in most other commodities. This is why healthcare is more or less completely collectivised in all developed countries outside the United States – and even there it is largely collectivised. And it has little to do with a conventional taxonomy of market failures. The justifications for public provision arise from a widely shared consensus about the nature of society which can find expression only through political and social action and not through individual choices in the marketplace.

The notion that some economic choices are essentially collective, and cannot be described as a summation of personal preferences, strikes at the heart of the market failure doctrine. While it is at least possible, though I think mistaken, to argue that the output of a health system might be measured by health outcomes – mortality and morbidity – the output of an educational system is plainly multi-dimensional: average attainment levels are important but not the only indicator that matters. *Microeconomic Reform* acknowledges the multiplicity of educational goals: 'Imparting basic skills to children, preparing them for work, instilling ideas of citizenship and fostering emotional growth. Although they are not contradictory, these goals compete for resources.'

Up to a point. Imagine the debate which would establish those priorities. I think that emotional intelligence is crucial, you emphasise workplace skills. How do we resolve our disagreement? By democratic vote? Or perhaps these objectives should receive weights: 40 per cent to one, 30 per cent to another. If we can only describe all the objectives, and agree on the weights, we might construct an index of educational attainment. But no one imagines that policy is, or could be, determined in this way. The multiple objectives of education are neither compatible nor conflicting, but ultimately incommensurable.

The term 'incommensurability' is anathema to economists, for whom it is an article of faith that there are always trade-offs. The existence of such trade-offs makes optimisation possible. The market failure model supposes that a social welfare function can be defined, and that it should be the basis of policy decisions. The existence of such a function requires that not just for individuals, but for society as a whole, there exists a coherent, consistent preference ordering which politicians must first define and then maximise.

But this formulation is a misunderstanding of the nature of choice in a democratic society. There is no plausible means of constructing such a social preference ordering – neither by the aggregation of individual preference, which gives rise to no coherent result, nor by the imposition of some leader's conception of a general will, which is not an acceptable solution in a democracy. Modern politics always involves a process of mediation between largely compatible but sometimes conflicting views on specific policies and programmes. The modern political context is one in which a balance must be struck between conflicting purposes. Sometimes we have moved too far in one direction, sometimes too far in another. Education policy might have emphasised emotional growth too much at the expense of preparing students for work. A decade from now, these issues will no doubt look different. The politician who enters this inevitably messy debate with 'clear priorities' is a figure with whom one can sympathise, but whose instincts are properly restrained by the institutions of a pluralist democracy.

The economic theory of the centre-left must accommodate collective choices and must also acknowledge collective actions. But just as the market failure model interprets collective choice in terms of the aggregation of individual choices, so it interprets collective actions as the aggregation of individual actions. But if the approach to collective choice misunderstands modern politics, the approach to collective action misunderstands modern economic organisation. Armies, production lines and hospitals, railways and schools function because people work as teams. The notion of the business enterprise as a nexus of explicit contracts, in which people negotiate new agreements with each other every day, misses the features that made corporations necessary and distinctive.

Issues of incentives are relevant but only part of the story. There is a very large middle ground between the excessively utopian belief that everyone will do the right thing once they perceive what it is, and the excessively cynical assumption that everyone is principally driven by the prospect of personal financial gain. It is in that middle ground that both the public and private sectors of modern economies function.

People have many motives for work – money, of course, but also pride in the job, the respect of colleagues, family and friends. Employment contracts are most successful when they make use of all these motivations. The time-and-motion precepts of Taylorism in the workplace failed: even in the automobile industry crude incentive systems proved unsuccessful and were abandoned because workers had no concern for the quality of the product. Purely instrumental motivation created dismal workplace relations, and negotiation over the terms of the bonus schemes proved interminable. And in the last decade Taylorism has failed in the boardroom too, for essentially similar reasons. The elaboration of complex incentive systems for top managers distorted motivation – both among those who benefited from the schemes and among those who did not – and attracted into executive positions the relatively small number of people for whom personal greed was indeed an overriding motivation. The boom and bust in structured credit markets and the consequent losses for financial institutions show how in the long run these structures have failed even in their own materialistic terms.

People make careers in education and medicine at least in part for non-materialistic reasons, and we want it to be that way. The motives of those who deliver treatment matter, because what we want from a health system is not simply pills and surgery but the

ministrations of people who care. Much medical treatment is not
very cost effective in terms of health outcomes, and a high proportion
of total expenditure goes on the last year of life; but the economic
approach to health policy, which measures output only in terms of
'quality-adjusted life years' gained, fails to recognise that even in
matters of life and death we care about processes as well as outcomes.
The provision and receipt of healthcare is, by its nature, a social
activity. The misapprehensions that put financial incentives at centre
stage explain how, as in the mishandling of GP contracts, the public
sector has spent so much more money on health services only to
reduce further the morale of those who work in them.

The market failure doctrine, dedicated to reforming the world
in line with the model, has led to inappropriate policy prescription
for public sector reform, to policies that burden consumers with
information they do not want and cannot understand instead of
ensuring that the trust they wish to place in their suppliers is well
founded. The proliferation of targets and incentives fails to recognise
that people value freedom of action for its own sake, and not just for
associated financial incentives. The attraction of fund holding to
some GPs, or of school budgets to many headteachers, is not just that
they might make a few bob out of it, but also that these mechanisms
give them greater autonomy. The market failure approach directs our
attention to secondary issues of information asymmetry and fails to
recognise the more fundamental ones – the primacy of collective
decisions and collective action – that make unmoderated market
forces inappropriate means of providing health or education.

Moreover, the policy relevance of the market failure doctrine is
limited by another, perhaps more subtle, problem of connection
between the model and the world. The resources and endowments
which economic agents trade are not given by nature, as the model
implies, but established through social process. In the simple models
of exchange I used to teach, apples grow in my garden, pears in
yours, and since I want some pears and you some apples there is
room for mutually beneficial trade. The tax and benefit system might
take some of my apples, or give me your pears; but there is no room
in this model for argument either about the definition of apples or
pears or about our initial entitlements.

But few exchanges in modern economies have this simplicity.

The nature, as well as the distribution, of property rights is a matter of social construction and political debate. The majority of contested economic policy issues reflect disputes about the nature of entitlements, or they occur when parties look to the government to fill in the implicit terms of imperfectly specified contracts. Arguments about whether goods are in fact apples or pears, and whether they grew in my garden or yours, are not peripheral: they are a major part of political debate. Below is a list of recent policy issues, each of which concerns either the nature of the default position – what rights do individuals have when they begin the market process of exchange? – or the content of complex relationships, in which it has proved impossible to specify every contingency in advance, and one or both parties looks to a political process to resolve their entitlement.

- **Top-up fees:** What rights of access do individuals have to higher education, and on what terms?
- **Problematic issues in retail financial services:** What were the implied terms of endowment mortgages and defined-contribution pension schemes? What responsibilities at Equitable Life or Northern Rock does the government assume for a regulatory agency which is – perhaps inevitably – inadequate in monitoring the solvency of financial institutions?
- **Funding the long-term care of the elderly:** If the costs associated with uncertainties of medical treatment are largely socialised, how does this judgement apply to costs associated with longevity in general, or to abnormally costly longevity?
- **Executive remuneration and corporate governance:** What is the proper balance of rights and responsibilities between managers and other stakeholders in large corporations?

Not one of these questions, which are typical of everyday debate in micro-economic policy, can be resolved either by saying 'leave it to the market' or by identifying a market failure from the conventional list. Each arises because property rights are not an external 'given' but socially constructed. If government is called on to define entitlements, or to regulate agreements which have not worked out as planned – and this is a large part of what economic policy is about – then there is no alternative to a pragmatic, issue-specific assessment of how best to achieve the simultaneous goals of efficiency and equity, and the attempt to separate these objectives must fail. The economist who brings to questions such as those above his standard toolkit of individual rationality and market failure is not wrong, merely irrelevant.

Yet the most serious weakness of the market failure doctrine is that its model provides not just an inadequate account of how markets fail, but an inadequate account of how they succeed. The model provides a partial explanation of one of the most striking features of market economies – their capacity to achieve coordination without a coordinator. It is remarkable, and wildly counter-intuitive, not only that the question 'who is in charge of the supply of bread to New York?' has no answer, but that the supply of bread to New York is better managed by a system in which that question cannot be answered than by one in which it can.

But the endemic deficits and surpluses of a planned economy which is unable to effectively coordinate large quantities of information in a rapidly changing environment are only part of the failure of central planning. Similarly with the suppression of incentives: in reality, few societies have offered as wide a range of incentives as the Soviet Union, from the privileges of the nomenklatura to the perils of the gulag. The main failing of planned economies was that they could not accommodate the flexibility needed to cope with an uncertain future. This issue is not one the market failure doctrine can easily recognise since the underlying model does not recognise innovation and uncertainty, except in trivial ways.

If the partial genius of market economies lies in their capacity to achieve coordination without a coordinator, the greater genius lies in their ability to innovate and adapt in an environment of uncertainty and change. The sustained achievement of market economies comes from their pace of innovation – in products, technology and organisation – derived from the ability of market systems to undertake small-scale experiment, to watch the results, to mimic what works and discard what doesn't. This is the mechanism which I describe as 'disciplined pluralism' in my book *The Truth about Markets* – a mechanism which allows a multiplicity of small-scale experiments and in which the successful experiment is quickly imitated while the unsuccessful quickly folds. Such disciplined pluralism is an inherently inefficient process. It relies on constant displays of irrational optimism, and most of its experiments fail.

Rationalist bureaucracies detest such pluralism. They are run by micro-managers, people at the centre who feel able to set clear priorities in education and who believe that the information asymmetries inherent in healthcare can be addressed by nationalising its provision. Centralisation with targets fails to recognise the pluralism which is the market's central strength.

The historic error of Old Labour was to conflate the need for collective choices and collective action with central direction and political control. A successful team achieves common goals via co-operative activity effected through individual decisions. This process, neither market nor hierarchy, characterises the effective sports team or school, workshop or military unit. The trick that disciplined pluralism – decentralised choices with accountability – achieves is to replicate that combination of free choice and coordinated outcome throughout the economic system. That insight – the economics of Friedrich Hayek (concerned with the dynamic capacity of a market economy to experiment and innovate) rather than of Milton Friedman (concerned to promote the allocative efficiency of competitive markets and to attack all kinds of state intervention) – is the lesson the left needs to learn from the right.

In New Labour's acceptance of the market, there has been something of the zeal of the convert in the readiness to believe in market efficiency – especially in the efficiency of financial markets, an area in which the alignment of social and private interests is especially weak. Taken as a whole, market economies have proved far more effective than planned economies. But this does not imply that every individual market outcome is superior to every individual planned outcome.

A centre-left economic policy should recognise the primacy of the market neither as an ideal nor a necessary evil, but as the best pragmatic solution to a wide range of economic problems. Efficient production and allocation is a mixture of individual and collective choice and action. The shape of our transport infrastructure needs to be a political decision, but the railways need to be run by professional managers accountable to customers rather than political appointees responsible to ministers. Major inequalities in health provision need to be addressed but ministers cannot know and should not decide which treatments should be provided. Education requires public funding but no one has the capacity, or should have the power, to 'set clear priorities'.

The market is a tool, not a fount of wisdom, and earnings are not a measure of desert. On balance, open capital markets are beneficial, but that does not mean that every foreign takeover benefits the British economy. Free trade is superior to its alternative but entails job losses and wage reductions for specific groups unless policies alleviate the consequences. Mergers generally have more to do with management egos and investment banking fees than a better allocation of economic resources. Markets do not do the basic research, or the training that isn't job specific, on which the innovative capacity of economic systems depends.

The list of market failures is a guide to some common problems in economic policy. But it is no more than that, and it does not provide a proper account of the limits of markets or their strengths. The notion that the boundaries of markets can be precisely defined by regulation and contract has been common to both the New Labour left and the right in the last decade. But a precise definition is not always possible. There is, and should be, a large grey area in which disciplined pluralism, the 'decentralisation with accountability' which is the strength of market organisation, coexists with political control. In that world, educational goals are not determined either by central state direction or by the simple aggregation of individual choices. Both are relevant but neither is sufficient. Multiple goals emerge, are different across different parts of the educational system, and evolve over time, through an interactive process between those who provide the service and those who pay for it. In a similar way, medical treatment must be managed through trust relationships between politicians, professionals and patients.

The reason for giving a choice of provider in health and education is not that consumers see inherent virtue in choice, but that the ability of consumers to exercise choice raises standards. There is no wide disagreement about what constitutes a good school or hospital. That is to say, there is wide disagreement about what makes a school good or bad but much less disagreement about which schools are good and which bad. That is what makes exit so much more effective than voice. And so the most effective means of getting a good school is to be able to reject a bad one, and individual choice is far more effective in achieving this than collective choice. The reason for promoting competition between providers is not that conflict is better than cooperation, but that recognising success and failure is indispensable to innovation and imitation.

Incentives matter: but it is not only individual incentives which matter, and the failure to recognise this has given us both corrupt corporate bosses and demoralised public sector workers. So long as market organisation is equated with individual greed and jingling cash registers, the limits to markets will in practice be set by the determination of the public to keep them away from those areas of human activity – such as health and education – that matter most to them. And that would, indeed, be a market failure.

6

Democracy, community and culture

Melvyn Bragg

Democracy, community and culture: the Three Graces of civilisation. There are, I believe, essential connections between the three in our country today and these can be both deepened and extended over the next decade.

The key combining factors I propose are *the future of the creative economy*, *the extension of access* and *the growth of participation*. Through increased participation in the variety of strands which make up the culture, new communities could be created, more traditional ones reinforced and the idea of a community itself redrawn. And following the strengthening and kindling of communities, a local, social and a national sense of democratic conversation and involvement could (I believe will) grow.

There is a widespread sense that the mechanisms of our democracy, though essential and full of service, are rusty and too limited in their reach. For too many they come down to a couple of votes every five years. But there is a much deeper role for democracy, for that release towards equality of opportunity, for that liberation which comes from having a voice and a say in what impinges on your everyday working life and on the lives you can live through imagination. This is and will continue to be an expanding role, though only recently pursued for the majority. This is not to bypass politics but to enrich the political landscape and to increase the decisive choices available. It could add to the individual citizen's control over more of his or her life. The interconnectedness of community and culture not only feed into this idea of a much more fully and widely realised democracy, they are its greatest engines.

The brief for this chapter allows that future judgements can be 'informed by closeness to the events of the last decade'. For which, relief. . . For though I wholly agree with the guiding notion – to look at what we think should happen and not spend the pages on an assessment of what has happened – I think that in this case a glance at the last ten years (at least) will provide a necessary platform and important proofs for what should happen in the next ten years.

The most salient features have been the recognition and dramatic expansion of the 'creative economy': the creation of communities clustered around culture; increased participation in culture; increased access to and in some areas marked developments in cultural education. Alongside that the dynamics of popular culture – in music, fashion and popular entertainment for example – have helped drive the creative industry and in some cases have been near the heart of it. It is difficult to portray with statistics the relationship between the old-time 'popular' and the old-time 'traditional', but in the last ten years there has been a steady, influential confluence between these two streams until at times the old 'popular' is now happily labelled with the word 'classic' (popular music of the 1960s) and the once wholly traditional demands to be called 'popular' (the Proms).

In 1997 our creative economy accounted for less than 4 per cent of UK gross value added (GVA). In 2007 it stood at 7.3 per cent of UK GVA, growing at 6 per cent per annum compared with 3 per cent for the rest of the economy. The Work Foundation estimates that the UK has the largest creative sector in the EU and, relative to GDP, probably the world. It employs about two million people – many highly skilled specialists who can and do travel the world with their crafts, like the more scholarly of the mediaeval monks – and this economy now contributes just over £14.5 billion to our exports. The chief curiosity about that brief roll call is that in many panelled corridors and oval-tabled boardrooms this burgeoning, feisty part of our national life is still regarded as a sideshow. Yet the overall impact of British theatre alone is £2.6 billion annually from a subsidy of £120 million. If the creative economy continued to double in value and its size reached 16 per cent in 2018 – which is not at all fantastical – then a number of our worries would be over. For inside those figures are maps and routes that could take us to new worlds far from the Gradgrind grime of the Industrial Revolution but no less inventive, no less dependent on multiple skills and great numbers, though a great deal healthier, more cerebral and more 'power to the people', but this time to individuals. The 6,000 employees in Birmingham's magnificently rejuvenated Jewellery Quarter, for instance, are mostly niche craftsmen who can command a world clientele.

Many causes could be found for this remarkable surge in activity. Government can take much credit, from CEMA (the Committee for the Encouragement of Music and the Arts) which came out of the Second World War, to the injection given to the power of the Arts Council by Jennie Lee, to the key targeting of some of the lottery money to the arts under John Major, to the foot on the accelerator which came two or three years into the 1997 Labour government. In the last ten years government funding has gone up by 73 per cent. Free admission to some galleries and museums has seen visitor numbers rise by 87 per cent – at the British Museum from 4.8 million in 2006/7 to 6.0 million in 2007/8. More than 100 new arts buildings have been opened, more than 500 refurbished; one million young people benefit from the Youth Music Programme; the lottery has directed over £2 billion into capital projects transforming the infrastructure. It is plausible to be starry eyed. Cultural tourism accounts for 37 per cent of world travel and is growing at 15 per cent a year. London has more such visitors per year than any city save New York.

Private support has come into the arts – partly through tax breaks, partly through philanthropy – rising from £448 million in 2002/3 to £530 million only two years later. Of course there are shortcomings and missed opportunities and the British sound of moan is sometimes justified. But fair's fair. There has been an overall success, even triumph, in culture and the arts during the last ten years and it has been one of the best-kept secrets in the UK. And what the infusion of mostly well-positioned funding did was to uncork a jeroboam of talent. It was the talent that did it, does it and is willing and able to do much more.

By and large – despite legitimate cries and murmurs, despite the dual afflictions of incompetence and over-bureaucratisation, which are not uncommon, it seems, along the waterfront of the institutional UK – there is now a confident, proven, foundation for growth and influence in the arts. 'Culture' is no longer an embarrassing word.

Much of this is down to Andrew Neil, when as editor of the *Sunday Times* he chose the word for the title of his arts supplement. The combination of public and private money works and there is clear evidence that across the board funds are carefully deployed and monitored. The engagement of the government at a higher level has been key but would not by itself have done the business: it was, and must continue to be, the great enabler, with the lottery at the fore, to bring in private money both with the partnership guarantees it can offer and, as time goes on, with the ever-increasing allure perfumed by success. For better and sometimes, purists believe, for worse, the creative economy is now bringing riches to the mind, to the wallet, but most importantly, to the many.

Over the next ten years this cultural upsurge should continue. There is now a creative cluster which is of a significant and world-challenging size. Its possibilities are unbounded. In developed and developing countries more leisure time is released and in the luckier countries there is money to spend in it. Tourism, as mentioned, has increased, is increasing and, unless all forecasts become void due to some planetary disaster, will increase even exponentially – especially from the east – in the next ten years.

The cultures of this country are a strong attraction. There is the stately-home culture, well refurbished over the last generation; the numerous World Heritage Sites; the incomparably varied and brilliantly portrayed and described British countryside; the galleries and museums; great dance and theatre companies now in London and several other British cities; and a gargantuan web of the arts spread out to entrap all that flies. The only problem may be that when the Chinese, the Indians, the Koreans and others follow the Japanese, the Americans and the Scandinavians, London will become not only the most polyglot city in the world but the most crushingly overloaded polyglot city in the world. Tourism is now one of our leading industries and culture drives it.

Tourists increasingly form a new global community seemingly forever on the move. In the more blest countries, early retirement, prudent or lucky financial management and a determination to see much more than Naples before dying have resulted in a loosely knit group whose members see themselves as part of a community of cultural travellers. Much energy goes into this and travellers, often literally in the same boat, become part, however fleetingly, of what is an increasingly adventurous set, even sect, which finds in foreign travel not only the satisfactions of intellectual curiosity but also the comfort of companionable strangers and that feeling of belonging which on their home turf might seem to have been eroded. 'I belong to cruises.' Although this may seem at the moment only a little lamp, tourism is well on the way to becoming a new community replacing the old: a community of preoccupations rather than a community of location.

There is a legitimate fear that part of what some commentators see as the malaise of the UK (though far from unique to it) is this erosion of what were seen as the traditional, binding, place-defined communities of old. We can track it back to the mediaeval village and beyond, of course, but the mediaeval village subtly morphed into a Victorian idyll that can still beguile us. The thatched cottages, the squire in his hall, the vicar in his rectory, the blacksmith, the basket makers, the sturdy and contented army of a bold peasantry – Thomas Hardy at his lightest perpetuates this. It was rarely thus but it remains one of the dreams and all across urbanised Britain, avoiding the motorways and the flight paths, sometimes even spared the through traffic, this vision still clings on. And it can still seem that it is this vision that keeps England in shape as England.

A more popular and more recent example of a community still yearned for by some and now thought to have gone to the dogs is the industrial towns, numerous in the north and the Midlands, often built to serve a single manufacturing process – coal, steel, cotton, shipbuilding. These were communities not only set in a constrained location and organised according to the practical inventions of those whose ideas Richard Arkwright filched and given intellectual respectability by Adam Smith, but made culturally cohesive, even vibrant, by a network of unions, clubs, churches, chapels, societies, choirs, the Co-op, brass bands, little shops up for 'tick', pigeons, whippets, football, cricket, rugby, allotments – mostly male associations, but as long as the males bonded, the culture was thought to be secure.

I would suggest that despite evidence in fiction, documentary and oral histories that there were times of savage unemployment, despair, hunger, thwarted fury, waste and the barely treated diseases which were the inevitable consequence of congested habitations and filthy hard work, this industrial community too somehow remains an idyll in the UK. Go to those industrially broken steel towns and pit villages today, often plagued by drugs, and there is not only a nostalgia for the work that maimed as much as it nurtured those who did it, there is also a conviction that the values held in that society are now gone to the loss of all: decency, helping each other out, not getting above yourself, being proud to be who and where you were planted. These are values which George Orwell found in his *Road to Wigan Pier* and D. H. Lawrence evoked despite his own hatred of what he saw as the enslaved subservience of the industrial masses. It is widely felt that since the passing of the mills and the coalfields, the shipyards and the iron ore mines, there has been a decline in social capital, in the very notion of decent interdependence which is still hungered for as a better way to live than what, by contrast, is often described as the anonymous, alienated, consumer-driven life of today, in the Big Cities, with the globally rich increasingly cutting themselves off from the 'little people' and forming themselves into an alien aristocracy of lucre. Yet the phoenix has been at work here over the past few decades and it is Culture, a new, non-localised, non-hermetic culture, together with a growing property-owning democracy which is transplanting and could further transplant those old tight, settled community advantages into the new looser arrangements of today.

Just as the rather extreme example of tourism was chosen to illustrate how a 'community' can be global, floating, on ships that pass in the night, based in world-beckoning brochures rather than in local bars, happy in fleeting friendships, finding pleasure in arrivals and equal pleasure in departures, so the refashioned cities, cleaned up inch by inch, are feeding into regenerated ideas of community. Culture is the choicest instrument. Parts of our great cities and towns – the rich parts – have always fortressed a culture. Much bigger parts – the poor – have lain outside those city walls and when the great labour-intensive and skill-demanding manufactures petered out they were abandoned. The arts have reached and can reach more successfully there.

To take one example: recently *The South Bank Show*, in the course of making a film on the violinist Tamsin Little, went with her to the Gallions Primary School in Newham, east London. She did several workshops with the children and performed for them and with them. The team reported:

> The school is an inspiration. It opened eight years ago – and took in children from multiracial and multilingual and very difficult backgrounds, including sink estates. Nearly all the children had failed in previous schools and both they and their parents were disillusioned with the concept of education. To begin with it was chaos and the children were disruptive to the point of actually throwing the school furniture around.
>
> However, the staff had all been recruited because of their own arts expertise and they developed an ethos of arts education which would have an impact on the children's attainment, achievement and overall happiness. They obtained funding from J. P. Morgan and invested in musical instruments for the entire school. Every child studies music and plays an instrument. Immediately behaviour improved. They also introduced philosophy classes and created a curriculum where National Curriculum objectives in foundation subjects are sorted into research projects and delivered through art, dance, music and drama. It has all been a great success and the school is a delight to visit.

This is one of an increasing number of examples demonstrating the power of the arts to inspire those who have abandoned or been abandoned by the normal curriculum. It is something that Andy Burnham, the current culture secretary, is practically evangelical about. I interviewed him in April 2008 for this piece. He had no doubt that the benefits of culture – a poetry or music workshop, transporting the subsidised arts world into schools – had a direct beneficial effect. In that world, children could find self-confidence, learn skills, realise that it was acceptable to explore your imagination – in short be unleashed from the poverty of ambition and the curse of miserable expectations. Burnham linked this with the free entry policy to galleries and museums, an opening up of the mind that cannot be found anywhere else.

The in-between part, the suburbs, below the salt of the moneyed elite but out of and above the slough of the poor, created their own communities through a culture of clubs and games with a touch of the village – tennis and bridge, Scouts and Guides, church and tea, lawns, gardens, neat shopping parades and space for the kids. Yet the culture in middle-class suburbs today has become more complex, even demanding, with art galleries, reading groups, musical performances and numerous school-connected events. The suburbs have, in many cases, despite the eerie emptiness of the daytime avenues, managed to retain a particular character and given those old idylls a real purchase on the modern world. And there is little sign of them losing their grip. Culture becomes them. The notion of a leisure life spun around a cultural axis is part of the suburban contract which could intensify: festivals, for instance, which have brought many thousands of blooms to British life over the last twenty-five years, are just as likely to be in a suburban hall as in a city centre and just as likely to be well attended.

In the wider sense of the city, that metropolis which can appear chaotic, it is increasingly clear that what pulls it together, gives it its buzz, its beat, its pulse, its character is culture, and the aspiration for more culture. Barrack blocks of housing serving the factory down the road remain but the factory down the road has gone. Old divisions of class are ignored and the number of culture seekers grows as their wealth and leisure grows, as they approach the condition of social freedom which capital and education has given to their betters for centuries. They want it too and would like it now. It is around the cultural communities that the enlarged middle classes and more confident old-style 'working classes' identify themselves. Culture gives them a sense which takes them beyond earning, work and domestic imperatives.

The new communities are more and more to do with individual choice and equal participation. They come out of a belief that theirs is the culture now, they do not have to accept what they are given unless under the financial cosh: they can pick and choose and vote on their style of life by participating in it. The internet is a powerful instrument in enabling this behaviour and just as powerful a metaphor.

This can lead us to a bewildering number of cultures of community. Far from there being a decline in social capital I would argue that there is a recent and accelerating trend to shore up social capital. But it is only rarely in the giant block style of the old industrial mass or the landscaped rural jewel.

Club football has become a force of community and looks set to increase its attraction for millions of supporters and players who may well be participants in other communities in parallel, in which leisure, money and confidence in the right to participate mean that more people find community not just in one or two, but in several groupings. If club football seems a rather eccentric illustration, I would argue that it adds up to a community, deriving from though different from the old cloth-capped assembly down the road every Saturday at 3 p.m.

I stress *club* football. It retains the old notion of 'place' common to village, factory, pit and shipyard. It is a place of assembly on a regular basis, not unlike a church in that respect. It is a place of sufficient tradition – many of those clubs hark back to the late nineteenth century, when the English invented football as it is played today, as they did so many other games. Yet support for a modern football club comes from a very different community than that which obtained until fairly recently when the squad of men (almost all men) who worked in factories a few streets away swung into line at the turnstiles as orderly as they might have been in an army.

The big football clubs now are increasingly national and inter-national communities and the game itself – global, immensely wealthy, a great engine in the worlds of television, radio, newspapers, magazines and merchandising – is now reaching for and sometimes achieving levels of skills which draw it near the tempting phrases hitherto reserved for the arts. Most significantly, a club such as Manchester United has a following from all over the United Kingdom. Not only those who listen and watch – those who will drive or take a bus or train 300 miles or more on a round trip to see 'their' club in a city not their city, watching players often not of their nationality. Moreover the following of Manchester United extends around the globe with active supporters' clubs and merchandise purchasers – the shirt, the tracksuit, the cap, the boots – everywhere. It has irradiated. A recent league game between Manchester United and Arsenal (not a final or a vital fixture) drew in a world-wide television audience of 1.3 billion viewers.

Two years ago in South Africa I was talking to a number of young black people who were supporters of and experts on Liverpool, Manchester United, Arsenal and so on. It is unlikely any of them will ever visit the ground of their team of choice. Television coverage has made this community public. If you support a great club you have instant access to friendly gossip with your community wherever you go. You belong. Talk of football, with men and increasingly with women (twenty million of whom now play regularly and more and more go to the games), and you enter into sport's lingua franca. Moreover, its heroes come from the democracy of talent, though their success can bring them great wealth; often, confusingly, this catapults them into the nest of plutocrats and cuts them off. The intertwining of democracy, community and culture in a way which sockets into global trade (among players for example) and capitalism redefines both the notion of culture and the notion of community.

There are other examples in sport, none as big but all sharing in the new trajectory of successful world sport which is creating global communities and employing many of the outward and visible signs of the traditionally more acceptable faces of culture. The new football stadiums are often called the new cathedrals. Fans are 'devoted'. Money is paid weekly, tithe-like, subscription-like; there is a wonderfully refreshing equality of opinion whoever you are. Bad times are to be endured, good times are an occasion for festivals; in extremis the club is something the fans will war over. Golf, tennis, rugby, cricket, sailing, equestrianism: these and other sports now have world-wide communities and will become ever more attractive, profitable and, for millions, an absorbing part of our culture – the way we choose to spend some of the best free hours of our lives.

The football stadiums are often in or near parts of the city which have never really known good times and are now either struggling to survive or hopefully seeking gentrification. They are part of the rolling acres of brick and concrete which in many cases desperately need regeneration. It is here, unexpectedly, that the arts have proved over the past ten years to be surprisingly effective. There is no rejuvenated city or large town in the UK which does not acknowledge its debt to the arts as a catalyst for growth and a new focus for the reassembly of communities blighted by poverty and transported to outlying estates yet now revisiting old haunts in the city centres in what had frequently become ghost towns tipping into dereliction. Not now. Well cultivated, this could burgeon.

To take one example – from many – of the way that the arts have restored and redefined community, we can look at the Gateshead/Newcastle development along the Tyne and see it both as a dynamic project in itself and as a template for the future, probably just the first step on what could be a long, enriching journey. By the alchemy of government grant, lottery manna, private contribution, public consumption and all the spin-offs and add-ons, what began as encouraging art, supporting high culture, recognising the world of the pursuit of beauty has come to encompass the mass, or at least the many. Now, bred from an idealistic vision, there is, in parallel, the pursuit of pleasure, another sort of high culture involving alcohol, dancing, desire; a full house of Greek gods, Dionysus, Aphrodite and Pan all in evidence most nights on the banks of the Tyne.

It all began in Gateshead town hall in the mid-1990s, when the council of a battered, gutted, in some ways despairing town in the north-east, nurtured by heavy industries which then collapsed, decided that art would be the answer. And so it has proved. The monumental Baltic Salt Mill became a monumental art gallery. On an abandoned mound of land overlooking the river Norman Foster built a space-age hall fit for concerts classical, popular, young, strange and local. A beautiful new swing bridge connected Gateshead and Newcastle and to stroll across it and see the blaze of life which this institution has brought to the banks of a riverside so recently lost in misery at the passing of its great shipbuilding days is to see the future.

Those cultural institutions are being backed up by inner-city eating and drinking developments, but the evidence shows that the more imaginative and bold they are and the more they stick to the arts as the fructifying core, then the idea of the city centre as a community in itself, a community of cultural pleasure, will in turn drive on commerce, which in its turn can help bankroll the community.

It is often difficult for those of my generation fully to understand how the arts can become such a generator of wealth. I think that we can once again invoke the triumvirate in the title of this chapter and see that culture helps form a community which, when owned by those who come of their own free will and vote strictly according to their own preferences, democratically, provokes a benevolent fusion, a virtuous spirit and spiral. This, now proved in many cities – Glasgow was one of the first, Liverpool the most recent – then leads the way to what with luck and steady support from government, the lottery and the locality can and probably will make British cities (outside London, which is sui generis) at the very least a match for the great European ones whose cultural infrastructure we have envied for so long. Books do furnish a room, wrote Anthony Powell; galleries, museums, theatres, concert halls, craft centres, publishing houses, pubs and winebars do furnish a city, it seems, and an opulent one. And full of surprises. Bloodaxe Books, for instance, founded in Newcastle, are the biggest poetry publishers in the world.

I wrote 'will' in the case of culture and the city because its success so far has been so striking that the UK's local and governmental bodies have already eagerly accelerated from their usual conservative crawl where culture is concerned, like a late-awoken herd of elephants, smelling a new watering hole, now heaving across the industrial deserts to seek out its benefits. What also will, I think, happen is yet further expansion of that movable city, the festival. There are analogies with the legendary Victorian fairs, but the festival culture is not solely sensation; it aspires to and reaches other, often impressively intellectual and demanding, goals. It is difficult to know where to begin, but let us use as an example Cheltenham, where my good friend the late bookseller Alan Hancox was critical in starting up the literary festival about forty years ago. Then it was a quiet, modest affair: a few writers, a few days, a frugal assembly of readers and perfectly satisfactory. Now the Times Literature Festival takes place over two weeks in autumn: event is layered on event; about 80,000 people turn up; writers travel there from all arts and parts; and in spring there is a Science Festival rapidly approaching the same numbers. Hay on Wye has the aspect of a mediaeval tented encampment for two weeks in the summer. Edinburgh, from beginnings even more modest than Cheltenham, entertains more than 200,000 visitors to its literary festival. And so it goes. Cities, towns, villages and hamlets, so many now have their festivals, literary, musical, theatrical, operatic – the Glastonbury Festival, the Pitlochry Autumn Festival, the Southwold Literature Festival, the Lake District International Music Festival, the Wigtown Book Festival.

This thirst will not, I think, be appeased. It is part of the still largely unsung recent story of the arts in this country, and indicates a determined and increasingly numerous minority who will travel and pay and seek out that which satisfies their intellectual passion. In part it grafts on to old traditions of self-help and the quest for intellectual improvement – back to the great literary and scientific institutions with their well-attended and uncompromising lectures. Once again there is a mix of funding here – part subsidy, central and local, part private, part box office. Soon all Britain in summer will be as tented as the fields of Agincourt, the battles all in the mind.

What should and without great outlay could happen in the next ten years is the improvement of cultural skills in schools. In terms of information, it will have to fight for its place in the curriculum. A greater emphasis on the history and variety of culture and cultures would be very useful. But skills, for the individual and for the community, occupy a different area – that of active participation, as in sport. One of the key reasons for the popularity of football and some other games is that children play when young and know how hard it is to be good while enjoying the game at their own level. Having played the game, forever after they have an informed view of it. Now the one million children currently enjoying the Youth Music Programme (YMP) by playing in orchestras or bands as well as singing in choirs will have an inside knowledge and understanding which should be branded into them as deeply as learning to ride a bicycle. The rewards that come from learning an instrument, playing alongside others, making the sounds that make up wonderful music, are very great. It teaches discipline and also the satisfaction of knowing you can master something difficult. There is a sense of communality and learning, and not least pleasure, the doing of it, being inside a force of music with others, together making the one sound.

The promotion of cultural skills has made a sound start and it is possible to pinpoint a number of achievements, such as the aforementioned Gallions Primary School or on a bigger scale the YMP. But this is territory still waiting to be opened up. However, this target has been brought into much sharper focus recently with Margaret Hodge's work on the role of culture in promoting shared values and Andy Burnham's proposal that there should be a mandatory five hours a week of culture introduced into schools. This would match the five hours prescribed for sport.

In both their cases I think that they have come to a conclusion which strikes at the root of the title of this chapter, as attempts are made to reach deeper into our lives, not in the much resented area of micromanagement or ceaseless poaching on privacy, but in a decent democratic effort to give more choices to more people. The opinion that people have of their own capacities, as well as the opportunities provided to realise those capacities, becomes the key agenda. What Burnham cannot sufficiently emphasise is that through the arts, through the practice and performance of the arts, through engagement with others in pursuits of pleasure and welcomed tasks of difficulty, a significant and long-neglected stratum of society can be lifted out of its too imprisoning sense of 'place' and given the self-confidence to set itself up for a much fuller life in that society. It is to do with self-worth – not an easy thing to measure but, according to teachers and others close to the case, not difficult to observe when it happens. This policy in my view is right and good.

The 'old' communities are not gone but they play a restricted role now. Tribes remain – the aristocracy, the new immigrants; communities of interest – educational tourism, sporting fidelities – are growing. And much more. But to go to the root of the matter, to bring together the Three Graces of this chapter's title, you need engagement, the engagement of everyone willing and able, the formation of a generous, open, democratic country of culture. This has to begin in schools and this will be the biggest challenge over the next ten years.

As we try to move on towards a wider and finer culturally literate future, we need that reservoir of cultural skills which will provide both activists and audience. Education is part – in my view the essential part – of access but the drive to provide more access should not start and stop in schools. More can mean better. A better-educated population, a better distribution of the too frequently curtained-off masterpieces, will give us a better society which can feel strengthened by the opportunity, for too long mooted as a privilege, of luxuriant and ample choice. Tax-free access to museums and galleries – a magnificent achievement by the then secretary of state, Chris Smith, against very fierce odds – has resulted in a spectacular rise in attendance figures which must be related to the extraordinary crowds queuing for hours to see the Terracotta Army at the British Museum.

I wrote 'more can mean better'. In a country stratified for as long and as deeply as ours, the habit of keeping the majority out – of power, learning, affluence, culture – is hard to break and it will never be entirely eroded. Moreover there is a point here, a point made by the previous culture secretary, James Purnell, and taken up by his successors, in emphasising the importance of excellence. This was salutary. Imperative though the arguments for access and much wider participation are, they cannot be uncoupled from the acceptance and knowledge of the central importance of quality, the difficulty of achieving high quality, the difficulty in deciding what is of high quality and therefore the necessity for a critical body.

The arts in this country in 1997 were in much the same state as other public services – there had been a fifteen-year run-down and it took about ten years to pull them back and redirect them. Now there is a sense of arrival – in mass, in quality, in ambition. And the great future tasks include an attempt to introduce the guiding need for excellence. This is not easy. It never has been. But, given that it is accepted as part of the equation, the odds are that it will get through as it has done, by and large, over the centuries. The important factor is that it should be keyed into the overall policy and become a basic assumption.

Much of what I have written, though, could be faulted in the fullest terms of 'democracy' and 'community' as being still too heavily skewed to the privileged. The haves are having more, as are their offspring, and although many '*nouveaux* haves' are coming to the table, much of the arts is jointed into the community of the well educated. Privilege and good education are in short supply for at least 50 per cent of our population and yet, to achieve our potential and to allow and help people to lead fuller lives, the arts are already for some and can be for many the best ladder.

One statistic will do: since some galleries and museums ceased to charge, there has been a 21 per cent increase in visits from socio-economic groups C2, D and E. A small step, perhaps, but not insignificant. An indication, certainly, that what holds people back is not lack of native intelligence but lack of cash and social nurture. My father's generation and his father's generation and far back were every bit as intelligent as my own. It was the trap of their social context which took them from school at fourteen, put them in coal mines or on the land, allowed for no further education, adjusted them to the bottom rung and made sure by subtle and not so subtle means that they stayed there. This is not to lay all blame on the class system: there was some movement, but little and painfully gained. There is now the chance to change that radically, to burst out.

So we should intensify arts access even more – to galleries, museums, theatres, concerts. The examples of outreach work done by the 300 small touring projects and the great theatres are a beacon, as are the recent efforts at the Old Vic, to take one example, working stoutly in the unrich environment in which it is situated. The response to exposure to culture from children given little chance by their background is invariably, touchingly, not only positive but often remarkable. There is no way in which our society can compete in the increasingly high-status world of brain and talent power unless it marshals all its resources. That is the bottom-line argument. We will not have enough who are good enough in a world where migration of people and outsourcing of increasingly sophisticated work is commonplace and intensifying. All we have to use is our brains. This country needs its people to be highly educated, as well as savvy, eccentric, seizing on their own idiosyncratic talent. The problem is that this sounds like wishful thinking or mere whistling in the dark. Yet if you had said, in 1957, that fifty years on instead of 6 per cent of school leavers going to university there would be almost 50 per cent, you would have been accused of being a Pollyanna or an anarchist. But that is here. And despite Cassandra and all her jaundiced camp followers, it is energising, lifting, bettering our country.

We should make the priority the lifting of the next 50 per cent – although not into university necessarily. The denigrating of technical education has been a bad consequence of the drive to universities and it is encouraging to see that denigration beginning to be remedied. But only beginning. Skills are still seen as the recourse of those 'outside': how many public schoolboys (able in so many ways and well taught) are plumbers or would dream of being? Yet this 7 per cent are often thought the educational elite. But through the arts we can bring out, lead out, educate, young people who currently feel wholly unempowered, unwanted by society. There are already numerous and positive examples of outreach programmes, touring companies and imaginative teachers using drama, dance, poetry, music to kindle enthusiasm and ambition in those whose poverty begins in fear of imagining a life in which riches can be found and cultivated without material wealth. This too needs to be given a more coherent strategy. To do this, to give to those who so eagerly wait to be given a decent chance, to be given at least a fair portion of the going excess, to be nourished with a slice of the action, enough to show a route they can take: that is the challenge we have to assume. This will fulfil the democratic promise of release from a contemporary form of bondage for the millions denied, through no fault of their own, access and skills to be part of the bounty of opportunities out there. This is not asking for a miracle. This is what has happened for centuries to the few who have been given the chance: the door opens. We can make it happen much more now. And culture is the best key of all: practical, peer-impressing, seeking out nerve and dependent on talent.

Cultural activity in the country should be increasingly supported for its unarguable social benefit. In hospitals, in the care of mentally ill patients, in prisons, in neglected estates, in tough schools: wherever arts commandos have moved in the evidence is convincing. Music, painting, drama, singing, dancing – each in its way helps to alleviate pain, to build confidence, to uncover talent, to forge ideas of small community interdependence. Nothing is the one panacea, but enough 'experiments' have been done to show proof positive that those on the margins, and those who seem destined to a life of compound poverty including the poverty of ambition, can be rescued, even redeemed, by participation in the arts.

It may seem trivial to employ the wording of an advertisement for beer but the evidence does show that the arts can refresh the parts that other methods cannot reach. What is lacking now is the money to follow through, to set in place structures which will not be at the whim of short-term and minimal funding. Better call it an investment, which is what it is: investment in a stronger, more thoughtful, more able society, fit for the twenty-first century. It may seem odd that the arts should be seen as part of the drive to root out the multiple causes of social deprivation. There is sport, of course, and social work and clubs and the enabling nature of self-generated, self-reinforcing activities such as bands and choirs which have a part to play, and underpinning it all must be the attempt to construct jobs. But culture counts. Who would have thought that culture would make London the most visited city in Europe? Or that Glasgow, so battered by the collapse of shipbuilding and manufacturing, would rebuild itself around the notion of being selected as the European City of Culture?

I suppose it seems odd because culture has been seen for so long as by no measure central to the lives of the majority. Therefore the idea that it has come down from that pedestal and has not only engaged in social commerce but has itself become a commercial force still seems a little surreal. But that is the fact. The musicals of Andrew Lloyd Webber and Cameron Mackintosh tour the world and bring in profits simply unheard of in any other age and in any other country, including the United States, even today. The two of them started out as kids on the block doing the thing they loved and ended up as major employers of a wide range of talent.

The waters have been further stirred by the popular arts, which now have access to posterity through CDs and DVDs and, because of that access, availability for the constant critical re-examination which refines much popular work into 'art'. Mozart would have approved. Dickens would have revelled in it. Today's new generation take it entirely for granted. You play the cello in a youth orchestra – of which there are now many in this country – and you moonlight as a blues guitarist with the local rock group.

The theatre should continue to receive subsidy over the next ten years. Without it, the serious work available in our theatres would be much reduced. As it is today, whenever the grant is cut, the cast numbers go down, and we end up with two-handers or one-man/woman shows, whereupon the theatres reach out for pantomimes, or the crowd pleasers that pleased the crowds half a century ago. It has been proved, during the last fifty years, that a steady infusion of money from the state, put in the hands of talented people, will attract private investment and audiences, preserve the greatness of the classics and cultivate the classics of the future. The Royal National Theatre, the Globe, the Royal Court, these and other venues in London alone demonstrate – as nowhere else in the world – the vitality which comes from that mix. The same principle should continue with opera and dance and film, though film stands rather apart from the others in that the Anglo-American character of our studios, the transatlantic conduits of talent and the riskier financial climate in film making bring in opportunities and problems of a rather different order. But once again the film industry is a forger of skills, a high-quality niche industry, and part of what should be Culture Britannia riding the arts waves.

I am aware of a consistent optimism in this chapter which some may find jarring. And although I think it possible to prove and fair to claim that the 'health' of the arts has improved over the last decade, is improving and can improve further, there are difficulties.

The first arises from success. Like the National Health Service, the arts appear to know no frontiers. The older the more of us grow, the more we need from the NHS; the more effective the developments in drugs and surgery, the more we can claim from the NHS. It is a bottomless benefit. The arts are not dissimilar. Once groups have gathered together to set up a theatre group, orchestra, dance company, they seek the core enabling subsidy. Once obtained it is hard to let it go. As I write, Arts Council England's decision to cut back on the number of its clients in order to seek out new companies and shore up the more successful ones has led to demonstrations, outrage and U-turns. Yet last year it announced investment of £1.3 billion for 2008–11, not insubstantial.

But this will continue to be a problem. The genie is out of the bottle. More access and more energy in the creative economy attract more people who have the skills to go for subsidy. There arises the vision of these islands as thicketed with the arts as it once was with heavy industry. Not an unattractive vision, but given that the key to so much of this has been core funding from national and local resources which are entering into what could be a long period of belt tightening, the outcome and the input could be on a long course of confrontation.

And as the economy slows down (I am writing this in 2008), there are clear signs that private or business philanthropy, which have played a sustaining role in the institutional arts, is receding. This would be a blow. In 2005/6, for example, private sector support of the arts reached £529.5 million. It would be a setback if these horns of plenty were to be drawn in, but the evidence suggests they will follow the market rather than the arts. However, the most energising thing is that this government is much more enthusiastic about arts subsidy than it was in 1997 and much more aware of its 'investment' role in skills, in jobs, in niche industries. When tighter constraints come in there may well be a recognition that overall, the arts are making an unquestionably strong contribution to the strengths of this country. It's in the DNA of governance now, no longer an optional extra, though for some it will continue to be thought a minority preserve.

I have left books and broadcasting to the end partly because, being heavily involved in both, there is so much to say and partly because broadcasting is the big beast in the jungle while the book, for me, is the best indicator of cultural health.

What broadcasting should do over the next decade is to preserve what has been called public service broadcasting. This phrase has not worn well. It smacks of Whitehall, nanny and the grumpy prescription of the agonised Lord Reith. Nevertheless it will have to serve. No one has come up with a better one and to change it would inevitably be to dilute it or, by some stroke of re-branding genius, wholly obfuscate it.

'Public service broadcasting' means the making and transmitting of programmes which commercial companies would hesitate to make or might flinch away from: programmes which take an unashamedly considered and thought-through view of political, current and social affairs; programmes which take on board the cultural, historical, religious and intellectual heritage of this country and of other countries; programmes which call in the best available talent to work on them and seek out the widest possible audience without threatening the integrity of the subject. If that sounds dull, I suggest you think of *Channel 4 News*, *The Death of Yugoslavia*, the serialisation of *Bleak House*, David Attenborough, the dramatisations of Jane Austen, *Dispatches*, ITN and any number of fine contemporary dramas and documentaries. That is just in television. In radio perhaps the shorthand for public service could be Radio 4. And there is more – steady supplies of classical and popular music, more and more narrowcasting on digital channels.

There is so much more. What is going on with the technology is as big a change as under Caxton. In one leap we have gone from spectrum scarcity to 'infinite' availability. The broadcasters no longer control the spectrum: the powers that be would have to struggle all the days and nights they have to exercise any meaningful control on the broadcasters. We have a waterfall of choice. Regulation – that old-time religion which served the BBC, ITV and Channel 4 so well – may soon be no more than a finger in the dyke. The internet, which announces itself as taking over the world, is 80 per cent pornography and much of the rest is house sales. Where is the kernel of public service in that? The idea of a community of broadcasters planted in the BBC or ITV or Channel 4 whose talents were various but whose unspoken oath of allegiance was to deliver high quality to the public and acknowledge that at the heart of the matter was this contract to serve the public with the best in all aspects of information, entertainment and education is being dug up at the root. The very notion of linear attention to television and radio is challenged by the multiplication of outlets overwhelmingly offering cheap fodder. Do we fit our culture to the shape of available technologies? Do we go with the flow of market forces, globalisation, primacy of choice, information overload, and the necessary advance of the lowest common denominator? Do we give in to Gresham's law? This matters because, to stick to the UK, broadcasting is the biggest cultural mover and shaker in the land.

What should happen here over the next ten years is as follows: first, the government must ensure that the population has access to proper information. In the United States for instance, home of some of the greatest broadcasting, news and opinion, patriotic bias and shock-jockery are becoming fused. A healthy democracy needs powerful, objective, well-reasoned, independent news services, and more than one of them. Second, broadcasting must oil the wheels the economic system does not – which is where the phrase 'public service broadcasting' is useful. We as a society are testing the driving potential of market principles sometimes, it seems, to destruction. There has to be a counter-force, in democratic political terms an opposition.

At the moment, we are, comparatively, well placed here in the UK. The BBC receives a licence fee of about £3.5 billion a year to spend on programmes and their distribution, and this alone, apart from the top-ups which come to it through its commercial enterprise, put it on strong ground. This licence fee is currently guaranteed for about ten years, which would seem to solve the problem, but I'm not sure it does.

The BBC is nothing if it is not the guardian of public service broadcasting. On the whole, programmes thus described garner lower audiences than entertainment, game shows, talk shows, reality television, quizzes – all crowd pullers which inhabit every other channel as the competition becomes frantic in pursuit of a remorselessly fragmenting audience. There is a diminishing loyalty to the traditional terrestrial channels and therefore competition becomes more frenzied. If the BBC sticks too closely to its public service remit, it risks broadcasting to a minority and therefore the majority of the population which pays the licence fee (the very old excepted) would legitimately ask: What am I getting in return for my contribution? This is already asked but, thankfully, the recent settlement saw it as a murmur rather than a roar and reinstated the licence fee. But it is a question which will not go away and is always potentially available as a rousing vote winner.

The BBC in the case of BBC1, the channel on which it spends most money, is already accused of ducking its obligations, and there is a body of opinion, in which I find myself, which thinks the corporation would be better advised to tough it out now, to stick to its guns now, to take on the big battle while it has ten years in its reserves – the big battle being an outward, visible and unflinching dedication to public service broadcasting, even on BBC1, its most popular channel; especially, some would say, on its most popular channel.

But it is important to state that the BBC does not have a monopoly on public service broadcasting. Over the last few decades ITV and then Channel 4 have given the BBC strong competition in this area. Commercial pressures on those channels are currently unremitting and yet they too should be enabled to carry on with public service broadcasting over the next decade. This will be a tough fight. One way to do it, it has been suggested, would be for the licence fee to be used exclusively for public service broadcasting and become a sum parts of which other broadcasters could bid for. I think that would be dangerous. Once the BBC licence fee is spread all over the place its justification is surely weakened. The BBC has guarded the licence fee well for more than eighty years. It is a magnificent, world-class organisation, perhaps at the moment taking up too many opportunistic options for its own good. But it has been encouraged in this country to represent the best we can do and any tinkering with its democratic base, which turns the whole country into a community supporting the national culture, would weaken it fatally.

Another thought is that a separate sum be set up for which, again, commercial broadcasters could bid to facilitate their public service output. This could be a runner. We wait and see whether these will be options but the imperatives are that public service broadcasting continues, that it is not the monopoly of one channel, that it sticks to its guns.

For not only does our broadcasting provide for several communities, it is itself, for those employed in it, a community, the media community, a large one now. And it is also a crucial arena for directors, writers, actors, production staff and technical staff – again an impressive number of niche skills which fit in well with any realistic idea of a prosperous future for the UK. And there are the communities which form themselves around a popular programme – *Coronation Street* is the prime example – and use it as their village street, their garden gossip. Broadcasting is also, at its best, a strong guarantee of our democracy. In its public service mode it reports on it, examines it, criticises it, investigates it and by doing what it does is itself part of a wider democratic process.

If I end with the book it is partly because this is one, and rather fancifully because our particular British contribution to civilisation began with a book (The Lindisfarne Gospels) and found its apogee in four collections of books, those of Shakespeare, the Bible, Newton and Darwin. It is also because, so far, despite prophecies that 'The End Is Nigh' from the late nineteenth-century arrival of the cinema to the advent of radio, then television, then the web, and more to come – books still remain the best conscience and revealed consciousness of what we are. They are totally new tech – mobile, silent, always turned on, independent of all fallible power sources and uniquely convenient to have and to hold. They allow every individual to exist on equal terms with any other individual who has written anything and to take to and from the page whatever strikes the imagination or reason. Authors have their own communities of readers; readers increasingly have their own communities of other readers. While the content of books seems as threatened by mass supermarket demands as the content of farms, there still appears to be an unfazed resistance movement which reveals little sign of panic; they will, we will, find the books we want to read and in the search discover others we had never heard of.

But this should be underpinned by a rigorous and positive reassessment of the public library system. That is democracy, culture and community in action. It is a noble and bold idea but over the last few decades the book side of the libraries has not been given the support it deserves. Its internal indecisiveness has not helped its own cause. But it remains crucial and needs constant support. This is not crying 'subsidy, more subsidy!' for a cultural institution yet again. A free library service is critical to the basic need of a proper democratic system which serves its local and national communities with the richest fare available. Books hold great treasure. Free libraries are the guardians and the link in a most valuable and vulnerable chain between mind and mind. A society in which anyone at all can walk freely into a library and order any book on any subject and take it away to possess alone for the time it takes to read and absorb it is a society that understands and values one of the essential tools of a fulfilled and examined life. Libraries should be organisationally over-hauled and given more resources and guaranteed their role as the citadels of thought and imagination available to each according to his need. This should be a priority.

The creative economy can and should be developed and encouraged to the hilt over the next decade. It is a proven performer, as a pillar of the cultural tourist trade which has so much potential, as an educative and inspiring force for young people, as a conduit of skills and self-confidence in schools and community centres, as a high-quality niche industry in a country which must develop such specialist strongholds if it is to flourish, as an employer of a vast range of talents and not least as a source of gaiety to the nation, a focus of imagination to a people who want to reach out to one another.

Part III

Equality, society and family

7

A progressive agenda in relation to family, gender and generation

Mary Daly

Today's family is enormously varied – diversity is so prevalent that sociologists have stopped using the definite article and now refer to 'families' or 'family-related behaviour' rather than '*the* family'. Incomplete households, informal cohabitation and more than one marriage throughout the life course all change the landscape within which family policy (and public policy more generally) operates. When it comes to relationships, a greater emphasis on individual needs coexists with identities and standards of living deriving from family. While it might be somewhat premature to proclaim the disappearance of the housewife, the counterpoint to increased employment among women has been a decline in the traditional household form of a male breadwinner and female homemaker and a growth of households where both partners are employed and where children are cared for primarily outside the home. Globalisation is, therefore, not just (or even) an economic phenomenon – as a term it can and should be used to refer also to profound changes in values and practices around individual behaviour and family life. This has been the stuff of much sociological theorising and much conjecture.[1] From the point of view of this chapter, the key questions centre on how policy in the UK is linking into these and other changes and what constitutes a progressive agenda for family and gender relations as we look towards the future. 'Progressive' is of course a contested term. As used here, it refers to a new family agenda for the social democratic project. This will involve valuing family life as well as making for greater equality in regard to individual autonomy, and undoing the structures of inequality, especially as they derive from relations of gender, class, generation and ethnicity.

The chapter is organised into three parts. The first outlines the main elements of the New Labour approach to family and gender, against a backdrop of the changes and challenges in British society. The second focuses on the model of family life that underlies reform and the strengths and weaknesses of the New Labour approach. In the third section, elements for a progressive approach are set out, mindful both of the limits of regulation and of people's real family lives and their wishes in that regard.

Policy reform/developments/trends

Unlike in the past, family is now a strong motivator of policy reform in the UK. New Labour has not just prioritised family performance and welfare but has unfolded a programme of support and regulation for (some) families and sectors of the population. The reforms have been tightly organised around a number of goals.

As is well known at this stage, people's economic behaviour has been a primary concern. From the beginning of its tenure, New Labour represented receipt of state benefits as a form of 'dependence' that was socially and morally undesirable. This conviction authored a sustained programme to move people away from a condition that was perceived as passive (benefit receipt) towards one seen as active and enhancing (self-sufficiency in the marketplace). While the resulting 'activation' measures were primarily focused on individuals, they had a strong collective cast too. The notion of 'workless households', which quickly took hold in the policy lexicon, is meant to convey the idea that a household or family in which nobody is employed constitutes ipso facto a social problem. And so such households, and the behaviour of low-income parents especially, were made the subjects of a range of increasingly interventionist programmes, designed to both push and pull targeted groups into the workforce. In the process, the nature of the public support system for families and individuals was transformed. The range and generosity of benefits available was altered (typically tied more closely to employment but some, such as the universal child benefit, were increased in value) and a broad-ranging system of family-based tax credits, designed to make employment more feasible and attractive for families by topping up wages, was introduced to take over major functions in regard to income support. A strong goal throughout was to synchronise the economic and other behaviours of family members.

Work–life balance, a social policy idea that has its main origins in the OECD and the European Union, is another dominant frame of family policy in today's Britain. The idea draws upon two roots: the wish to better accommodate work and family life, and gender equality. It places lifestyle changes on the policy agenda – in a nutshell, men are to become more domesticated and women more 'professional'. Conscious of tensions between economic and social objectives, over the course of the last decade New Labour has put in place a series of more generous and extensive leaves from employment for family (actually childcare-related) purposes that target both mothers and fathers. The amount of paid maternity leave has been extended (to thirty-nine weeks from fourteen), for example, catapulting the UK into the lead position in Europe in terms of maternity leave duration. The leave has also been made more generous (doubling in value in ten years) and part of it is now transferable from mother to father. In addition, paid paternity and adoption leave have been introduced and plans are afoot to extend both to twenty-six weeks. Another innovation has been the introduction of a right to request flexible working for parents of young and disabled children. While it is at the discretion of employers, the fact that workers are given a right to request the leave is far from trivial given the otherwise strong voluntarist tradition in UK industrial relations.[2]

Greater policy focus on children and young people is a third anchoring idea in the New Labour social programme. The impulse here is to improve children's existing welfare and human capital resources, with a view especially to enhancing their future chances and performance. To effect a better childhood and especially adulthood for today's children, improved services have been the major target in a programme that has had three main lines of action: a huge expansion of early childhood education and care, a drive to address child poverty and a sustained programme to streamline and improve support services for children and families. Some £21 billion has been invested in early childhood education and care services since 1997, doubling the stock of childcare places over the period.[3] Although it still falls behind the very best provider countries in Europe, the UK can no longer be depicted as a laggard in childcare policy.[4] Better financial assistance for families with children has also been a goal – the level of financial support for families with children has almost doubled in the last ten years. There has also been another set of interventions which target young people in disadvantaged areas, this time oriented to increasing discipline and supervision and attacking 'the anti-social'. The interventions include a number of measures that on the one hand target young people and their families by criminalising behaviours deemed to be anti-social and on the other 'activate' young people for the purpose of employment and training. Part of the latter intervention has been the introduction of financial incentives in the form of direct payments to young people to remain on in school as well as a host of New Deal-type programmes that seek to improve young people's chances of getting a job.

This focus on children and young people is complemented by a focus on families, especially those that live in what are considered risky areas. One of the most sustained aspects of New Labour's social policy has been a move to expand and streamline general services for families and via that and other measures improve social order. This was effected in the first instance by the SureStart programme, which began in 1998 (modelled on the US scheme Head Start). The aims of this programme lie partly in better governance and a desire for neighbourhood renewal but they also extend to effecting better family practices and outcomes. The policy momentum is to gradually roll out on a wider basis measures which upon initiation are focused on children from disadvantaged areas. The anchoring goal is to ensure that families living in the 20 per cent most deprived areas have available to them in their locality a range of child- and family-centred services, including health, family support and outreach and early learning, so as to improve the standard of parenting and as a by-product promote parental employment. Conceived of as a one-stop shop, SureStart, and the Children's Centre programme that has replaced it, which will oversee the establishment of a much larger network of 3,500 centres by 2010 (trebling 2006 provision), are firmly anchored both in anti-poverty objectives and in social inclusion. The government itself speaks of a 'personalisation' of services for children, using this term to represent its preference for targeting children from the worst-off homes and tailoring services for different types of problem.[5]

Strengthening family relationships and family performance has, then, been a fourth axis or aim of British family policy under New Labour. By 2010 all schools will offer a range of parenting support, including information sessions, alongside more specialised support for parents whose children have problems with attendance or behaviour. As well as services focusing on children, there has been investment in relationship support (delivered through the third sector) and also support services for resolving conflict between parents whose relationships have broken down. An authoritarian under-current sits alongside the more paternalistic measures. Parenting orders, for example, have been introduced to compel those parents whose children have come to the notice of the authorities through behaviour that falls within the rather wide and loose classification of 'anti-social' to attend parenting classes and fulfil other requirements deemed necessary by the court for improving their child's behaviour. In addition there are parenting contracts, which are two-sided voluntary agreements between parents and the local authority (or other bodies) to address children's behavioural or attendance problems.

How should these reforms be assessed, especially in the light of the conditions that make for balance between individual and collective interests?

Risks or tensions inherent in the current reforms

Family is notoriously complex – policy has to balance many different considerations, some moral, some pragmatic, some ideological. Not only this, but family consists of a 'community' of members whose interests are potentially in conflict (for example along gender and/or generational lines). Family policy, therefore, needs to work simultaneously to a number of goals. The work of Franz-Xaver Kaufmann and Thomas Bahle among others identifies a fine-grained set of actual or possible motives for family policy:

• the natalist motive: the importance of demographic reproduction

- the economic motive: improvement of the stock of human capital
- the socio-economic motive: balancing employment (self-sufficiency) and support for the family
- the societal motive: the significance of the family as a form of social stability and social capital
- the socio-political motive: compensating for the costs of having families
- the institutional motive – to protect the family as a valued institution
- the gender equality motive
- the children's welfare motive.[6]

This serves as a useful template against which to think about a progressive agenda for the UK.

While some elements of each motive are to be found in the contemporary UK scenario, it is clear that the economic and socio-economic motivations are the most firmly embedded. When framed against the diverse policy portfolio identified above, family policy in the UK appears narrow in several key respects: its commitment to crafting a particular family/work interface, its focus on family dysfunction and the proclivities and practices of low-income families, its prioritising of children and young people over other target groups, and aspects of intergenerational relations. What is de-emphasised? Gender equality, the protection of the family as a valued social institution, and compensation for the costs of having children (what Kaufmann terms the 'socio-political' motive and what economists call horizontal redistribution). As I will explain in a moment, while there are elements of each of these in the UK scenario, they are not driving goals of policy reform.

One could point to an underlying unidimensionality in the New Labour approach. A very specific type of family life and family structure is being promoted. It is in the first instance the economic family, where the family is seen in terms of income procurement and exchange, and in the second the working family, where both parents are employed, where fathers as well as mothers take leave from their jobs when a new child is born and where children, once they reach the age of two or thereabouts, receive their care and education primarily outside the home (some of it in publicly provided services but most of it from private, potentially for-profit providers). There are real questions about whether the 'dual-earner couple' model is consonant with the diversity of family norms in our society. The quite singular promotion of the dual-earner couple does not sit well either with the preferences among some ethnic groups and sub-sectors of the population for a different family model (for example matriarchal families, male breadwinner families, 'reconstituted families' of various types). Apart from the normative level, there are questions also about the well-being of lone parents in this model. Their welfare and income standard constitute a potential weak point in the two-earner system.

There are particular preferences exercised by current policy, especially when it comes to gender. The gender equality thrust of the past has been replaced by a more gender-neutral model which, to the extent that it problematises gender at all, is oriented to differences (or similarities) between women and men rather than inequalities. The assumption is that women and men can now act as economically independent worker-citizens. A sameness model prevails wherein women's life courses are expected to increasingly resemble those of men, outside the home anyway. Women have little or no choice about this; if not the state, then the economy and/or society prevails on them to be economically active. Within the home it is a different story. Here the meaning of equality is much more contingent, an artefact of the expectations, ideas and (power) resources that each member of the couple brings to the relationship. What the British state asks of fathers is that they bond with their new-born children for two weeks in their early lives (as evidenced by the duration and conditions of paternal leave) and that they be 'responsible' in financially supporting their children. For women 'responsibility' is defined in terms of being prepared to be employed (and in the process giving up the personal care of their children, especially when they are past the toddler stage, to others). There is a double (and to some extent contradictory) loop for women: they are being 'defamilialised' when it comes to employment but 'familialised' when it comes to unpaid work.

Looked at from the perspective of how individuals are treated, a further risk in the current reforms is that people are seen only or primarily in terms of their functional utility. Instrumentalism is a consideration highlighted especially as regards the focus on children. Measures to improve the life conditions for families with social problems and the cognitive performance of children from these and other backgrounds are of course always welcome. They also tap into an international seam of thinking which holds that generous parental leave, high-quality subsidised childcare and organised after-school activities significantly enhance life chances and counteract social inequalities.[7] The New Labour approach has its particularities, though. Ruth Lister suggests that in it the child is a 'cipher for future economic prosperity'. 'Children matter instrumentally, not existentially,' she says.[8] One of the main weaknesses of the move towards children's policy is that it fails to realise a broad-based and existential citizenship for children and is not sufficiently concerned with a good childhood (as distinct from a satisfactory adulthood) for today's children. A mirroring question at the collective level is whether family is or should be for policy purposes more than an economic unit or an instrument of social control. This raises the matter of the extent to which family life is valued per se. While policy is always instrumental to some degree, issues of economic functioning (rather than, for example, any number of goals or objectives in relation to social and family welfare understood more broadly) appear to be more dominant now than they were in the past. Is the real goal of 'work/family balance' policy to craft a more employment-friendly form of family life, to alter the nature of family life such that it is rendered compatible with the rhythms and exigencies of economy and employment, or to improve the quality of family life? And where does the balance lie? There are also other doubts about the underlying approach. 'Work/family reconciliation' rests on a very restricted and conventional understanding of 'work' (and even of 'family'). Julia Brannen and colleagues point out that the concept assumes an opposition between work and the rest of life, that it has a one-dimensional view of time, focusing mainly upon the present, and that it assumes time to be a commodity which individually each of us can manage (in the sense of having the skills and capacities to do so).[9] Their research on how people actually manage work and care shows that employment and the rest of life are not separate domains but are closely interwoven over the course of people's lives across generations and that people struggle to balance them.

Set in its context, there is something genuinely new underway and there is more family in British social policy now than there ever has been. The strong focus on children is noteworthy here, as is the concern with the quality of family relations and the roles of family members and (some) family practices. Yet while there is no doubt that New Labour has opened up new frontiers – seeking to target cultural and cognitive inequalities as well as the most entrenched of economic inequalities – it has done so through a particular and particularistic approach which itself carries significant risks.

Towards a progressive policy agenda

How much the state should ease the passage of families is an open and difficult question. Arguments against an interventionist approach are easily marshalled. If families are left to their own devices they might be better able to weather whatever storms they encounter. Interventionist policies may also be charged with the taint of social engineering. However, counter-arguments are also compelling, not least the claim that the development of a family policy is integral to the future of European market societies, given the need to find an equilibrium between economic and social objectives. In any case, intervention is already underway. New Labour's reform process has had strong moral and normative undertones, not just led by increased state purview and regulation of behaviours heretofore considered 'private' but also prosecuting distinctions between good and bad, deserving and undeserving, troubled and troublesome.[10]

Among the large issues that have to be addressed as part of a progressive agenda is whether to take a universal or a targeted approach. New Labour has tended towards the latter, effecting a policy for some families rather than one for all families (and thereby continuing the selective approach that has for long dominated in the UK). In effect, New Labour plans for the problem family, the failed child and the incompetent parent. I am of the view that both a universal and a targeted approach are needed. One of the signature achievements of the New Labour policy approach has been the attention to alleviating the conditions of poor families, with particular emphasis on the life chances and situations of children living in such families. This targeting is essential, if inequalities and dysfunction are to be reduced. The grounds for complementing this kind of approach with a concern about quality of life for all families lie in the kinds of concerns I raised above about family as a valued domain of life and a potential source of social stability and social quality. One could make a strong argument that, when it comes to the family anyway, endorsing the positive is as likely to be as effective (and perhaps a lot less expensive) as seeking to address the negative. Policy makers need to adopt a perspective which takes family life and its quality as its starting point. This would mean moving away from the perspective of family as problem – including the kind of instrumentalist approach whereby the primary orientation of policy is to address particular 'problems' of family culture (mothers' (under)employment, paternal irresponsibility, poor parent–child relations, family instability, social disorder) – and towards an approach that considers family as a valued domain. There are several elements to this.

A first element is what might be said to be the essence of family life – the activities and relations involved in care as it applies not just to children but also to elderly and other family members. Considering the activities and relations involved as 'care' confirms them as holistic, recognising that they extend right across the lifespan and know no real boundaries between home and elsewhere. We have to ask whether the recent mass movement of care out of the family has acted to downgrade it. It certainly runs the risk of devaluing care provided in a family setting as well as those who provide it. I am of the view that giving greater recognition and value to caring should have a firm place in a progressive agenda. How to actually achieve this is remarkably difficult; however, I suggest a number of steps.

In the first instance, care should be viewed as a need and a responsibility that potentially affects all individuals and many institutions. Hence it requires interventions at different levels, from individuals, through households, civil society, state and market.[11] There should be no monopoly of care, either within the household or outside it, and social policy should actively seek to redistribute care (in much the same way as income redistribution is accepted as a legitimate social goal). Of course care giving has to be resourced – for this purpose the concept or idea of 'care capital' might be a useful frame. Giving payments for care is one way; these already have a place in social policy provision. But such payments will work only if set at a sufficiently high rate – excessively low payments run the risk of ghettoising the activity and confirming it as a low-wage, low-skill, low-status activity. For example, low payments act against gender equality, incentivising women but not men to undertake caring activities. But payments on their own are an insufficient response – recognising the value of unpaid work extends beyond remunerating it.

A second element of valuing care relates to rights. We are more familiar with the duty elements of care but actually rights are vital to giving and receiving good quality care. The movement towards granting home carers pensions and other entitlements serves to strengthen the rights basis of care. Equally, granting those who are at the receiving end of care, such as children or older people, rights around access and quality is important.

A third essential element is services. The need for services is already widely accepted and under New Labour the range and volume of services associated with care has been widely extended. This should be continued, informed by a perspective of partnership (especially between employers and employees and between the state and the market) and of collective provision.

A fourth element is time; actually the root resource conferred by employment leave (along with income replacement). The Netherlands has recently gone one step beyond employment leave, introducing a scheme whereby Dutch workers can trade time for money by building up a time and income bank, resourced from part of their normal wages and salary and unused leave time, which can later be used for goals such as more income, day care for children or reduced hours of work.[12] The Dutch government is also making a deliberate attempt to redistribute the existing volume of both paid and unpaid work by actively improving the quality of part-time work. We await the fruits of these measures – at the present time the division of paid and unpaid work continues to have a strong gender cast in the Netherlands.[13]

Empirical research indicates that the variety of ways in which people would like to and can maintain a work–life balance means that the goal of policy should be flexibility, so that workers and employers may arrive at combinations that suit their particular needs. Rather than absolutely reduce their working time, people express a preference for greater control over it and also show enthusiasm for time-saving schemes (whereby overtime is saved up and taken as extra time off, as in the Dutch model).[14] This is an important meaning of 'flexibility' in today's Europe. Options that involve a reduction in income, such as career breaks and early retirement, are generally less popular. The adequacy of existing policy is called into question by the fact that, when it comes to preferred options to balance home and work, there is in many cases a mismatch between preference and availability. People's preferred options to balance their work and family life are not available to them in sufficient quantity.[15] Options paid for by employers (such as paid leave to care for relatives and for study purposes) tend to have low availability although they are popular, whereas the reverse is the case for unpaid leave.

Focusing on the dynamics and quality of care might also serve to address some of the complex moral issues involved in the domain of family, especially as they relate to interpersonal relations. Policy often either ignores or misunderstands felt obligations and responsibilities among kin. One compelling insight of research is that for women the relationship between employment and family is an active one in the sense of being a site of fine-graded decision making and careful reasoning, in which morality plays a large role.[16] Mothers in the UK have typically tried to find employment that 'fitted' around the family.[17] We now know that there is some trade-off for women (for example between work and family) in all European social policy systems.[18] The scale of the trade-off matters, as does its sign (for instance, a negative trade-off between women's labour supply and fertility is commonplace in Europe). Even the Scandinavian countries are discovering that gender equality is more intractable than was assumed. Nabanita Datta Gupta and colleagues have identified the emergence of a new male-breadwinner society in these countries whereby mothers self-select into relatively low-paid jobs in the public sector, where it is easier to combine a career with family responsibilities, while men tend to locate themselves in the private sector.[19] The results of this and other research raise doubts about potential 'boomerang effects' of policies on women's position in the labour market.[20] In effect, gender equality is something of a moving target in that measures intended to alleviate it, once in place, appear to encounter or even lead to new 'glass ceilings'.

There are certainly real limits to gender equality understood in the sameness model – mainly because it leaves underlying structures and stereotypes unchanged and fails to adequately meet people's wish to be closely involved in the care of their relatives. We have to hold policy to a higher standard than this. As Nancy Fraser has said, the goal is not to make men and women identical to each other but rather to promote a universal caregiver model, whereby care is shared not just between women and men but also between the state, employers and companies, the voluntary sector and the community at large.[21] We must cleave to employment and career as a goal for the majority of women. Furthermore, we have to be careful of neo-familialism, which does little more than 'modernise' traditional arrangements. This does not necessarily mean depriving women of the choice to rear families or to care for their ill or elderly relatives themselves, but it does mean extending that choice in a real way to men as well.

These to me are two essential conditions of gender equality at the present time: that it be the norm for women to be employed (one might even think of setting benchmarks in this regard because, without a critical mass of women employed, stereotypes of women as unreliable and casual workers will continue); that it equally be the norm for men to undertake caring-related activities. This in turn, and the latter especially, leads to a third condition: better sharing of unpaid work. The movement of women into the labour force has not resulted in a significantly improved sharing of home-based work between women and men – the average woman does between two and three times the amount of unpaid work carried out by men.[22] The present arrangement works only because it rests on a gender division of opportunities and costs. This, the failed revolution, has to appear on the policy radar in the UK as well. Paternity leave as it exists in the UK – of only two weeks' duration and restricted to the period around the child's birth – is not especially oriented to over-turning this source of inequality; it is geared more to the father–child relationship than to mother and father sharing. It is a step in the right direction, however. The conditions as always are crucial – the experience of other countries makes clear that men will, or can afford to, take paternal or parental leave only when it has a high wage replacement ratio and that services to supplement and at times replace parental activities are crucial. For those worried about population renewal – and this has to be a concern of any future policy given the strong tendency right across Europe in the direction of fertility at less than the replacement level – the evidence suggests that countries with higher gender equality have higher fertility scores than those where women face difficulties in reconciling an independent life with family obligations.[23]

When it comes to unpaid work, the appropriate response is not to mandate for equal sharing in the narrow sense – parents with task charts ticking off who does what – but rather to place greater value in and on the sphere of care and associated activity. In the spirit of the measures outlined above, it means treating home and work as interconnected. Gillian Pascall and Jane Lewis speak of a logic of gender equality in carework, income, time and voice, as well as in paid employment.[24] Miriam Glucksmann's concept of the total social organisation of labour is also relevant here. With this approach she has in mind the manner in which all the labour in a society is divided up and allocated to different structures, institutions, activities and people.[25] In practice, this kind of approach means developing an entire environment favouring more equal sharing between men and women across spheres and resources: in paid work, carework, income, time and voice. It might also be worth thinking through what is the desired end when it comes to better sharing between women and men – better sharing of what? Housework? Child rearing?

The approach taken to children and young people is especially important in all of this. Recent developments, such as anti-social behaviour orders and parenting orders, undermine a rights approach to children and young people. Their focus is the child's behaviour rather than his or her welfare.[26] Such measures also tend to individualise children and young people. While children have been made a prime consideration in the contemporary policy constellation, the extent to which policy targets a good childhood is limited. For Lister such a policy for children qua children means focusing on two inter-related elements: their well-being and their citizenship.[27] Taking a citizenly perspective allows policy makers to have a guiding frame-work which underpins children's membership of society, namely in that context their rights, their responsibilities, their status, respect and their level of recognition vis-à-vis other sectors of the population.[28] The family life of children and young people and their right to high quality in that regard has to be a consistent priority.

Staying with the investment paradigm which has been so prevalent in recent years, there is an argument to be made for the beneficial effects of increased parental involvement with children. Research now suggests, for example, that the passing on of cultural knowledge and appreciation (cultural capital, if you will) from parents to children is vitally important and may even be a stronger predictor of subsequent cognitive skills and development than household income level.[29] That said, any new measures have to complement and be rendered compatible with continued efforts to improve the living situation, life chances and social mobility of children from low-income backgrounds. Without more effective action towards this end, two long-term consequences are likely: a decline in intergenerational mobility – already visible in the UK[30] – and a decline in the number of families (as young people postpone the move to family formation). There is also the matter of financially compensating families. Having children is associated with income constraint and economic dis-advantage in relation to other sectors of the population. Considered as an issue for policy, the critical challenge here is redistribution and achieving a balance between horizontal and vertical equity. Given the ever closer relationship between large family size and low income, there is a need for policies to focus more closely on vertical equity. In addition, as Jens Alber and Tony Fahey and others have pointed out, measures must also have a horizontal cast (in terms of redistributing resources and opportunities between those with children and those without).[31]

Central to the 'demographic problematic' also is the issue of the chances open to young people and the extent to which the implicit promises to them as the next generation – of a career in gainful employment and fulfilled choices in their private lives – can be realised. Opportunities for today's young people vary widely across

Europe but in many cases young people are experiencing a relative loss of autonomy compared with former generations. Getting a foothold in the labour market can be especially difficult for them, with consequences relating to job security and quality, the prospects of a progressive career, dependence on family and even the chances of founding a family of their own. Recent research on globalisation and its social consequences underlines both the need for flexibility and the fact that young people with low skills and education are disproportionately negatively affected by globalisation.[32] In this context I suggest that we have to look again at the risks we cover with our social and other services and see them as a challenge. At the present time the risks that we cover are few, mainly because the energies of the social support system have targeted the 'behaviour' of young people rather than their underlying situations and future chances. This is a relatively shallow approach to progress; at its heart there is a silence about underlying causes, needs and the heavy hand of social circumstances.[33] It is especially necessary to bear in mind that a widespread consequence of globalisation (understood both as the impulses towards a global market and as the policy responses to them) is that it shifts uncertainties and risks to certain social groups, such as labour market beginners, returning women and unskilled workers.[34] An approach to policy, then, which rests on the belief that people's own behaviour is what is placing them on the periphery is inadequate.

Transitions are normal and must be thought of as such by social and other policies. The ideas of the German policy analyst Günther Schmid are of relevance here. He has pointed out that people are most at risk when they move between activities – unemployment to employment, education to work, work to caring, caring to work, work to retirement – and that to best manage the risks requires taking the whole of their life course into account.[35] Schmid developed the concept of transitional labour markets, which involve clear rights and practical support for people to move in and out of the work-force as their needs and circumstances change. People could vary their work commitments in the light of caring responsibilities, their need for further education and training, or because at certain points in their lives they may be more involved in community or non-profit activity.

Overall, a progressive agenda around work and family means being open to change on many fronts, being mindful of the need to protect individual welfare but also to balance this with exigencies and concerns about collective well-being.

8

Social justice in a changing world

Towards a fairer Britain

Patrick Diamond

Introduction

The debate among social democrats about the definition and meaning of 'social justice' has been dominated for the last fifty years by Anthony Crosland's seminal text *The Future of Socialism*. It is the finest work of political theory ever produced by a serving Labour politician, and the standard by which all subsequent theoretical contributions have been assessed. Indeed, Crosland's work is a reminder of what genuine 'renewal' entails. It urges us, in R. H. Tawney's words, 'to treat sanctified formulae with judicious irreverence', and remains the most thorough and unapologetic presentation of the social democratic revisionist case.

The argument of this chapter is that the strategy elaborated in *The Future of Socialism* is based on an ideological world-view and a set of assumptions that are likely to be quite inadequate for the future. This does not mean that social democrats have nothing to learn from Crosland's writings, or that they should be oblivious to the achievements of past Labour governments. The challenge, however, will be to develop a set of governing principles that might frame a new politics of social justice. This should draw on a clear analysis and critique of the condition of Britain, as well as providing a renewed sense of guiding purpose. It will need to acknowledge key social changes including the rise of diversity, complexity and time poverty, the emergence of new family forms, the changing labour market and the shift to a 'post-consumption' society. The chapter then explores how such governing principles might practically shape the progressive agenda in the years ahead.

Social justice and equality

New Labour favours greater social justice. It has sought to create a society less unequal than that which it inherited from the Conservatives. But there has often been confusion about how equality should be defined and about the types of inequality that could feasibly be reduced in a world characterised by global markets and rapid technological change. An open and honest debate about the nature of social justice and equality is vital if Labour is to devise an approach that transcends the limitations of both old-style social democracy and market liberalism.

At the outset, it is necessary to clarify how terms such as 'equality' are to be understood. This chapter refers to the notion of economic inequality as the term has traditionally been used: inequality between individuals in respect of income, wealth and other factors that produce differences in disposable material resources. The traditional notion of equality may be somewhat limited, however, in the emerging narrative around social justice, and there is a need to take into account a broader range of dimensions that involve distributions, opportunities and procedures, as well as rights and needs. The relative distribution of material resources is not the sole factor in determining social justice. The chapter therefore deals with an account of social justice rather than 'equality' per se.

The central principle of a new politics of social justice is that social change cannot be imposed from the top down, that the purpose of reducing inequality is to enrich and strengthen personal freedom, and that achieving social justice is as much about shifting the terms of political argument as finding technical solutions to long-standing policy dilemmas. The ultimate aim of this new politics must be to liberate people, not to create a larger state. While centralised government intervention can of course fail, the state remains an important instrument of progressive change and reform. Where the left seeks to use the state as its chosen instrument of equity and efficiency, it needs to show that the state can function efficiently. The coming agenda for politics will be how to give people greater choice and control over their lives. That shift will aggravate current inequalities if it is restricted to a form of negative freedom in which people are merely free to buy and sell in the marketplace. Instead, it is important to develop a more compelling vision of freedom and social justice – the right to human dignity and fulfilment through the opportunity and security afforded by an empowering state.

Inequality in British society

In the immediate aftermath of Labour's 1997 victory, a fierce dispute broke out about how far and in what sense the Labour Party remained committed to the traditional aim of equality of outcome. Some have decried New Labour's abandonment of egalitarianism as a formal objective of party policy, but the arguments tend to under-estimate the extent to which traditional social democratic approaches have in fact remained influential.

Labour since 1997 has been the most redistributive government in modern British history. Since 1998/9, the number of children living in poverty has fallen by half a million and is now at its lowest level since the early 1980s. Some 1.5 million individuals have been lifted out of poverty, where poverty is defined as living under 60 per cent of median income. Absolute poverty has declined steadily: the numbers living in poor households fell from 13.9 million in 1996/7 to 12.4 million in 2002/3.[1] In fact, between 1996/7 and 2001/2 income inequality rose on a variety of measures to reach its highest ever level since comparable records began in 1961, according to the recorded Gini coefficient. Since then, income inequality has repeatedly fallen, a trend recently confirmed by the OECD: since 2000 poverty and inequality have fallen faster in the UK than in any other OECD country.[2]

Median incomes have also grown by 2.6 per cent since 1997, compared with 0.7 per cent in the Major years and 2.1 per cent during the Thatcher governments. Income transfers to poorer families have risen by nearly 1 per cent of GDP since Labour came to office.[3] Since 1996/7, the fastest rises in mean and median incomes have been among lone parents and single pensioners.

Gordon Brown's pursuit of redistribution through a higher rate of economic growth directly parallels the strategy elaborated in *The Future of Socialism*.

In many respects Britain has become substantially fairer in the last decade. Until 2008, the economy experienced steady growth, employment rates increased and registered unemployment fell. Significant progress was made towards the government's aim of eradicating child poverty, with tax credits and support for finding a job as the central planks of government policy. Life improved for the very worst off and Britain was healthier, living longer and experiencing less crime than in the 1990s. There was far greater optimism about the capacity of policy to resolve major social problems than was the case in the 1970s or 1980s, although the recent economic downturn may reverse that effect to some degree.

Of course, Britain is still a long way from being a just society, and there are major structural drivers that threaten to aggravate and heighten inequalities over the next decade.

Social justice in a changing world

As Geoff Mulgan, the former director of the Strategy Unit, has noted, many features of poverty and exclusion have actually changed depressingly little over the last century.[4] The places in Britain most at risk of deprivation are the same as twenty or forty years ago: the major industrial centres and former mining areas. Within cities, most of the same neighbourhoods have remained poor for very long periods. The UK remains a relatively immobile society and family background is still the most significant predictor of poverty. At the same time, new challenges for social justice are steadily coming into view that are often more differentiated and fine grained than in the past.

The first is that Britain is an increasingly diverse society experiencing rapid migration and demographic turbulence. The ethnic minority population will continue to grow from 9 per cent of the population today to at least 11 per cent by the end of the decade, but the life chances of minorities are heavily dependent on class background and the social and cultural capital they bring with them to the UK. Almost all minorities continue to lose out on jobs and wages relative to their qualifications, but the pattern is complex, as Indians and African-Asians, for example, have quickly overtaken the white majority in school performance and earnings. Another issue is the potential conflict over resources between ethnic minorities and predominantly white communities, from the supply of housing to funding for community regeneration initiatives.

The second challenge is the growing number of people living with a disability, owing to rising levels of mental illness and stress-related conditions, with many drifting into a permanent state of worklessness. This draws our attention to debates about the balance between rights and responsibilities, and the extent to which those outside the labour market ought to be incentivised to return to work given the social and economic consequences of long-term inactivity and unemployment. An even more profound question is how far the state ought to impinge on basic moral freedoms in seeking to change deeply ingrained patterns of personal behaviour, including public health and family life.

The third challenge is that the shift towards a service-based economy with flexible labour markets, accompanied by rapid technological change, has further polarised real incomes. There are more service sector occupations and jobs that need higher education qualifications and skills: a million new jobs will be created by 2012, three-quarters in education, health and personal care. Yet the proportion of workless households has barely changed over the last decade, and a large number remain trapped in 'dead-end' low-skilled service jobs with few opportunities for progression. Low levels of numeracy and literacy often go undetected, leading to reduced rates of economic activity, and these problems are exacerbated by poor transport infrastructure and inadequate childcare.

The fourth challenge is the forms of inequality that cut across the traditional class-based divisions of post-war society, including life-cycle and intergenerational inequality. For example, there are already 9.4 million people in Britain over the age of sixty-five and that figure is expected to increase to 12.4 million by 2021. By 2026, the demand for informal care for the elderly will be nearly double what it is today, but our current infrastructure will not be able to provide adequate human or financial resources. We must also consider the decline of the male breadwinner model and the polarisation of 'single' and 'dual' households, with major consequences for child poverty and family stability.

The new challenges of social justice are very often a reflection of the new patterns of risk and insecurity that individuals encounter when they reach major transition-points in their lives: from school to employment, work to caring, caring back to employment, work to retirement, and so on. The post-war welfare state designed by William Beveridge and John Maynard Keynes has often performed badly in enabling people to negotiate their way through life course transitions.

The pursuit of social justice continues to be influenced by changing patterns of income and wealth distribution, and the relative allocation of material resources remains of decisive importance. Of course, several pre-eminent forces have restructured capitalist economies since the 1950s, exacerbating existing income inequalities.

Then, capitalism was industrial; today it is financial. In derivatives markets, financial returns are accumulated far more rapidly than in industrial goods markets, with rising rewards for top managers. Then, capitalism was relatively standardised; today it is post-industrial. Large enterprises have steadily disappeared, while work itself has become more atomised and individualistic with the notable disappearance of collective wage bargaining and corporatist institutions. Then, capitalism was national; today it is global. Rising returns to technology, demographic change, and the fluidity of international capital, product and labour markets have dramatically increased the earnings dispersion.

The impact of these trends on income distribution can be illustrated with several salient statistics drawn from Britain. In 1979, the richest tenth of the population received 21 per cent of total disposable income. This figure rose throughout the 1980s and 1990s to reach 29 per cent by 2002/3. More than half of this increase was accounted for by the top 1 per cent of income earners – most of it by the top 0.5 per cent. Two-fifths of the total real increase in personal incomes between 1979 and 1999 went to the top 10 per cent of earners. The rise in wealth inequality has been even more pronounced, while the changes at the bottom have been equally clear cut. In 1980, the poorest tenth of the population received roughly 4 per cent of disposable income. By the end of the 1990s, this share had fallen by more than a third to just over 3 per cent, where it has remained until recently.

Against this backdrop, it is hardly surprising that the debate about economic equality is high on the agenda. The Institute for Fiscal Studies and the Fabian Society have recently published major studies on life chances and social justice. There has been a steady flow of academic research, from John Hills's empirical work at the LSE on inequality and the state to Richard Sennett's treatise on respect.[5]

Why has the debate about equality arisen now? There has been continuing frustration at levels of progress in tackling inequality and its consequences – especially child poverty – since 1997. The rate of decline in the number of poor children was not sufficient to meet the government's target of reducing child poverty by at least a quarter in 2004/5. This figure will have to fall by a further million to reach the current target in 2010/11.

There is also growing anxiety about the status of the 'super-rich' in the industrialised countries, driven by transformations in the nature of global capitalism. Evidence of corporate excess, the rise in earnings differentials and the dominance of winner-takes-all global markets fuel this anxiety. The bonuses paid to City financiers in the UK, for example, had the astonishing effect of raising the average increase in wages in the three months to April 2008 from 4.2 to 4.4 per cent. If City bonuses were excluded, the growth in earnings would actually have slowed, from 3.9 per cent to 3.8 per cent. The *Economist* has reported that the 'rich have been pulling away from the rest of the population, as the returns to capital and talent in a global market have increased'. The pay and benefits package of the average Goldman Sachs employee comes to more than $500,000. Yet the wages of the typical American worker in the very middle of the income distribution have risen less than 1 per cent since 2000.[6]

Finally, there are concerns about the cycle of intergenerational disadvantage in Britain. There is increasing evidence that multiple deprivation produces higher crime rates, worse public health and faster neighbourhood decline. Others observe the steady collapse of social mobility in the UK since the Second World War.[7]

The future of social justice: new governing principles

In reality, developing a credible conception of social justice for a changing world requires a new set of governing principles that can give definition to the idea of an empowering state. As the Oxford philosopher David Miller has argued,[8] the core idea of social justice is contained in the following four principles:

- **Equal citizenship**: every citizen is entitled to an equal set of civil, political and social rights, including the means to exercise those rights effectively.
- **The social minimum**: all citizens must have access to resources that adequately meet their essential needs and allow them to live a secure and dignified life in today's society.
- **Equality of opportunity**: a person's life chances, and especially their access to jobs and educational opportunities, should depend only on their own motivation and aptitudes, and not on irrelevant features such as gender, class or ethnicity.
- **Fair distribution**: resources that do not form part of equal citizenship or the social minimum may be distributed unequally, but the distribution must reflect relevant factors such as personal desert and personal choice.

The four principles elaborated by Miller are ambitious: a society that genuinely fulfilled these ideals of social justice would look very different to Britain as it does today. Nonetheless, an element is missing from this analysis: the ability of people to lead a freely chosen life and to control their destiny. The link between social justice and personal freedom needs to be made more explicit. Miller's principles articulate a convincing theoretical framework, but what is needed is for theory and practice to be drawn together coherently to develop a new politics of social justice, as this chapter argues.

The first governing assumption of that new politics of social justice is that equality has to be defined as the means to an end, not as the value to be privileged over all others. Equality is the basis of the good society, rooted in fellowship and cooperation, solidarity and freedom. The thrust of past approaches to social justice has tended to focus on the Rawlsian conception of equality, in which egalitarian values are sustained by individual calculation and

rational self-interest, with the aim of securing the most disadvantaged a larger share of the economic cake through taxation and
redistribution.[9]

This 'zero sum' approach to equality proved to be a fragile basis
for an enduring political settlement, leading to the defeat of the
Labour government in 1979 and the rise of Thatcherism as a
response to the exhaustion of post-war social democracy. This helps
to explain Labour's reticence towards progressive taxation since the
early 1990s and its reluctance to develop a set of moral arguments
that might have preceded more imaginative efforts to address the
distribution of income and wealth. It is imperative that these ethical
and moral foundations be restored to our account of social justice.
This should draw strength from emerging debates about quality of
life and subjective well-being in market democracies, demonstrating
the limits to increasing life satisfaction through rising personal
incomes alone.

The second assumption is about defining the relationship
between equality and personal freedom: the real issue in a modern
politics of social justice is not equality of 'outcome' versus equality
of 'opportunity', but how to give people more choice and control
over their lives and how to expand positive freedom as envisaged by
the Nobel prize-winning economist Amartya Sen through the concept
of 'capabilities'.[10] This is the case in relation not only to income but
also to social and cultural capital. That requires a fundamental shift
in the conventional terms of the egalitarian argument.

Equally, a single generalised conception of social justice is unlikely
to generate widespread public support, since any application of
the principles of justice is context specific and rooted in particular
situations, procedures and distributions. These principles may often
conflict so a robust concept of social justice would recognise the
importance of pluralism and difference and the need to take into
account institutional variation and complexity, as the philosopher
Jon Elster has acknowledged in highlighting the limitations of grand
theories of equality and justice.[11]

The third governing assumption of the new politics of social
justice is the recognition that equality is concerned with human
flourishing and individual difference, not retreating into narrow
uniformity. This draws on Sen's highly influential capability theory:

it is about giving the individual sufficient power to become the author of their own destiny. The promotion of equality should be focused on what Sen terms the 'capability set' – the overall freedom a person has to pursue his or her well-being. Disadvantage should similarly be defined as 'capability failure' – not only the loss of resources, but also the loss of freedom to achieve. What matters is not economic deprivation as such, but the consequences of such deprivation for individuals' well-being. This demands a new conception of social justice more profound than simply equalising the distribution of material income.

The fourth assumption is that social justice is best achieved by developing an increasingly nuanced conception of the relationship between states and markets – not through subjugating the market and enlarging the size of the state and the public sector. Social democrats need to understand the limitations of the centralised state as much as competitive markets, and they need to think radically about the future of the state itself. The needs of service providers must never be put before those of service users. At the same time, the state is expected to do more and more in contemporary society, solving an extraordinary array of problems, but citizens appear to have less faith than ever in its capacity to deliver.

The next challenge is to develop a new definition of public value that can accommodate ways of allowing individuals to choose and exercise more control, while advancing the claims of social justice. That will probably require forms of self-government in local communities and public services that offer a genuine alternative to the traditional 'command' model, the 'managerial' model and the 'market' model alike. It is imperative to demonstrate that non-market provision can be efficient and responsive to the needs of individual citizens.

The fifth assumption is to recognise the implications for social justice of the shift towards the post-consumption society: merely creating the scope for redistribution through higher rates of growth will no longer be an adequate strategy for the future. In fact, new agendas for the state are emerging focused on individual well-being that go beyond issues of material need to address quality of work and quality of life. This includes the balance between work and other activities, the redefinition of traditional gender roles, and judgements about what capacities an individual needs to live a full human life. This cannot be reduced to a financial calculus, and also draws our attention to the limits of markets.

The argument of this chapter is that social justice is best understood as the means to effective freedom and self-actualisation, going beyond Miller's four principles of equal citizenship, the social minimum, equality of opportunity and a fair distribution. Progressives should recognise that egalitarianism itself cannot be sustained by economic intervention and redistribution alone. They should focus on the broader distribution of power and cultural capital in society, as well as how best to uphold the public interest through states and markets, and the fulfilment of human needs in market democracies as a core aspect of the new social justice agenda.

The new policy agenda

These governing assumptions must be refined into a new political and policy strategy. Where should progressives turn their attention in the coming years? The challenges facing Britain in 2020 will not be those of 1997 or 2001. The sharpest debates in the 1980s were about resolving Britain's economic weaknesses. In the 1990s, they were concerned with restoring the efficacy of public services, reforming the British constitution and devising an equitable response to globalisation. The focus of debate will inevitably shift again: the ideological terrain of the early twenty-first century will be about approaches to individual and collective self-fulfilment, as well as the need to combat social polarisation.

The key is to offer a fresh, dynamic vision for the country that gives a renewed sense of guiding purpose. The right's answer is to make the state smaller in the name of greater freedom. Progressives must show that their agenda empowers people – enhancing freedom not merely in the economic realm but in every sphere of life, given the rise of complexity and diversity. In some areas, such as tax and education policy, Labour needs to refine and sharpen its current strategy. In others, such as cultural capital and emotional well-being, it needs to advance new frontiers, extending the reach of public policy through a genuinely empowering state that can strengthen and deepen social justice. This may require large-scale institutional reforms, but it is equally about a culture of disciplined pluralism based on frameworks that permit a degree of experimentation, forging new forms of ownership, association and personal control.

Education in a free society

In a knowledge-driven economy, access to education and skills is one of the central determinants of individual life chances and key to reducing inequalities. For social democrats this is a vital arena in strengthening the individual's capabilities and advancing social justice.

Economically, education is now more important than ever. It fulfils two traditional elements of the social democratic ideal. It enables each individual to reach their productive potential, narrowing the gap in under-privilege created by what Gøsta Esping-Andersen terms 'social inheritance': parental status and children's destinies are no longer as strongly tied together.[12] Education, however, should not be reduced merely to what is economically advantageous, either for the individual or for society. It also helps to strengthen self-fulfilment and the chances of leading a full human life, as well as the scope of personal freedom.

Labour's future education agenda cannot simply argue for higher investment. Resources and reforms need to complement one another. If Britain were to develop as a genuinely classless society we would match the European norm, where only a tiny minority attend private schools. Yet more than half a million children were in private education in 2008. In London nearly a fifth of parents go private – many more say they would do so if they could afford the fees.

The controversies that have arisen over the government's education reforms illustrate how limited debate in the Labour Party has been since the mid-1990s. A genuinely diverse and sophisticated secondary system would best meet the great variety of talents and needs of all children. But Labour has not yet shown how this chimes in with a modernised conception of social justice. A future Labour government will have to provide a far sharper vision for 21st-century education.

The commitment of 5.4 per cent real terms investment in the

2003–6 Spending Review was impressive, although this has fallen to
2.8 per cent in real terms between 2007/8 and 2010/11. The amount
spent per pupil in the state education system will have doubled from
1997 to 2008. This is still far less in real terms than the UK spent in
the 1970s, and it will be wholly insufficient in the next decade given
the scale of under-funding in educational infrastructure that
occurred in the 1980s and early 1990s. The decision to give the NHS
priority over education in the last three Spending Reviews was
highly questionable and should be reversed. Another investment
step-change is required along with imaginative decisions on expenditure priorities.

In raising standards of attainment, improving the quality of
teaching is at least as significant as structural changes in school
governance. A more intensive focus on literacy and numeracy is vital
given that more than 40 per cent of pupils leave primary school
without mastering the basics of English and mathematics. It is also
counter-productive to teach the full National Curriculum to pupils
at Key Stage 3 who have not yet mastered the core subjects. Extra
tutorial support for these pupils is essential. The brightest, ablest
teachers are still not recruited into the most challenging areas.
Stronger incentive structures are required – while central government
has to give greater freedom to the front line if it is to attract the best
young people into the classroom. The rigid and over-prescriptive
National Curriculum needs reform. The present structure fails to
promote individual progression, while it severely under-emphasises
the central focus on learning for life. A baccalaureate system –
such as that advocated in the Tomlinson review – would be more
advantageous to pupils and the nation alike.

There has also been too little experimentation to help the poorest
schools. Funding should be explicitly weighted towards those pupils
with the most challenging needs, as occurs, for example, in the
Netherlands. This could be used to dramatically reduce class sizes in
the least advantaged areas. Otherwise, desirable measures to promote
parental choice will further erode the position of the least advantaged.

Further education colleges and adult learning also remain badly
neglected, to the benefit of the higher education sector, where a
substantial proportion of post-16 expenditure is still allocated. More
modern apprenticeships, offering high quality part-time education

above level 2 (equivalent to five good GCSEs), are vital. The bias of lifelong learning is still tilted away from the least advantaged, precisely the opposite of what a Labour government should seek to achieve given its social justice aspirations.

Extending asset ownership

A wide-ranging strategy for tackling inequality and advancing social justice requires more than a sharper vision for educational reform. Establishing Britain as an asset-owning democracy is another key challenge. Over the last decade – originating with Michael Sherraden's work in the early 1990s[13] – there has been a growing interest in the role that assets play in extending opportunities.

The ownership of assets provides a buffer in times of crisis. This can give people a real stake in the future, enabling individuals to act independently – making their own choices, not being solely dependent on market-generated incomes. Indeed, there is a proud labour movement tradition that champions self-help, not only state aid. The tradition of Robert Owen, the early friendly societies, the cooperative movement and the Workers' Educational Association should inform future policy formulation as much as Beveridge or Crosland.

Wider asset ownership opens up a new front in strengthening social justice. The Child Trust Fund is an exciting and welcome venture. But we must go further if we are to get Britain moving socially again, dramatically raising the initial sums invested in the CTF for the poorest families to increase financial independence. The government was right to commit to increasing home ownership as an explicit goal of its policy, including the wider availability of equity stakes in social housing. Widening employee share ownership in private companies should be another objective. New incentives are required to encourage profit-sharing schemes modelled on those such as the John Lewis Partnership.

The UK is a post-industrial economy in which 52 per cent of the workforce is employed in small and medium-sized enterprises (SMEs) with fewer than fifty employees. Whereas widening share ownership was problematic in the larger conglomerates of the industrial economy in the 1950s, today's SMEs should provide incentives to motivate the whole workforce. Rules are required that favour the broadest distribution of share options, instead of being restricted only to senior company executives. When corporate profitability is strong, it is right to encourage the spreading and sharing of wealth.

Widening asset ownership will promote greater independence, self-reliance and aspiration. Another area of assets policy is strengthening human capital, raising skill levels and improving access to specialised knowledge. The path to a better-rewarded job is complex and difficult in the tax credit economy and there are still major obstacles to progression, as this chapter has noted. A network of advancement agencies that work with employees and firms to improve skills – providing careers and not just jobs in a more dislocated economic structure – will enable people to have greater control over key decisions in their lives.

Redistribution: a progressive tax and benefits system

The critique of the traditional doctrine of equality of outcome is not, of course, a justification for abandoning redistribution. A country will have a higher level of average happiness the more equally its income is distributed – all else being equal. An extra pound gives more freedom to the poor than the rich, as the economists James Meade and James Mirrlees have argued. A full frontal attack on poverty in families with children is an essential tool in the pursuit of more equal opportunities and social justice.

The tax system in Britain is deeply iniquitous because of the burden it imposes on the lowest paid. The rich enjoy generous tax relief. The poor pay a high proportion of their income in indirect taxes and the lowest earners pay the highest effective marginal rates. Labour should establish a progressive tax commission to consider the fairness and efficiency of the tax and benefits system. This could make recommendations in particular on cutting tax for the poorest; the balance of incremental decisions about tax structure should be to reduce the share of the tax burden borne by those on the lowest incomes. Another reform that the commission might revisit is tax–benefit integration under a negative income tax arrangement, combining means-tested benefits and direct taxation in a single income assessment – resulting in a net payment or receipt administered through the tax system.

In whatever guise, the tax and benefits structure has to assist individuals in dealing with new social risks – as well as more predictable life events such as unemployment and retirement. This is central to the new politics of social justice in Britain. These new social risks include relationship breakdown, single parenthood, mental illness – and the challenge of economic restructuring and skill obsolescence. For example, individuals might be entitled to claim periodic tax breaks through adverse life cycle transitions. The government could also return to the concept of an integrated Individual Learning Account for use throughout life – but avoiding the administrative deficiencies of the original scheme.

There is of course no justification for indiscriminate tax-and-spend policies. The impact on social injustice is what counts – the ability of fiscal policy to enlarge the scope of human freedom. This means that how resources are used is as significant as the level of resources raised. Labour must ensure that its tax and redistribution policies fit with everyday sensibilities about morality and desert – that they accord with the reality of public understandings of justice. As the philosopher John Rawls concluded towards the end of his life, conceptions of justice must be political, not metaphysical – individuals are more likely to agree on their application than the fundamental principles from which they are derived.

Changing structures of work and welfare

A social democratic agenda for the future must go far beyond educational reform if it is to expand happiness and human freedom. Life chances in Britain today are powerfully determined even before a child's first encounter with the school system. Meanwhile, many adults are unlikely ever to re-enter formal educational in their lives, which suggests a limitation to a social justice policy focused too heavily on effecting change through educational institutions. A new social democratic agenda must broaden its scope. It must attack inequalities in access to cultural capital – in the family and beyond – if social justice is to be strengthened.

As Mickey Kaus argues, the public sphere should be used

> to incubate and spread an egalitarian culture . . . The institutions of
> that sphere would drive home the point of social equality – and the
> ultimate moral arbitrariness of capitalist success – through the crude
> expedient of treating all citizens equally and the more subtle tactic of
> providing a part of daily life actually enjoyed by various economic
> classes on this equal basis.[14]

Plato recognised the impact of the family when he proposed that
intelligent children of 'uncultured parents' should be removed from
it. Our aim should be to seek to equalise the cultural and cognitive
resources of all families. This is partly a question of time and
improving the work–life balance. The extension of time sovereignty
– statutory changes in workplace culture that give workers greater
control over their lives – strengthens family stability as well as
intrinsic human satisfaction. This should enable people to better
reconcile work with caring responsibilities, which, given the rapid
change in the number of women in the workforce, is an urgent issue.
In the United States in the 1950s, 20 per cent of mothers went out
to work. Today, the figure is over 70 per cent.

Similar, if less dramatic, changes have revolutionised the structures
of work, welfare and family in Europe, including that dramatic
increase in the female employment rate. But gender mainstreaming
policies have still not yet brought enough highly skilled and talented
women into the labour force. Full-time day care for children below
school age is an essential prerequisite. The erosion of the traditional
family is a matter of concern – not only on moral grounds, but also
for instrumental reasons. The role of the state in family life has always
been a matter of dispute. But the rise in divorce rates, for example,
imposes costs on the rest of society that are not borne directly by the
individuals themselves – and it is therefore a legitimate focus of
public policy to seek to compensate for the effects if not to reverse
the trend.

It is vital to strengthen and bolster the emotional intelligence of
children. Controlled trials have shown that well-designed courses –
an hour per week for one year at school – help them to acquire
inner strength and gain greater consideration for others. The 2005

report *Transitions* by the Social Exclusion Unit rightly recommended more lessons in basic life skills such as anger management. It is true that personal, social and health education is presently taught to all 5–16-year-olds – but there are too few specialist tutors, and its aims are not sufficiently radical.

The key dimensions of social capital – such as trust and membership of voluntary associations – contribute greatly to human satisfaction and therefore expand the scope of freedom beyond the rewards that can be earned in the market. A strong predictor of low crime rates is how many friends people have within fifteen minutes' walk of their home. Governments should bolster social cohesion by creating many more volunteering opportunities, as the Russell commission recommends. Labour might also develop a citizens' participation agency – a national body with a neighbourhood presence designed to encourage and support greater public involvement in every aspect of the running of the state: health, education, criminal justice, economic development, leisure and so on. Meanwhile, communities generally should have far greater access to culture and the arts.

But the largest single cause of misery and restraint on human freedom in the industrialised countries is mental illness. 'It explains more of the variation in happiness than income does, even after we allow for the interrelation between poverty and depression.'[15] Yet only 13 per cent of total health expenditure in the UK is directed at mental illness. The majority of those who are ill get no treatment. For example, it is estimated that only 40 per cent of patients who are likely to benefit from talking therapies are able to access them.

Major developments in psychotherapy and cognitive behavioural therapy have ensured that there is now effective treatment. The NHS should train 10,000 more psychological therapists by 2015 and create a network of specialist treatment centres to improve access, as Richard Layard proposes.[16] Meanwhile, investment in science should ensure that psychiatry in Britain becomes a far more prestigious branch of medicine. In the 1980s, Layard worked exclusively on unemployment. Today, mental health is the central focus of his research – itself illustrative of the shift in priorities and the opening up of a new frontier in the politics of social justice.

Conclusion

Modern social democracy has to paint a compelling picture of the good society if it is to inspire enduring electoral support. In *The Future of Socialism*, Anthony Crosland envisaged an age when economic and social change had gone so far that attention in politics would shift elsewhere – to personal freedom, happiness and cultural fulfilment. Those issues are very much alive in our politics today, yet far from indicating that a more equal society has been achieved, inequality and social injustice are still major challenges for Britain, and are set to grow more so in the future.

The ultimate aim of the new politics of social justice should be to expand the scope of human freedom. That will still require major reforms to social and economic institutions, but one of the most potent lessons that the left ought to learn from the right is that a strategy of 'micro-change' can be critical to engineering progressive change. That emphasis on pluralism means paying attention to the detail of how institutions are designed, the rights and opportunities available to individuals and groups, the frameworks that can allow a degree of social experimentation, and new forms of ownership and association.

This point about the significance of 'disciplined pluralism' is intrinsic to the politics of social justice. It is about enabling people to lead a full human life, not retreating into narrow uniformity. On that basis, social democracy in the next generation can develop a compelling agenda for the future. Indeed, it will attain a new vibrancy if the centre-left is prepared to think anew, adapting to new opportunities and new challenges, establishing a plausible and credible connection between means and ends.

9

Identity in Britain

Hannah Jameson

Introduction

Looking forward, we can expect two trends currently visible in the early twenty-first century to continue and to challenge many of the assumptions upon which policy and political debates currently rest. The first trend is greater diversity: easier movement of people and migration policy set at the international, rather than national, level will lead to fewer and fewer people being able to define their British citizenship through British ancestry. The second trend is transience: emigration partners immigration, ensuring a continual population 'churn'. Even within Britain, movement of people from one region to another is greater than ever before. This poses a challenge to progressives. How do we ensure that greater diversity and transience do not induce greater inequality and fragmentation?

So far greater diversity has not just created new dimensions of inequality, it has also challenged progressives to rethink the very meaning of inequality. Immigration from the Commonwealth in the 1950s and 1960s challenged the existing understanding of equality as equality of opportunity accompanied by redistribution and drove an extension of the conceptual boundaries to include freedom from harassment and discrimination. Increasing diversity in Britain today, and in particular the accompanying changes in identity, will again challenge our notions of equality to expand and adapt. Progressives will have to ask whether the ideas dominant at the end of the twentieth century will be able to deliver meaningful equality in the twenty-first. Already there is a sense that current notions of equality have given undue prominence to the differences between us, in a flattening-out model, but have failed to articulate a vision of what we have in common. It is this need for a vision of a shared community that was at the centre of Anthony Crosland's depiction of the good society in the 1950s, and it has arisen more recently in the backlash against multiculturalism.

Greater diversity has changed not only the ends of social democratic thinking but also the means. The political context in which social democrats operate has been altered by the increasing importance of identity and its growing prominence in the public sphere. The broad collective identities of class on which social democrats have traditionally relied have long been on the wane, and more individualised identities have come to the fore. But in recent years the rise of new group identities, most obviously along faith and ethnic lines, has challenged a predominantly secular left, committed to anti-racism but uncomfortable with the role of faith in public life. Issues of race and immigration, which regularly top the polls of British concerns, do not divide the electorate along neat party lines but provide a new cultural axis that political parties must negotiate. The landscape of British politics has been changed by diversity and identity, challenging social democrats to rethink their approach.

New Labour's response to diversity and identity has been largely piecemeal. The desire for increased immigration to support a flexible labour market and drive economic growth has meant having to reassure the majority over migration fears, often by deploying tough rhetoric, while simultaneously finding ways to incorporate new citizens with their new identities into representations of the nation. The two have not always fitted easily together.

This short-termist approach, however, does not adequately respond to the fundamental way that diversity and identity affect the social democratic project. In a number of parts of Europe, including the Netherlands and the Scandinavian countries, identity is changing the political landscape and it is often the parties at the edges of the political spectrum who benefit at the expense of social democrats. The response cannot be to ignore identity, or to call for a return to the class politics of yesteryear. Identity needs to become central to what social democrats do and how they think. Social democrats will need to re-examine the meaning of equality in the twenty-first century, rethink how they do politics and find new ways to address the anxieties that arise from rapid change and transient communities.

I would argue that the social democratic response to diversity and identity must be to find ways to foster new collective identities, and in particular, a renewed civic identity. Identities are not free-floating; any attempt to strengthen our civic identity can only come through a reconsideration and reform of social democratic citizenship. Equality as a process of levelling between competing claims, as redistribution or freedom from discrimination, is essential in a diverse society, but it has little to say about what we have in common, how we can use that equality or how we relate to one another – in short, the good society. Citizenship, in its fullest sense, captures this. It enables egalitarians to address not just material equality but the equality of esteem that makes a shared society feasible.

This chapter is structured in four parts. The first section describes identity in Britain today, looking at the identities that have come to prominence in the last ten years, as well as those that have remained unchanged. The second suggests some of the implications of these trends, and the role of identity more generally, for the social democratic project. The third looks at New Labour's approach to identity over the last ten years, and the fourth suggests how a social democratic approach to identity might develop in the future.

Identity trends

Immigration has dramatically altered the picture of identity in Britain, introducing new identities and changing the meaning of more established ones. But equally significant are the ways in which those identities are used; the process of integration has often helped to decide which identities groups adopt as political identities. At the same time, social and economic change in Britain has altered established identities, resulting in the decline of collective identities such as class and the rise of certain individualised ones. Political change has brought to attention the popularity of national identities and the resilience of Britishness.

Religious identities emerge as one of the key areas of change over the last twenty years. Against an overall picture of secularisation, and the decreasing importance of organised religion in daily life for the majority, a substantial minority remain attached to their religious identities and are utilising them in new ways. Religious identity, once seen as the glue of a shared national identity, has been increasingly portrayed as a threat to cohesion, whether through the supposed divisions of faith schools or the foreign allegiances associated with some faiths and denominations.

For some groups, notably Muslims, religion has become a significant marker of identity in the public realm. The 2001 citizenship survey revealed that for Christians, religious identity came seventh in a list of identities that were important to them, but for Muslims, Sikhs and Hindus, their religious identity came within the top three along with family identity and ethnicity.[1]

But what does 'religious identification' mean? What should be made clear is that a rise in a public religious identity does not necessarily denote a rise in religiosity.[2] For example, for some, particularly vulnerable new migrant groups in Britain, the rootless nature of religious identities may make them especially important identities in times of upheaval, providing a continuous form of security and belonging. For others religious identification in the public realm, particularly 'Muslim', has become a preferred political identity too. One study found that 'Muslim' has become the most important form of identification for Pakistani and Bangladeshi groups who are active in British politics.[3] Race and ethnicity were the favoured political identities for many through the 1960s, 1970s and 1980s, bringing people together under the grouping of 'black' and subsequently 'black and Asian', but the 1990s and 2000s have witnessed more visible and audible political religious groupings. It presents a particular challenge, ideologically at least, for a British left dominated by liberal secular traditions and a British constitution with unclear guidance on the role of faith in public life.

Among this picture of change are certain continuities. Even at a time of greater transience, geographical identities retain their prominence for many. Once seen as great uniting forces, geographical identities such as national identity have, according to some, since declined into irrelevance. For others, they are viewed as holding fixed meanings that may threaten, or support, progressive ends. So while Europeanism is associated with a progressive and cosmopolitan outlook, nationalism has struggled to shrug off its association with the politics of the right.

Perhaps most surprising is the extent to which national identities have retained high levels of support. Although fewer respondents to the British Social Attitudes (BSA) survey in 2005 chose 'British' as the best way to describe themselves than in 1996 (44 per cent as against 53 per cent), it still remained relevant to a great number of people. When asked to select from a list the identities that describe the way people think of themselves, 'British' was selected by 67 per cent of respondents in 1996 and 2005, peaking at 71 per cent in 2001.

However, over the same period, identification with Britain's constituent nations has also altered. There has been an increase in identification with Scottishness, Welshness and Englishness, arguably at the expense of Britishness. The increase in support for Englishness has been notable: between 1997 and 2003 there was a 5 percentage point rise in those identifying as English and not British.[4]

Much of the debate around identities may focus on the national, but local identities have remained popular, and of all the geographical identities, the locality remains the strongest point of identification for the majority of Britons. Although popular among all groups, and across the generations, locality is listed by people from black and minority ethnic groups as more important to their identity that any other geographical identity, including country of origin.[5] Integration is often thought of at a national level, but this evidence suggests that it is a more complex process occurring at different levels.

In a world of greater people flows and easier access to communications technology, it might be expected that national and local identities would decline, to be replaced by continent-wide, or even global identities. Indeed, a stronger European identity has long been the great hope of social democrats in Britain. Yet identification with Europe remains low at 10 per cent, and has remained at this level for some time.[6] Identification with Europe, or international identification, is more likely to be expressed by those with experience of higher education, and European identification in particular is more likely to be expressed in London than in other regions of the UK.[7]

Regardless of the levels of support for geographical identities, there remains scepticism that they can be useful for progressive politics. Underpinning the hostility to national identity in particular is a presumption that geographical identities have fixed meanings. But a multicultural society in Britain has clearly forced a reassessment of what it means to be British. An urban elite may associate British-ness (negatively) with the politics of Enoch Powell, but combined identities such as 'black British' retain high support, suggesting that the meaning of Britishness for many has changed dramatically. Although there are still those who retain an ethnic understanding of Britishness, an increasing number understand it as a more inclusive, values-based civic identity. Moreover, there is little evidence to suggest that British national sentiment is associated with any particular political positioning; it does not split easily along the left–right or libertarian–authoritarian axes.[8]

Below the surface of the new identity politics, more established identities remain. It is often assumed that race and religion have replaced class in British society, but the British 2003 BSA survey revealed that overall, class remained the second most popular choice of self-definition. Probing further into that figure, the vast majority of those identifying with class were identifying as working class, and further still, among men, 'working class' was the most popular identity. As one sociologist summarises, 'Working-class was the most popular choice for men, those with no qualifications, those in the petty bourgeoisie, the "working class" (occupationally) and those in manual occupations.'[9] The classless-society politics of the last ten years or more may have managed to erase class from mainstream political discourse, but for men with no qualifications in manual work, class identification is often as relevant and as valid an identity as it was in the past. These stubborn remains of the 'institutionalisation of class feeling within a framework of industrial conciliation', which Peter Clarke traces back to the mid-nineteenth century, lead us towards a narrative of the overall decline of class influence in Britain, masking, one suspects, the emergence of a new framework within which today's class feelings are institution-alised.[10]

At the same time the BSA survey reveals the extent to which 'parent' or 'mother/father' have become dominant identities. In a survey of almost 2,000 people, where respondents were asked to choose the three identities most important to them from a list, parental identity was by some margin the first choice of self-description. Perhaps reflecting the dramatic shift in paternal contributions to childcare over the last thirty years and wider cultural changes in parenting, when broken down by gender, parental identity remained within the top three most popular identities chosen by men.[11]

Gender and parental – the more individualised and reflexive identities – were all more likely to be offered as self-descriptions by the relatively privileged than by those from lower socio-economic backgrounds in the BSA survey.[12] Those with fewer resources, including education, were more likely to opt for class. What then, one might ask, is necessary to 'be' a parent, or a woman, or British? Those identities which are apparently available to all are in fact not, on closer examination, or at least are not equally available to all. What implications does this have for shared identities?

The resilience of class identities and their apparent relationship to structural factors such as employment and education challenges another assumed identity trend in recent years: namely that cultural identities, supposedly unrelated to socio-economic factors, have overtaken others as the dominant force in public life. This picture presents two interrelated problems. First, while it may be true that conceptually race and class are now understood more in cultural than material terms, assuming a 'culturalist model' obscures the powerful role of material factors in shaping the meaning of race and class and the extent to which both cultural and economic resources are required by the individual in the formation of identity. Second, presenting these identities as cultural incorrectly suggests a far greater role for individual agency and choice in identity, and a far greater conceptual malleability of that identity.

The implications of identity change

Identities in Britain are changing: ethnic diversity is increasing, religious identities are becoming more prominent, the number of people identifying as parents is growing significantly, and Englishness, Scottishness and Welshness are on the rise. These changes can be seen against a backdrop of continuity: a high level of identification with locality, a persistence of class identification among those with little education and few skills, and a resilient, but somewhat looser, identification with Britain.

So what are the implications for social democracy in Britain? I would like to suggest three ways in which identity change matters and is likely to impact on the social democratic project. First, a wider range of identities will stretch our current model of equality beyond meaning, reducing its popular resonance and threatening its likelihood of becoming a majority project. Second, progressive political parties may struggle to build the broad coalitions necessary to effect large-scale social change, as they have done in the past. Third, at a time of greater transience and a heightened awareness of risk, a lack of common identities will make it difficult for politicians to formulate an urgent response to the need for belonging.

The concept of equality has been forced to evolve and adapt, often to fit with popular conceptions of fairness, throughout the last century. Already, the identity changes outlined above are generating demands for further legalistic expansions of the equality framework. Most notably, a rise in religious identities has challenged the existing provision. Blasphemy laws developed for a different age are deemed inadequate, an established church places power in the hands of one denomination which no longer holds the consensus, and race equality laws fail to capture the likely evolution of discrimination along ethnic/religious lines. Further, the categories by which equality is judged are challenged by increasing diversity; ethnic categories, for example, struggle to capture the complexity of ethnic identity and particularly the rapid growth of those who identify as mixed race.

At the same time, ever greater diversity has complicated the picture of inequality, with higher levels of poverty among certain ethnic minority groups, concentrated in deprived urban areas where resources are scarce and competition is great. The policy response is often to try and target resources on smaller and smaller groups of people for maximum effect. But as allocation is shaped by need, and needs vary between different ethnic groups, some are seen to get more out of the pot than others. The unintended consequence is the politics of competitive grievance – a clear separation of equality policy from a common sense of fairness as resentment between communities festers over resource allocation.

Critics identify the policies of multiculturalism as a key contributor to this situation, claiming that multiculturalism tied resource allocation to identity, entrenching difference and fuelling inter-group conflict. A fairer criticism might be that 'corporate' multiculturalism as practised by the state reflects the stretched limits of equality; it is unable to provide the framework and guidance within which the majority can engage in a conversation with one another about how much equality is needed, which equalities matter, what the trade-offs of greater equality will be and where the balance of fairness lies. It leaves people where they are, reinforcing a sense of group identity as fixed, immutable and without compromise.

Identity groups understandably argue for changes in legislation to protect against the discrimination they experience, or changes in equal opportunities criteria, or state funding to gain recognition of their identity and parity with other groups. But does this deliver the meaningful equality that they are aspiring to, or merely a freedom from inequality? Does it make them integral to society, or just not directly excluded? Furthermore, does equality that is understood as a gradual expansion of legislation to protect minority groups ever hold the potential to fully engage the majority, such that they feel they have an equal stake in the project?

It is not just equality but also the politics that deliver equality that are threatened by identity change. The second way in which identity change is likely to impact on social democracy in Britain is through social democrats' ability to build coalitions for social change. Historically, progressives relied on a certain level of common identity in order to organise and sustain political responses to social challenges. It is the connection with that identity that saw people vote against their direct economic interest and respond to the argument that improving one's individual situation will be of little value if those around you remain as disadvantaged. From the 1906 Liberal government, which drew together a radical working class and 'the progressive professional man',[13] to the post-war class and nationalistic campaign for the welfare state, an ability to speak to people as part of a wider grouping – to offer them new ways of belonging – has been crucial in bringing about social change.

Greater identity diversity, and particularly the use of those identities politically to advance separate group interests, will challenge this approach to progressive politics, as will the rise of more individualised identities. Without the broad group identities of class or nation, common problems faced by those in similar circumstances are masked. The poverty experienced by both the white working class and their Bangladeshi counterparts is hidden by a veneer of cultural difference. The residential clustering in response to poverty, scarce resources and insecurity is read as a meaningful choice to segregate rather than a rational economic choice. Moreover, mobilising for change in the context of narrow identity politics risks becoming a matter of finding the lowest common denominator, rather than a process of compromise between self- and common interest.

New inequalities are likely to require the left to organise again for social change. That may involve agitating for new legislation and resources to abolish child poverty or climate change, or highlighting the need to build a new settlement for the welfare state. Social change has happened and will happen when those with a direct interest in change are brought together. But demonstrating common cause and shared responsibility will be made more difficult in a society where narrow identity politics dominates.

Third, the increasing plurality of identity and the relative decline in importance of shared identities could well inhibit social democrats' attempts to sustain support for migration and diversity and to facilitate integration. Social democrats have traditionally focused on delivering a fairer and more just society, and yet the rapid pace of change in Britain over the last fifty years, and its effects on the structure of society, have made belonging – to community, family or nation – an issue of political importance. It is not a choice between priorities, as Michael Ignatieff argues; 'the question is not: can we make our societies fairer or more just? It is whether the pursuit of justice, fairness and efficiency can also deliver belonging, cohesion and community.'[14]

Identity provides an essential part of our security; it is our way of making sense of ourselves and our place in the world so that we can find a place to belong. But the need for belonging can easily drive people and communities towards insularity and introspection – a position readily exploited by political extremes – if social democrats are not able to articulate a narrative of change and a picture of the good society in which people can also find their place and belong.

The increase in diversity and transience that characterises globalisation can create feelings of insecurity and vulnerability that drive a search for security. Identity, and particularly easily formed essentialist identities, provide rapid security and an imagined solidarity in a vulnerable situation. Thus, immigrants may respond to appeals to shared origins, a homeland or a shared history, which becomes the essential truth of who they are. Worryingly, Paul Gilroy argues that although individual identities are seen as being constantly negotiated, collective identities are increasingly seen as being fixed and immutable, based on essential elements. The consequences of such an approach are not hard to imagine. For both the established and the new communities, a hostility to change can damage race relations, integration and cohesion.

Without a way of speaking to people as part of a wider community, politicians struggle to explain the changes that people experience and see around them. Globalisation is experienced at the local level, and rapid change makes places seem unrecognisable to those who have lived there for a long time. Without a national story about who we are and, crucially, who we are becoming, that individual or local experience cannot be put in context. Change becomes a threat, rather than a process in which people have a stake. Without an alternative, established communities are left to construct a narrative of decline from a community and solidarity that probably never was.

Identity and New Labour

Following the social and economic change of the 1980s and early 1990s, New Labour was forced to respond to a new configuration of identity unlike that seen by any previous Labour administration. Class identity did not exist on anything like the scale it once had, and in its place stood a new range of identities, on the whole more individualised, accompanied by a new configuration of political identities including ethnic/religious ones. New Labour did not fundamentally challenge individualisation, nor the economic structuring that gave rise to it, but instead sought to complement it with a return to the idea of community as a way of reintroducing the value of collectivities into the political structure. Influenced by the New Democrats and their communitarian strand of thinking, New Labour in the early years placed community prominently in their policy and rhetoric. Community appeared in the context of 'safer communities', the 'Muslim community' or indeed a more amorphous 'community' used to evoke a moral 'us' against undesirable behaviour.[15] Its use said a great deal about New Labour's imagining of where power lay and the relationship between the citizen and the state, but the evasive nature of the term also had significant implications for identity in Britain and the role ascribed to it.

It is the relatively recent use of 'community' to describe those following a particular faith which has proved most controversial. This was, perhaps, an unsurprising response to the growing prominence of religion in public life, and a reaction in particular to the political self-representation of many south Asians in Britain as Muslim. Characterising faith groups as communities incorporated them within New Labour discourse and policy. If a community was a legitimate body within the body politic, then conferring the status of 'community' on an identity grouping extended that legitimacy. The problem was that those communities did not exist in anything like the way they were described. There were pleas from the outset from British Muslims to pluralise the phrase to 'Muslim communities', to reflect the diversity among those who identified as Muslim. At the same time, the primacy of one identity implied by the term 'community' did not fit easily with the multiple identities held by many.

Even though, since the Rushdie affair, the number of people identifying as Muslim had steadily increased, conceiving of those people as a coherent group created problems. New Labour was heavily criticised over its early approach to engagement with Muslims, relying on one, undemocratically constituted, organisation to represent Muslims in Britain. The breakdown of that relationship drew Labour towards other, equally unrepresentative, groups in an attempt to find more compliant partners. But the idea of identity groupings as communities has had further-reaching implications. They have become objects of policy, responsible for implementing civic education, denouncing criminal activity, contributing to local development forums and regeneration initiatives. There has been little questioning of the legitimacy of this, or of the capacity of an identity group to fulfil this role.

The debate about the relationship between the state and identity groups has been most vividly played out in discussions of public funding. The stated aim, to strengthen communities, translated into funding available from central government, often for community development work. But as the tide turned against an idea of a multicultural citizenship that demanded recognition of difference, and crucially, public support of that difference, funding criteria rapidly changed. Amid criticisms, particularly in the wake of the London bombings of 2005, that the government was 'funding difference', policy altered to prioritise funding for those undertaking integration work, and later still, the funding of single ethnic community groups was temporarily halted. The association between identity and violence since 2001, and particularly 2005, has blurred government objectives. Funding integration is closely aligned with preventing extremism, and the strengthening of communities in the public narrative has become about resisting the influence of violent extremism among Muslims.

At the same time as New Labour was considering identity in relation to communities, it was also looking to the national picture and the potential of a new Britishness. This was certainly uncomfortable territory for many on the left, who saw it as an agenda too closely associated with the right, and antithetical to the tolerance and diversity they valued. For others, it was without substance – 'flag waving', or at best a panicky reaction to devolution from a party that looked to lose out from any further constitutional reform. But for those within New Labour who sought to articulate what a new national identity might look like, it was a means of reframing traditional social democratic arguments around rights, citizenship and equality in a public debate that was dominated by diversity, integration and multiculturalism.

Although the idea of Britishness, and the role of government in advancing it, is still contested, it has led to a rich policy agenda, particularly around citizenship. There are now citizenship classes in schools, citizenship tests and ceremonies for new citizens, and more recently an effort to introduce the idea of earned citizenship, making clearer the expected contribution of residents applying for the right to remain. But, unsurprisingly given the ambitions of the project, other elements have been less successful. There is still a lack of clarity as to what the left's conception of citizenship entails, a lack of consensus on whether a values-based approach to identity is sufficient and a failure to fully connect the Britishness agenda with the integration and equality agenda.

A new approach to identity

Social democrats must rethink their approach to identity. Identity is already shaping the means and ends of progressive politics, redefining the meaning of equality in the twenty-first century and challenging progressives to find new ways of delivering it. The response cannot be to ignore identity, but nor can it be to uncritically accept its role in public life. If social democrats are to navigate the new identity politics, then they must develop a confident account of its place: when is it appropriate to consider identity and on what terms? As should be clear from the above, identity has the potential to both exclude and include, to extend opportunities to participate and to curtail them. A principled approach is needed, to ensure that identity is harnessed to generate a deeper equality through a new framing of a shared society, at the same time renewing the link between political and economic equality through a focus on equal citizenship.

   If these are the guidelines by which social democrats should approach identity, then what can they do proactively to respond to identity and channel it to progressive ends? Strengthening collective identities could provide social democrats with an important tool with which to tackle the problems arising from identity change in Britain. A British civic identity holds significant potential in that regard. A British identity is a civic identity for a multinational state. Not only does it meet the legitimacy test, but a British civic identity also has certain qualities that make it suitable to fill the role of a common identity. As we have seen, Britishness continues to resonate with the majority of the population, even after devolution. A British identity is, by its very nature, a plural identity and from its inception was always intended to work alongside other identities. This stands it in good stead for the task ahead; all accept that identities are plural, and that as we move into different spaces or situations, different identities come to the fore. What a civic identity has the potential to do is provide a recognised platform on which all are able to participate in the public sphere.

A civic identity, however, will be useful only if it is clear what it is trying to achieve. It has too often been the case that politicians will reach for identity at points of crisis, to paper over the cracks. I would argue that a civic identity can be an effective way of strengthening citizenship, and through that, finding new ways to make equality a majority project. Second, it can provide a way of representing a shared society and a guide to the integration needed to get there.

Equality for a diverse society must also speak of how we live together. The inequalities of modern Britain could too easily lead to fragmentation and isolation. A separatist approach to equality, with each group within society arguing for more rights and resources without considering how they may be brought together as a whole, falls far short of the egalitarian ideal and is out of step with popular notions of equality. Moreover, it undermines the social solidarity on which social democrats rely to maintain support for redistribution. Abolishing poverty and lessening inequality, while important in their own right, will not necessarily bring about the equality of esteem necessary for a cohesive, integrated and inclusive society. The little evidence we have suggests that when groups improve their economic situation, they will often move out of diverse areas, as with 'white flight'. We know that it is sustained interaction that challenges our preconceived notions of one another, laying the groundwork for greater solidarity, and yet it is not clear how a model of equality that in cultural terms is about equal treatment can facilitate that interaction.

Equality legislation, through the introduction of positive duties and reasonable accommodation,[16] and human rights law have both been gradually moving towards a positive notion of equality, in recognition of the limitation of equal treatment as an emotive account of the value of equality. The UN Convention on the Rights of Persons with Disabilities captures this vividly in its expectation that people with disabilities should have the right not just to freedom from discrimination, but also to independent living and civic participation. In short, the state has a positive duty to support all to fulfil their capabilities, not just as individuals, but as social and interdependent persons within society.[17] The imagining of the good society behind the convention is one characterised by solidarity and democratic participation; greater equality is the means of achieving it. That version of equality, however, does not mean treating everyone the same.

The legislation suggests a way in which equality can develop along a trajectory which is both more emotive, in that it reflects a values-driven approach to the good society, and also potentially more capable of responding to greater diversity. However, taking the Human Rights Act as an example, it is unlikely that legislation alone will be capable of effecting the cultural change that social democrats aspire to, and certainly not in the short to medium term. An alternative would be to approach the problem from the opposite direction: build a stronger civic culture – a more active citizenship through a stronger civic identity – to bring about the engagement and inter-action necessary for a shared society. It is as well to acknowledge that giving more weight to our citizenship will not automatically encourage all towards participation, as is their prerogative, but it can begin to shape civic norms that make opting out, not opting in, the exception.

What might some of the consequences of this shift be? A long-term commitment to using public funding to build shared civic spaces – whether they be leisure facilities, libraries or communal resource centres for civil society groups. The allocation of public funds by ethnicity, faith or even deprivation may have its place, but it needs to be balanced against the overall aim of creating a shared society with shared spaces. Similarly, while targeting resources at specific groups can be effective in addressing need, when resources are tight we must also consider the impact on cohesion. Procedural fairness and universal measures have the potential to reinforce a sense of common citizenship.

Citizenship is likely to be strengthened through the increased opportunities Britons have to 'be' citizens in day-to-day life and to be recognised as such. The idea of a national citizens' service scheme for all young adults, proposed by both the main parties, is one such example. But so is compulsory voting, argued on the grounds of civic duty. The introduction of citizenship education in schools is a welcome move towards a better understanding of what citizenship entails, but a natural extension would be to roll out the citizenship test to all British citizens, not just new ones. A commitment to building a common citizenship must also consider what it means to be a citizen at the sharp end. At present when people are out of work, receiving benefits or state support they are clients, or claimants, but not citizens. The language of the market was introduced to challenge the stigma of state support but it drew on a long tradition in British political thought; people were now citizens when they were 'independent' and contributing to the state, and clients when they were receiving support. This is not just a matter of semantics; the respect and dignity afforded to people claiming support, and their worth and ability to participate in society, are likely to be affected by their status.

More broadly, this is citizenship as a means of widening participation. Effective public services, stronger local democracy and better integration will all require a more participative democracy. Strengthening the legitimacy of the citizen in the public sphere has the potential to expand ways of participating far beyond our limited understanding of political life. There are currently thousands of Britons who volunteer on a regular basis, as a means of contributing to and effecting local change, and yet see this activity as quite separate to their citizenship. Challenging that distinction by recognising civic activism as a valid political contribution, opening up the political and policy-making process to allow grassroots initiatives to make the manifesto or ballot paper, and lowering the barriers for participation in political parties to enable looser affiliations might be important first steps.

Recognising individuals as citizens, as inherently political actors able to contribute in ways that they choose, is likely to change the look and feel of our democratic culture. It is likely to be messier, with plenty of disagreement and dissent. But it will also spread power more widely, giving more people a stake in the political process. It will be more bottom up, more deliberative and better able to accommodate the variety of needs arising in a diverse society.

The route to strengthening citizenship is far clearer than that of strengthening a civic identity directly. Indeed, there are those who argue that social democrats would be best advised to focus on citizenship and leave identity alone in the effort to achieve a greater civic culture.[18] The levers available to foster identities are limited, and often, though identity might be the intended outcome, approaching it indirectly is most effective. However, the level of engagement suggested by identification makes it a prize worth pursuing. Symbols and narratives are important, and have been in our understanding of Britain to date. As Linda Colley notes,

> National identity is not just, perhaps not even, mainly a matter of political allegiance. It is sustained by custom and by the texture and reference points of everyday life. So when Margaret Thatcher and John Major privatised those big, nationalised industries which inevitably had the word 'British' in their names, and when they wore down trade unions like the National Union of Miners or the British union of this or that, they were – whether they knew it or not – dismantling some of the mundane architecture of Britishness.[19]

Finding new symbols that represent the Britain of today, and renewing the symbols we have so as to make them best able to resonate with the majority of Britons, could be a first step. A better public representation of the story of Britain, which tells honestly of the past and of how those in Britain came to live here, would help to flesh out what it is we are to identify with. People must want to identify with something in order to form an identity, and although many on the left may wish it were true, citizenship, understood as a set of formal rights and duties, is unlikely to provide that incentive. But Britishness, an emotive and culturally sited representation of our citizenship, holds far more potential.

At this level, a civic identity can provide a valuable means of security at a time of greater transience, when migration leads to the movement of people to unfamiliar places, and areas subject to rapid population change can quickly become unfamiliar to those who live in them. A clear articulation of what it means to be British, the social norms, civic duties and rights, offers all an opportunity to belong. If people are not given this opportunity to find new ways of belonging, those in vulnerable situations risk clinging to narrow forms of identity, inhibiting integration and allowing the possibility of isolation. This is not just a matter for new citizens; a narrative that describes who we are as a nation and who we are becoming contextualises the change that people see in their locality and enables them to place themselves within that shared experience.

Identity, as this chapter has sought to show, is changing the social and political landscape in Britain, forcing social democrats to reassess many of their objectives and the means of achieving them. In particular, this chapter has challenged those who assert that diversity and equality have a negative relationship to one another, whereby increasing one must automatically decrease the other. Rather, increasing diversity and the identity changes associated with it will force equality to expand and adapt, as it has in the past. The threat of fragmentation has highlighted the weakness of a liberal, highly atomised, conception of equality that imagines each individual free from discrimination and disadvantage, equal to the next, but has nothing to say of the context in which that equality is made useful. Just as identity can threaten the social democratic project, so it can provide a way forward. A greater civic identity, based on a renewed conception of citizenship, suggests a way to articulate our relationship to one another and offers social democrats once more the opportunity to paint a picture of the good society in which all can belong.

Part IV

The constitution and
foreign affairs

10

Constitutional reform

Iain McLean

Introduction

What are the overarching principles of a progressive British constitution? Despite the fact that a profound transformation of the
British political system has been initiated, New Labour has not yet
developed a coherent account of the modern British state. The
historic opportunity for thorough reform of the state has not yet
been seized.

This relative failure perhaps reflects Labour's ambivalence about
constitutional reform. Throughout the history of the party, constitutional reform has risen to the top of the agenda only when Labour
has needed to broaden its constituency by bringing in the Liberals,
as in 1918, 1929 and 1997. Rarely has the constitution been seen as
central to the task of exploiting political democracy to gain greater
social democracy.

The reforms that have taken place since 1997 have largely been
incremental, leaving contradictions and a lack of clarity about
where power lies, making it likely that any future social democratic
government will have to address reform through practicality if
nothing else. Major outstanding questions remain such as the next
stage of House of Lords reform; how proportional and pluralistic the
electoral system should be locally and nationally; the ramifications of
the emergence of rival power centres in Scotland, Northern Ireland
and Wales, alongside significant regional disparities; the unresolved
question of the future of England in a devolved UK; whether elected
mayors can revive local government; and the wider impact of human

rights legislation on our society. Given limited space, this chapter can deal with only a few of these questions.[1] Instead it focuses on the principles that need to be at the core of the debate.

But there is a more compelling case for constitutional reform to be part of a social democratic project. Future reform provides the opportunity to embed much of the social progress gained in the last ten years, from the Human Rights Act to equality legislation. But the price of this, if it is a price, is to move power away from politics towards the judiciary – a proposition traditionally resisted by the British left. On one view, this would be a further step towards the weakening of traditional ideas of nation state top-down social democracy, which, as Vernon Bogdanor has pointed out, is under pressure from forces above and below – globalisation above and demands for devolution and the strengthening of local decision making below. Whether it is through the necessity of forming a new progressive majority, or the need to tie together loose ends, social democrats will need an account of power, the role of the state and its relationship to citizens.

This chapter asks to what extent constitutional reform in the future should be based on the traditions of civic activism or civic pluralism – in which liberty is defined as both self-government and active engagement in the public sphere. Broadly speaking, civic activism says: 'All power to the people.' Civic pluralism says: 'All power to the people under the constitution.' Under both, power flows from the people but following civic activism there are few restrictions. Civic pluralism, on the other hand, would place certain rights and institutions beyond a simple popular majority's ability to repeal them.

Each of the major political parties speaks of the need to bring power closer to the people. For each there will be different conflicts to reconcile. Labour may well struggle with the desire to devolve power and at the same time deliver the agenda they would want of social justice and equity in delivering public services. Since the Second World War, Labour has had a strong centralising tendency for exactly that reason, as epitomised by Aneurin Bevan's creation of the National Health Service, setting aside earlier traditions of British socialism as espoused for example by James Keir Hardie and his life-long commitment to Scottish home rule. But more recently figures within the Labour Party have begun to speak of the inadequacy of narrow redistributive approaches to social justice. The argument that power must be redistributed alongside material resources to allow individuals to participate fully in society and choose meaningful lives is gaining ground. But any future reform must answer two questions. First, how should power be diffused as widely as possible? Second, what checks and balances should be devised to ensure that power is not concentrated in an over-mighty central state?

This chapter proceeds as follows. The first section examines the constitutional reforms during New Labour's first ten years and the second considers where future social democratic governments can, or should, evolve towards civic activism or civic pluralism. I treat these two ideas as rivals, not complements. The third looks at the implications of these constitutional choices for progressive parties.

Constitutional reform 1997–2007

There was substantial but disjointed constitutional reform in the Blair years. It was, Tony Blair claimed, 'the biggest programme of change to democracy ever proposed'. The three main components, each done in utter isolation from the others, were devolution, upper house reform and the domestication of the European Convention on Human Rights. The programme had largely been formulated during the years in opposition and drew much from the Liberal and Liberal Democrat agenda of those years. Indeed, the Liberal Democrat and Labour Joint Consultative Committee on Constitutional Reform, established in 1996, heavily influenced the Labour manifesto of 1997.

Devolution
Devolution to Scotland and Wales was unfinished business that Tony Blair inherited from John Smith, whom he succeeded as Labour leader in 1994. Smith, a member of the Scottish political class, which had talked of nothing but devolution since the mid-1970s, had been closely involved in the Callaghan government's failed attempts to introduce a devolved constitutional settlement and was strongly influenced by the 1988 Claim of Right and the Scottish

Constitutional Convention. These events enabled Smith to claim that devolution was 'the settled will of the Scottish people'. Blair was much more sceptical, but the will was settled by the double referendum of September 1997. The people of Scotland voted by a large majority in favour of a Scottish parliament, and by a smaller but still comfortable majority for it to have the power to tax. A week later, the electorate of Wales voted by the narrowest possible margin for an elected assembly there. It was not offered the power to tax. The Scottish Parliament and National Assembly for Wales accordingly began work in 1999. Both of them were dominated by Labour in the first two assemblies, to 2007. In the 2007 elections, the SNP won a lead over Labour of one seat in Scotland, and in Wales, after some Liberal Democrat shilly-shallying, Labour formed a coalition with Plaid Cymru.

Devolution to Northern Ireland followed a quite different track. It had begun in 1922, when the six counties of Northern Ireland were excluded from the Irish Free State, whose independence the British had recognised in December 1921. They were then offered the home rule that their Unionist leaders had violently resisted since 1886. However, once they had what one of them described as a Protestant parliament and Protestant state,[2] they found devolution rather to their taste. However, Britain imposed direct rule in 1972 after the Northern Ireland government had refused to end internment without trial. No lasting attempt to restore devolution had succeeded. Blair continued the Northern Irish peace initiatives of his predecessor, John Major. Under New Labour, devolved government returned to Northern Ireland, then was suspended again, and finally (as of this writing) returned in 2007. The Northern Ireland arrangements approved under the Good Friday Agreement of 1998 impose compulsory consociationalism. That cumbrous word, coined in the Netherlands, means the formal recognition of rival communities which share power. In Northern Ireland, the First Minister and deputy First Minister must come from the two largest parties in the assembly. Hence the bizarre spectacle in 2007 of the Democratic Unionist First Minister, Ian Paisley, apparently cheerfully sharing power with the Sinn Fein deputy First Minister, Martin McGuinness. Thus nationalists share power in all three of the non-English parts of the UK, which means (if nothing else) that progressive politicians must revisit devolution.

House of Lords reform

New Labour has struggled with House of Lords reform. In 1996 Tony Blair made a speech saying that Labour had always favoured an elected upper house. Yet words failed to translate into action during New Labour's first ten years. The easy bit of Lords reform was the expulsion of most hereditary peers in 1999, although a backstairs deal with the Conservative Lords permitted ninety-two to stay for the time being. Efforts to complete the reform failed twice under Blair. In 2000, a hand-picked royal commission under the former Conservative chief whip Lord Wakeham recommended that the future upper house should be mostly nominated, with a small elected element. It should reflect the social, regional and gender balance of the UK. Sixteen Church of England bishops should continue to sit in it.

The Wakeham report was poorly received. Its recommendations were mutually contradictory. For instance, if the Church of England bishops were to stay, I calculated from official statistics that this would require the upper house to contain a total of seventy-seven representatives of faith communities.[3] Many or most of these would have to be female to satisfy the gender equality requirement, given that the Church of England bishops were all male. These seventy-seven would have been impossible to fit into a house of reasonable size.

Most people in the UK want an elected upper house. This was clear, and acknowledged, in the government's analysis of the response to Wakeham – but no government move ensued. Rather, members of both houses were invited to cast a free vote on Lords reform. Some Labour politicians see an elected upper house as a threat to the primacy of the Commons and have therefore been reluctant to support it. Blair was among them. The votes of 2003 on upper house reform were chaotic. MPs voted against all possible compositions of an upper house, including the status quo of an all-appointed house. But the result of the votes, contradictorily, was the continuation of the status quo.

The log-jam started to clear in 2006. Two committees of both houses were appointed, leading to white papers in 2007 and 2008.[4] These white papers picked up several reform proposals that Wakeham and earlier white papers had rejected. They proposed that elected members of the upper house should serve a fifteen-year non-renewable term, being elected by thirds at the same time as UK members of the European Parliament in the twelve standard regions, which are also the constituencies for European elections. At the end of their term, they would be ineligible for immediate election to the House of Commons. However, unlike the European Parliament elections, which use closed party list systems,[5] the government proposed that upper house elections should use a partially open list. The intention was that should voters feel that party whips were penalising independent or rebellious senators, they could rearrange a party's list. The existence of this sanction, it was felt (but not stated), would inhibit party whips from trying such a form of punishment in the first place.

Unlike earlier government proposals, the 2007 white paper proposed that at least half of the upper house should be elected (though it also proposed retaining the bishops). No party should have an overall majority, either in the whole house or among the elected members of the house.

When these proposals were put to a second free vote in the Commons, the results were very different to those in 2003. A wholly elected chamber won the vote by the widest margin, 338 to 226 (although it was widely suspected that the majority included some Machiavellian votes by people opposed to upper house reform who wanted an impracticably extreme proposal to be carried). An 80/20 elected/appointed split was also supported. Proposals for an elected percentage below 80 were all defeated. As in 2003, the unelected House of Lords voted in 2007 to stay unelected.[6] The 2008 white paper explores options for a wholly or largely elected upper house.

The European Convention on Human Rights

The Blair governments' record on human rights has been fiercely attacked from left and right. From the left, campaigners argue that under the guise of preventing terrorism, New Labour has overseen a huge incursion into human rights, for instance on compulsory identity cards. From the right, Conservative politicians and newspapers have complained that the Human Rights Act (HRA) has allowed travellers to break planning laws and prisoners to insist on hard-core pornography being delivered to their cells.[7] The attack from the right was renewed as this chapter went to press. When (actually incorrect) reports appeared stating that the HRA prevented murderer Learco Chindamo from being deported to his birthplace of Italy on completion of his sentence,[8] the Conservative leader, David Cameron, repeated his pledge to repeal the HRA in favour of a 'British bill of rights'. Lawyers point out, however, that if such a bill omitted any part of the European Convention on Human Rights, aggrieved parties could still appeal to the European Court of Human Rights, as before 1998, unless the UK were to withdraw from the convention, which it had itself drafted.

The European Convention on Human Rights was drawn up in 1950 in the shadow of the horrors of Nazism, largely by British lawyers. It guarantees a set of human rights broadly similar to those protected in the US constitution and Bill of Rights – rights to freedom of expression, assembly and religion, and procedural rights to a fair trial and against extra-legal punishment. Until 1998, individuals with a claim against the UK government or a UK public authority had to appeal to the European Court on Human Rights in Strasbourg. The Human Rights Act 1998 is widely stated to have 'incorporated the convention into domestic law'. What it actually does is more complex than that. It gives individuals access to the UK courts to complain that a public authority has abused their individual rights. If the public authority states in its defence that it was exercising statutory powers, the act requires the court to read the legislation 'in a way which is compatible with the convention rights'. If it cannot so read a UK statute, it does not (unlike, for instance, the US Supreme Court) have the power to declare a statute unconstitutional, although it may issue a declaration of incompatibility, stating that (part of) a statute is incompatible with convention rights. In the most prominent case, the Law Lords did so in 2004, ruling that part of the Anti-terrorism, Crime and Security Act 2001 was incompatible with convention rights. The part in question had allowed the Home Secretary to detain foreign terrorist suspects indefinitely. It was replaced by the system of control orders under the Prevention of Terrorism Act 2005, which was itself later declared

incompatible with the HRA. According to the (then) Department
of Constitutional Affairs, by December 2006 fourteen declarations of
incompatibility had been made by UK courts (and not overturned
by a higher court) since the act had come into force.[9]

The implications of change

All of these constitutional changes undertaken in New Labour's first
ten years were, as noted, done in isolation from one another, and
with complex interactions that are not yet tested or even necessarily
understood.[10] The tensions between reforms are already apparent; the
move towards popular sovereignty does not sit easily with measures
to introduce a human rights framework. Although Tony Blair stated
in 1996 that he wanted a 'new politics which treats people as full
citizens, gives them greater power over government', there was
not necessarily a consensus on what that meant in terms of the
constitution. Where did power lie – with Parliament or with the
people? Was there to be parliamentary or popular sovereignty?

Of the three sets of Blair reforms, two – namely, devolution and
human rights – chip away at parliamentary sovereignty. This has been
held to be the bedrock of the British constitution. But it is shattered.
If present or future progressive governments are to build a new
constitution, they need a new bedrock. I would argue that it should
be popular sovereignty. It is popular sovereignty that best reflects the
stated social democratic aim to give citizens sufficient power over
government, bringing power closer to the people. If and when an
elected upper house comes into existence, a new constitution based
on popular sovereignty becomes possible.

The constitution of the United States, written in 1787 and
ratified by the required nine states in 1787–8, opens: 'We the People
of the United States . . . do ordain and establish this Constitution for
the United States of America.' The people did not literally do so, of
course. Apart from anything else, neither slaves nor women were
'people' in 1787. Nevertheless, the constitution locates sovereignty
firmly with the people. It sets the conditions for its own ratification
(at least nine states – a threshold crossed on 21 June 1788) and
amendment (at least three-quarters of the states must ratify, either

through their legislatures or in a constitutional convention). If more than four states had not ratified it, it would not have come into force. The fierce debates around ratification, which gave rise to the famous *Federalist Papers* of Alexander Hamilton, James Madison and John Jay, were an awesome model of civic activism.

The concept of parliamentary sovereignty is most closely associated with the Victorian jurist and ideologue A.V. Dicey, who wrote:

> Neither the Act of Union with Scotland nor the Dentists Act, 1878, has more claim than the other to be considered a supreme law. Each embodies the will of the sovereign legislative power; each can be legally altered or repealed by Parliament; neither tests the validity of the other. Should the Dentists Act, 1878, unfortunately contradict the terms of the Act of Union, the Act of Union would be *pro tanto* [to that extent] repealed ... The one fundamental dogma of English [sic] constitutional law is the absolute legislative sovereignty or despotism of the King in Parliament.[11]

According to Dicey, parliamentary sovereignty is so boundless that there is only one thing Parliament cannot do, namely bind its successor. Public lawyers and others have been taking potshots at this doctrine for at least seventy years, but it still pops up in court judgments.[12]

What is wrong with parliamentary sovereignty? After all, the people elect Parliament, don't they? Well, up to a point. The people elect only one of the three houses of Parliament,[13] namely the House of Commons. Nobody elected the Queen or any member of the House of Lords.

This first objection to Diceyan doctrine could be met by electing the Lords and replacing the Queen by an elected head of state. In passing, these simple reforms could lay to rest the question of proportional representation that has divided the British left for a century. Out of self-interest, Liberals support it; out of self-interest, most Labour politicians oppose it. But rarely do debates go beyond this initial stage to consider how proportional representation would work in practice. Few on either side stop to think that Parliament comprises three houses. It would hardly be sensible for them all to be elected at the same time and by the same electoral system, as they would then be clones. Therefore either the time or the method of election, or preferably both, must differ across houses.

If electoral reform were to take place, a feasible option for the UK would be to adopt a similar system to Australia. The Australian lower house is elected by what the Australians call 'preferential voting', the Americans call 'instant runoff' and the British call 'alternative vote' or AV. In single-member districts, voters rank the candidates. The lowest candidate in each round is successively eliminated until one candidate has more than half the votes.

AV can be massively disproportional, and therefore the upper house must be elected by a system of PR. Australia uses the single transferable vote (STV) to elect its Senate, where the electoral units are the states, and each state has an equal number of senators. If adapted for UK use, the units should be Scotland, Wales, Northern Ireland, and the nine standard regions of England. Each should have not (as in Australia) an equal number of senators, but a number proportionate to their population. The PR system used should not be the debased Australian form of STV, where the option of voting for a party list, taken by almost all voters, turns it into AV and thus negates the balance requirement. But an open party list system should work.

There is only one head of state. Therefore, if directly elected, she cannot be elected by a PR system, since you cannot elect proportions of people to a single post. A head of state election should not use AV, but rather a Condorcet system with a tie-break.[14]

If Parliament were truly elected by the people in the way just described, could we then be content with parliamentary sovereignty? No; there remain two other fatal objections to Dicey. First, the doctrine of parliamentary sovereignty makes it impossible to give special status to any act, such as Dicey's example of the Act of Union with Scotland 1706 or the Human Rights Act 1998. Second, as Alistair McMillan and I have shown elsewhere, Dicey's own position is radically incoherent.[15] When Parliament did something he really disliked, namely legislating for home rule for Ireland between 1912 and 1914, he suddenly discovered that after all the people were sovereign – and that furthermore the will of the people was represented by the unelected King and Lords (who opposed home rule), not the elected Commons (where the pro-home rule coalition had a majority of about 120 seats). As philosophers like to say, *From a contradiction anything follows*. Dicey's views are radically contradictory. They should be jettisoned, and with them the whole idea of parliamentary sovereignty.

What would a constitution based on the ideal of civic activism look like? The US constitution, with its ringing statement that authority springs from the people, is one source; Scotland offers a second. As the presiding judge said in a famous case in 1953,

> The principle of the unlimited sovereignty of Parliament is a distinctively English principle which has no counterpart in Scottish constitutional law. It derives its origin from Coke and Blackstone, and was widely popularised during the nineteenth century by Bagehot and Dicey, the latter having stated the doctrine in its classic form in his *Law of the Constitution*. Considering that the Union legislation [of 1706–7] extinguished the Parliaments of Scotland and England and replaced them by a new Parliament, I have difficulty in seeing why it should have been supposed that the new Parliament of Great Britain must inherit all the peculiar characteristics of the English Parliament but none of the Scottish Parliament, as if all that happened in 1707 was that Scottish representatives were admitted to the Parliament of England. That is not what was done.[16]

The Scottish Claim of Right, published in 1988 and incorporated into the Constitutional Convention in 1989, celebrated by its name and date the tercentenary of an earlier important Scottish statement of popular sovereignty, the Claim of Right Act 1689, which set out the Scottish people's right to reject the reign of James VII and to offer the throne to William and Mary. Three hundred years later, the second Claim of Right was more explicit: 'We, gathered as the Scottish Constitutional Convention, do hereby acknowledge the sovereign right of the Scottish people to determine the form of government best suited to their needs, and do hereby declare and pledge that in all our actions and deliberations their interests shall be paramount.' However, unlike the US Constitutional Convention of 1787, the Scottish Constitutional Convention of 1989–95 was a purely unofficial body. Two of the main political parties – the SNP and the Conservatives – stayed aloof. The constitution drafted by the

convention was very largely adopted in the Scotland Act 1998; the
claim of that act to represent, in John Smith's phrase, the 'settled will
of the Scottish people' derived not from the convention but from the
referendum of September 1997.

Where next for Britain?

New Labour Mark II is led by a Scotsman with a PhD in Scottish
history. The green paper *The Governance of Britain* was one of the first
actions of the Brown government. It was issued in July 2007 over the
names of Prime Minister Brown and the secretary of state for justice,
Jack Straw. Ironically, because Gordon Brown had declared that he
was going to announce policy initiatives to Parliament and not to
the *Today* programme, it attracted remarkably little media comment.
But it is a startling document. It could propel New Labour down a
new road of civic activism. Or it could stop well short.

Why is it startling? First, because unlike most New Labour
documents, it is aware of its own history – Scottish as well as English.
To mention the English Declaration of Rights 1689 is remarkable. To
mention the Scottish Claim of Right as well is unprecedented, as far
as I know.[17] Second, and more substantially, because it announces the
government's voluntary withdrawal from several aspects of the royal
prerogative: 'The Government believe that the executive should
draw its powers from the people, through Parliament [paragraph 14].'
The most important such powers concern deployment of troops
abroad, dissolving Parliament, and the organisation of the civil
service. But the green paper also announces (at paragraph 50) that
Brown is abandoning the Crown's right to impress men into the
Royal Navy. Third, the green paper announces the government's
withdrawal from involvement in certain public appointments.
Symbolically, these include bishops of the Church of England. The
Brown government has quietly disestablished the Church, at the
same time denying that it was doing so. It has also withdrawn from
honours nominations, and promises to open more public appointments to scrutiny by Commons select committees.

Walking away from some powers is easy, and the government has
done it by fiat. Other reforms, including, notably, reform of the

House of Lords, are more complicated. The green paper announces that the government seeks consensus on this and other points that require legislation. On Lords reform it bluntly announces that it is 'committed to enacting the will of the Commons' in favour of a wholly or 80 per cent elected Lords. However, it notes that both the Conservatives and the Liberal Democrats fought the 2005 election on a platform that included a substantially elected Lords (paragraph 136). An elected upper house is an essential part of popular sovereignty.

Civic activism and civic pluralism are not the same thing. To see why they are different, look again at the hard cases thrown up by the HRA and by the UK's signature of the European Convention on Human Rights (ECHR). The core rights protected by the ECHR and the HRA are rights to freedom of speech, assembly and religion; and rights to a fair trial and against arbitrary detention. These rights only come to notice in hard and unpopular causes such as gypsies and other travellers, prisoners, asylum seekers and terrorist suspects. Furthermore, as the government's 2006 review of the operation of the HRA notes,

> many myths have grown up around the Human Rights Act since its enactment in 1998. Commentators have blamed human rights for a range of ills, but in particular for giving undeserving people a means of jumping the queue and getting their interests placed ahead of those of decent hardworking folk.

Often, it goes on, this perception arises because a member of an unpopular group announces an intention of proceeding under the HRA. The media do not then report that the application fails or is not even entertained. 'These sort [sic] of cases tend to bring the act unfairly into disrepute in public perception, and can only properly be countered by swift rebuttal of the false attributions when they appear.'[18] As noted above, the Conservative Party and much of the press oppose the HRA. It attracts none of the reverence that Americans say they feel for the US constitution.

This brings out that human rights protection is inherently anti-majoritarian. A government which announced that it was deporting terrorist suspects to home countries in which they might be tortured would be very popular. But that is absolutely (not, like most of the other convention rights, conditionally) forbidden under the ECHR and the HRA. The US Bill of Rights was designed to rule out the arbitrary power of George III. But as James Madison said in the *Federalist Papers*, the constitution must protect individuals against 'the insecurity of rights under the popular form of government'. Thus, some of the items in the US Bill of Rights – the first ten amendments to the constitution, ratified as a block – are explicitly anti-majoritarian. The first amendment states: 'Congress shall make no law respecting an establishment of religion, or prohibiting the free exercise thereof; or abridging the freedom of speech, or of the press; or the right of the people peaceably to assemble, and to petition the Government for a redress of grievances.' Many Congresses would have liked to have restricted freedoms in some of the ways described above – for instance during an anti-French panic in 1798 and during the McCarthyite 1950s.

That the US constitution is anti-majoritarian does not seem to bother most Americans, who revere it without knowing what it says. The UK Human Rights Act has no such protection. The Conservatives have promised to repeal it, although a simple repeal would not remove claimants' convention rights – only a withdrawal from the convention would do that. The issue then becomes the apparently arcane one of 'how far should a progressive government entrench rights and other constitutional statutes?'. 'Entrenchment' means 'putting something beyond the ability of an ordinary act to repeal', and it is therefore incompatible with Diceyan parliamentary sovereignty. If it entrenches them deeply, the result could be described as civic pluralism but attacked for giving unelected judges power over political decisions. If it entrenches them only shallowly, the result could be described as civic activism but may put unpopular minorities at risk from vengeful majorities.

The HRA is shallowly entrenched. As noted above, it gives the higher courts the right to declare that a statute is incompatible with it, but not the right to strike a statute down as unconstitutional. Recent court judgments have treated not only it, but also other statutes, including the Parliament Acts 1911 and 1949 and the European Communities Act 1972, as shallowly entrenched. A.V. Dicey said that if the Dentists Act 1878 contradicted part of the Act of Union 1706, then the Act of Union was to that extent repealed. That is not how the contemporary British courts read constitutional statutes. Therefore they have some de facto entrenchment. If an earlier, constitutional, statute overrides some later, non-constitutional one, then it is the later, not (as Dicey insisted) the earlier, that gives way. Thus a section of the Merchant Shipping Act 1988 was judged by the British courts to be incompatible with the 1972 act ratifying the UK's membership of the European Union – and it was the 1988 act that must give way.[19]

The lawyers' pressure group Justice has published a discussion paper suggesting how (and whether) a UK bill of rights might be entrenched.[20] At present, the HRA is semi-entrenched by the declaration of incompatibility procedure. The European Communities Act is entrenched by court judgments. A stronger entrenchment (e.g. by amending the Parliament Acts to make constitutional statutes unamendable by the Commons acting alone, or by requiring a two-thirds majority vote in Parliament to amend them) would swing the balance further towards civic pluralism. That is one of the many Pandora's boxes opened by the 2007 green paper. As Ernest Bevin allegedly said, 'If you open that Pandora's box you will find it full of bloody Trojan horses.'

New Labour, and any successor government, faces a choice. In a civic activism model, authority flows from the people with few restrictions. In a civic pluralism model, authority still flows from the people. But certain institutions remain entrenched even against a popular majority that would repeal them.

Both models call for an elected upper house and an elected head of state to replace the monarchy. The head of state could be elected either directly by the people or indirectly by both (directly elected) houses of Parliament acting together. Both models would recognise the separation of powers between the government and the judiciary. New Labour has already gone down that road in the Constitutional Reform Act 2005, which removes the government from the appointment of judges. In the 2007 green paper (paragraph 71) it offers to 'consider going further than the present arrangement'.

Both models would have to have *some* entrenchment. The three devolution settlements must be entrenched. Devolved government in Scotland, Wales or Northern Ireland should be abandoned only if the people of the territory in question vote to abandon it. It should be protected from abandonment by parliamentary vote. The Parliament Acts, governing the maximum length of a parliament and providing for lower-house supremacy over the upper house, must remain entrenched, which is the current practice of the courts *contra* Dicey.[21] Some other procedural acts should be explicitly entrenched, such as the Parliamentary Constituencies and Representation of the People Acts. These acts lay down the electoral system and the qualifications to vote. They should not be unamendable, but amendments must pass certain qualified-majority thresholds, so that narrowly partisan changes (such as removing the requirement for equal-sized constituencies) are made difficult.

A civic activism model would not entrench the Human Rights Act or other substantive rights. No guarantee of rights is majoritarian. It is not worth having if it is. But, as noted, the groups most likely to appeal to their substantive rights are those that the majority most dislikes. In these circumstances it makes it difficult to see how the Human Rights Act could overcome its popularity deficit. The drawback of civic activism is that minorities may be persecuted.

A civic pluralism model would retain or strengthen the entrenchment of the classic human rights to freedom of expression, assembly, religion, and family life. An advantage of this is that such things as the right to demonstrate in Parliament Square, restored in the 2007 green paper, would not be at the whim of governments. It could go further, for instance by entrenching equality legislation so that discrimination on grounds of colour, gender, religion (or lack of religion) and sexual orientation would not only be outlawed but super-outlawed.

There would be some drawbacks. Only the courts could deal with allegations of rights infringement. Especially if the HRA list were extended, they would have to deal with conflicting rights claims. (Consider, for instance, a religious believer who argues that being forced to treat gay job applicants equally with straight applicants interferes with her freedom of religion.) Some Americans (and British observers of American judicial politics) deplore the judicialisation of morality. Confirmation hearings of US Supreme Court nominees are usually taken up with rather primitive Congressional attempts to find out the nominee's position on the 'right' to an abortion, which in *Roe* v. *Wade* (1973) the court held to be constitutionally protected. Presidential nominations are driven by the same narrow imperative. Republican Presidents tend to nominate justices who they think will overturn *Roe*; Democratic Presidents, justices who they think will sustain it.

The 2007 green paper hints that New Labour intends to go towards entrenchment of rights. But this is never popular with the Home Secretary of the day, who would like to be able to lock up and deport terrorist suspects at will; and who may wish to deport released murderers to Italy. Ultimately the judgement between a majoritarian and a rights-based constitution is a value judgement. You cannot have an infinite amount of both majority rule and rights protection.

11

Foreign policy

Donald Macintyre

The international section, barely noticed at the time, of the new Clause IV of the Labour Party constitution approved in 1995 was written by Peter Mandelson. Presented at a late stage with a draft which retained much of the heavy emphasis in the old clause, composed in the third year of the First World War by Sidney and Beatrice Webb, on the peaceful resolution of conflict, Mandelson presciently scribbled a note in the margin: 'Won't a Blair government ever go to war?' Mandelson proposed that the text should read: 'Labour is committed to the defence and security of the British people and to cooperating in European institutions, the United Nations, the Commonwealth and other international bodies to secure peace, freedom, democracy, economic security and environmental protection for all.'

As an inevitably simple summary of British international goals at the turn of the century, the passage, which was published in a form almost identical to that drafted by Mandelson, remains valid. Yet what is striking about it is how far it fails to do justice to the central tenets of Tony Blair's foreign policy as actually put into practice, at war and in peace. True, the first three of the military campaigns embarked on by the Blair government, Kosovo (NATO approved in the absence of Russian support for a UN resolution), Sierra Leone (reinforcing UN peacekeepers) and Afghanistan (following a NATO invocation of its Article V to say that the September 11 2001 attacks on New York and Washington were an attack on the whole alliance), arguably conformed to the requirement of 'co-operating ... in ... international bodies'. But the war in Iraq, not backed by NATO, the European

Union or the UN Security Council, patently did not. Indeed, the most striking omission in the clause is of any mention of relations with the United States or the transatlantic alliance, the nurturing of which Blair repeatedly said – and demonstrated – during his premiership was central to his thinking. Moreover, setting as a priority 'cooperating in European institutions' failed to mention the other track of what was for Blair an explicitly two-track strategy, most often characterised as that of making Britain the 'bridge' between Europe and the United States. He defined it on countless occasions, but perhaps nowhere more clearly than in a speech to the joint houses of the Canadian parliament in February 2001:

> There are those in my country who say: . . . 'You can have Europe, or you can have North America, but you can't have both. Britain has to choose.' . . . It is an article of my political faith that I refuse point blank to do so. We will have the best of both worlds. We will give up neither relationship. We will make them both work.

This chapter will argue that the 'bridge' strategy is obsolete, and that global conditions no longer afford Britain the luxury of having 'the best of both worlds'. Britain's mystical belief in the United States' readiness to regard it as its closest ally – a readiness which is, to put it mildly, highly questionable – has blinded it to the reality that its hopes of influence, especially on the United States itself, rests on exactly the full-hearted engagement in Europe and its institutions which successive governments have repeatedly baulked at. While the Iraq War brutally exposed the failures of the 'bridge' strategy, it was already an anachronism by the time Blair came into office. Had the Labour leadership thought more profoundly about Britain's place in the world before coming into office, it might have more readily confronted this reality.

Ironically, it is possible to read the Mandelson clause as evidence that New Labour had recognised the impossibility of 'having the best of both worlds' and had resolved the dilemma in favour of Europe. In fact, omission of any mention of the United States from the text probably owed more to the short-term desire to avoid inflaming left-wing sensibilities than to any profound attempt to rethink the balance between Britain's transatlantic and European relations. For, as in several other areas of policy covered in this book, Labour did not perform an intellectually coherent and radical reappraisal of the fundamental global changes that had taken place since the party had last been in office eighteen years earlier, which a modern social democratic foreign affairs strategy required. The roots of the Blair government's foreign policy failures lay in that refusal to make a too long postponed strategic choice, all the more painfully so given Blair's undoubtedly genuine commitment to Britain having a leading role in Europe.

In determinedly seeking to reassociate Labour with the transatlantic alliance, of course, Blair was in good historical company among his predecessors, from Clement Attlee onwards. And in emphasising, as he did more or less throughout the ten years of his premiership, the need at once to stand 'shoulder to shoulder' with the United States and to put Britain 'at the heart' of Europe, Blair was drawing, whether consciously or not, on two overlapping doctrines, one ideological and the other governmental, dating back half a century.

The post-Gaitskellite social democratic tendency in the Labour Party had long combined a belief that Britain's destiny lay in the European Community, but with a robust Atlanticism (even if Hugh Gaitskell himself, to the disappointment of many of his younger colleagues in the early 1960s, was much less enthused by the first than the second). The latter was founded on a detestation of communism, a recognition that Soviet ideology conflicted directly with democratic socialist values (as they might have been called at the time) and that the United States remained the one international bulwark against its spread.

In seeking to combine a European perspective with a transatlantic one, Labour's 1950s social democrats were closely in line with the basic doctrine which evolved within the British (Conservative-run) government after the Suez crisis finally brought home the realisation that the United Kingdom was no longer a world power. Indeed, in one important sense they had anticipated it. Labour, led by Gaitskell, had already realised earlier and much more clearly than Anthony Eden and his Cabinet colleagues the dangers to Britain's relationship with the United States in the Suez misadventure; they were an important part of its arguments against it. The catastrophic attempt by the French and British governments in secret consort with Israel to seize back by armed force the newly nationalised Suez Canal from the Egyptian President, Gamal Abdel Nasser, in 1956 is now seen as a turning point in British foreign policy. It is to the lasting credit of Labour under Gaitskell that it resolutely opposed Suez, on the formal grounds, incidentally, that the invasion, like that of Iraq in 2003, was not sanctioned by the UN Security Council. The ignominious retreat forced on the Eden government by a deeply antipathetic President Eisenhower left the governing elites of Britain and France both confronting the same post-war realities. But while the effect was equally traumatic, the reappraisal in each country produced different results. For France, which signed the treaty of Rome a year later, it marked the beginning of a long effort to establish Europe as an independent force in world affairs. For Britain it meant, as Harold Wilson would write, that 'in place of imperialism, she turned inward to a preoccupation with her possible place in a West European grouping' – one that would not be fulfilled until Edward Heath took Britain into the EEC sixteen years later. But in Britain, recognition that its relative power was now inexorably on the decline led to a second post-Suez conclusion at least as potent, but by no means shared by its French collaborators in that doomed enterprise – namely that she could never again afford to find herself in opposition to the United States on an issue of strategic importance. The British goal, as defined in a paper by the Cabinet secretary, Norman Brook, in 1960, was therefore to maintain both projects in tandem. Brook argued that while 'our status in the world will depend largely on [the US's] readiness to treat us as their closest ally ... whatever happens we must not find ourselves in the position of having to make a final choice between the two sides of the Atlantic'. As the commentator Philip Stephens has pointed out, the Brook doctrine was closely echoed by the 'bridge' strategy pursued by Blair more than a generation later.

Nor was Blair the first British Prime Minister to discover that that such a doctrine was easier to state than fulfil. Indeed, at least two of his predecessors had been confronted with the painful choice Brook had wanted Britain to avoid, and found themselves, like Blair, opting for the transatlantic relationship when they were forced to exercise the choice. In 1962, Harold Macmillan, at once keen to pursue a 'special relationship' with the United States under President

Kennedy and to promote British membership of the European common market, agreed to buy Polaris nuclear weapons from the US. The offer to sell the same systems to France was rejected by President de Gaulle, who saw the deal as a means of extending US strategic influence in Europe. And the following year de Gaulle vetoed Britain's first formal application to join the EEC.

Five years later another Labour government would come up, if less momentously, against the same problems in reconciling the two primary goals of its foreign policy. The 'for your eyes only' telegram that Wilson sent to Kennedy's successor, Lyndon Johnson, describing his memorable tête-à-tête with de Gaulle in the immediate aftermath of the Six Day War could almost have been written by Blair to George W. Bush about his breach with Jacques Chirac over Iraq. Only a couple of months before the present crisis, the French President had been warmly congratulating Wilson on his pro-Europeanism, conceding that 'we had shown a willingness no longer to moor our British craft on the Eastern seaboard of America . . . but in the Channel'. But now, the Prime Minister reported to Washington, the French President – in his seventies like Chirac thirty-six years later – was feeling his age and bitter at Britain's continuous 'involvement' with the United States, which he believed had not only made it inevitable that it would 'be dragged into your wars' but also 'affected us damagingly in the Middle East where we were now suffering because we were regarded by the Arabs as indistinguishable from the [pro-Israeli] Americans'.

Wilson, of course, had – unlike de Gaulle – joined Johnson in supporting Israel in the Six Day War. Any hopes the British Prime Minister now had that de Gaulle would rethink his veto of Macmillan's application to join the Common Market were now dashed. With the great powers within the UN Security Council inevitably reflecting the Cold War, as Wilson (whose instinct, to be fair, would have been to support Israel even without the backing of Washington) would write much later, Britain was 'ranged on the American side and France seeking an intermediate but [for now] increasingly ineffective role'.

Faced with the threat that Chirac would veto a UN Security Council resolution sanctioning a US-led invasion of Iraq, Blair washed his hands of the most serious military power among Britain's

European allies and chose to support the US invasion of Iraq without the authority of a UN resolution. It was an extreme case, and a number of British officials believed that Chirac was not in fact threatening a veto in all times or circumstances, but was rather insisting that he would not support a further UN resolution until the UN weapons inspectors under Hans Blix had judged that they had completed their work. This was something they were not allowed to do, such was the build-up of US troops and the purported strength of the (mistaken) conviction in Washington and London that Saddam Hussein had weapons of mass destruction. Nevertheless, in preferring the United States to France at a critical moment, Blair was acting in accordance with half a century of conventional wisdom since Eden had – as disastrously – made the opposite choice.

Blair supported the US-led war in Iraq, of course, with much less reserve than Wilson had in the case of Vietnam more than a generation earlier. Indeed de Gaulle had been less than accurate in predicting that Wilson would be 'dragged into [the US's] wars'. By the late 1960s Wilson was persistently attacked from the left over his public support for the United States in the Vietnam War. Indeed, his biographer Ben Pimlott argues persuasively that it was because of Vietnam that 'intellectual fashion, most powerful of political motivators, moved away, and never returned'. Yet, as Pimlott also points out, Wilson's strategy was 'to give the Americans everything they wanted, short of what they wanted most, which was British troops in Vietnam'. This was by no means as easy as his critics on the left presumed. From his first visit to Washington in December 1964, Wilson faced persistent demands from Johnson to commit British forces. He resisted them despite a heavy economic dependence on the United States and a Conservative opposition whose leadership was willing to back the US right or wrong, like that which faced Blair, but which, unlike Blair's opposition, was still an electorally potent force throughout his first premiership. So while adhering to the post-Suez consensus, Blair went much further than Wilson had done by sending British forces to Iraq – and arguably under much less pressure, economic, domestic and from the United States itself. Indeed in contrast to Johnson, the most unilaterally inclined members of the Bush administration even appeared relatively sanguine about going to war without British troops, as indeed they would have had to do if Parliament had voted against war without a second UN resolution.

Debate will no doubt long continue over why Blair remained so resolutely in favour of doing so, even though it meant depending on the Conservative opposition to deliver him a parliamentary majority and even though there was – at the very minimum – considerable dissent within government legal circles over whether the war was legal without an explicit UN resolution of the sort that had endorsed the 1991 invasion led by George Bush Senior and Margaret Thatcher. (The attorney general's original opinion was that it was not; the Foreign and Commonwealth Office's deputy legal adviser, Elizabeth Wilmshurst, resigned because of her conviction that it was not.) It has to be assumed that Blair had long and sincerely believed that it was right to get rid of Saddam by military force and that – despite the grave intelligence doubts, particularly in the US agencies, which it has since emerged existed at the time – he believed Saddam had weapons of mass destruction, and that it was both Britain's duty as an ally after 9/11 and, as he has subsequently argued, in Britain's national interest to be steadfast in its support for the United States.

This may have been reinforced by other political considerations. The late Robin Cook, who resigned in protest at the decision to go to war, thought that Blair had entered the discussions on Iraq with an almost irrational fear of being outflanked by a pro-Bush right-wing Conservative Party, despite the latter's feebleness as an opposition. This in turn was closely related, in Cook's view, to the fact that Blair remained haunted by Labour's anti-Americanism in the 1980s and his determination that it should never again be defined as more hostile to the United States than the Conservatives. This may in turn explain why, through a decade during which there were sharp differences between the UK and the US – over Kosovo with Bill Clinton and with George W. Bush over trade and climate change, for example – Blair chose to minimise their impact, at least in public. Thatcher, for example, did have several high-profile confrontations with the Reagan administration – over the Falklands, where the State Department recommended rejection of her demands for help; over the invasion of Grenada; over Star Wars, which she opposed; and over the discussion of deep nuclear arms cuts with Mikhail Gorbachev in Reykjavik, which she also opposed. Thatcher had these disagreements but remained perhaps the United States' most trusted ally from among all recent British Prime Ministers; Blair by contrast may never have had the confidence that as a Labour Prime Minister he could be so trusted – either by Washington or by a domestic electorate being wooed, however ineffectively, by a virulently pro-Bush opposition.

But there is a painful irony here. Blair was entirely right to believe that Labour's hostility to the United States and its policy of unilateral disarmament in the 1980s had been a huge help in repelling electors who might otherwise have supported Labour. It had, moreover, been an important factor in sustaining the appeal of the Social Democratic Party during the mid-1980s. Yet many of those voters – spectacularly won back by Blair in 1997 – were among were the very ones who became disillusioned with Labour over Blair's support for the 2003 invasion of Iraq and its aftermath. Not only were the Liberal Democrats, whatever their other problems, in touch with the public mood by opposing the war; three of the old SDP 'gang of four' – Shirley Williams, William Rodgers and Roy Jenkins – had grave reservations about it from the start of preparations, long before the invasion itself. And even the most hawkish of the four, David Owen, though he supported the invasion, became seriously disturbed by the subsequent pursuit of it and lack of planning for the aftermath, accusing both Blair and Bush of hubris for not 'bothering to worry about the nuts and bolts' of reconstructing the country after the invasion and adding: 'Iraq is far worse than Suez and it will be felt for decades.' Echoing the judgement, Timothy Garton Ash, a commentator with considerable sympathy and admiration for Blair, eloquently summed up the failure:

> It would be difficult for things to be worse than they were under Saddam Hussein but they now are. Hundreds of thousands of people have been killed or maimed, and there is no end in sight. US intelligence agencies say Iraq has become a breeding ground for a new generation of terrorists. The hundreds of billions of dollars squandered on the war and occupation could have bettered the lives of many of the world's poor. Drawing away troops from Afghanistan when the job there was only half done, we have created two failures instead of one possible success. The Shia–Sunni rift has been inflamed across the Muslim world. The theocratic dictatorship of Iran has

been greatly strengthened. The moral authority of the US is in tatters, and that of the United Kingdom dragged down with it. Iraq has alienated Muslims everywhere, including our own fellow citizens. Need I go on? This is the most comprehensive British foreign policy disaster since the Suez crisis of 1956.

It is a matter of speculation how far the Conservative Party might have capitalised on widespread discontent among centrist, as well as mildly social democratic, voters had Kenneth Clarke, the only one of the Tory leadership candidates to have opposed the war from the start, led the opposition in the 2005 election. Either way it seems improbable, to say the least, that any British Prime Minister in the remotely foreseeable future will be able to support another unilateralist US military adventure.

Nor is this exclusively attributable to the worsening outcomes of the war itself. It was true that British support for the war declined rapidly (from 61 per cent in May 2003 to 43 per cent in March 2004, according to a Pew Research Centre survey) as it became clearer that WMD were not to be found, that post-war reconstruction (over which Britain, despite its nominal deputy headship of the Coalition Provisional Authority, was to exercise virtually no influence, as Sir David Manning, Blair's principal foreign affairs adviser at the time, has since attested) was proving a terrible failure, and that a protracted and bloody conflict was underway for which the allied war leadership had not remotely prepared the public.

But another reason was surely that the international context had altered beyond recognition – and very rapidly – since Labour's vote-losing foreign policies of the 1980s which had rightly appalled Blair. Part of the destructiveness of Labour's defence and security policy in that decade lay in the profound changes already underway in the real world. While Labour was espousing unilateral disarmament in the run-up to the 1987 election, Thatcher was on a historic trip to the Soviet Union, engaging warmly with a reformist Gorbachev – and endorsing his launch of perestroika – with a spectacular degree of success which was only enhanced by her forthright views on western security and the closeness of her alliance with Ronald Reagan. But by the time Blair became party leader in 1994, most of the changes which Thatcher had been among the first western leaders to foresee and – with the exception of German reunification – encourage had come to pass. Communism had fallen. Blair was the first Labour Prime Minister – and since some of the last death throes of the old Warsaw Pact were still being played out during John Major's first term, arguably the first British Prime Minister of either party – to take office in a wholly post-communist Europe.

This could hardly fail to have consequences for British perceptions of the transatlantic relationship. The bonds of language, culture and heritage remained – and remain – as strong as ever. Blair's instant reaction to 9/11 that Britain would stand 'shoulder to shoulder' with the United States – as well as his determination, much later to founder tragically in the case of Iraq, to ensure a multilateral response – perfectly caught the national mood. Nowhere beyond the United States more than in Britain – despite the memorable head-line in *Le Monde* the day after the destruction of the Twin Towers, '*Nous sommes tous les Américains*' – did the attack strike a greater chord or inflict a greater shock. But the Cold War British rationale for supporting a US administration of either political stripe right or wrong, the rationale that had led Harold Wilson's Labour Cabinet to back – though not join – the Vietnam War, no longer applied. That those realities had begun to change before Blair took office might not have been so rapidly exposed had it not been for Iraq, just as the post-World War II realities might not have been so rapidly exposed if it had not been for Suez itself. But they have changed; and nothing testifies to it more than the mounting hostility to the Iraq War and the US administration that launched it among those elements on the British social democratic left that in the past were most supportive of the United States.

This is important because it calls sharply into question the seductive view that the old transatlantic relationship – and with it the famous role of Britain as the 'bridge' between America and Europe – can simply be restored under the Obama administration. It is true that most hostility to the US in Britain is a function of the policies specific to the Bush administration. This chiefly means Iraq, of course, but also others including resistance to measures to deal with climate change, the loosening of the US's adherence to inter-national institutions, and above all, perhaps, an erosion, thanks to examples like Guantanamo, Abu Ghraib and the rendition of detainees for interrogation by ruthless dictatorships, of what precisely had helped to make the US an international beacon – including, however grudgingly to many in the Islamic world – namely its firm pursuit of the rule of law, including international law. It is true that Britain and the US – and indeed all the western powers – face common threats, most signally including security threats from militant fundamentalist Islam, though there is as yet little underlying transatlantic consensus on the priorities for dealing with it. And certainly Britain's goals, as the close ally to the US it will and should remain, will be all the easier to fulfil in light of a multilateralist Obama administration. But to assume that the 'special relationship' can simply be reinstated, or the 'bridge' rebuilt, is to misunderstand the profound changes in the transatlantic context.

These changes comprise not only the end of the Cold War – though that was fundamental – or the fact that Europe and a fortiori Britain are no longer as central as they were in Washington's world-view, increasingly preoccupied as it is with the Middle East and the emerging economic and strategic challenges from southern, eastern and south-east Asia, though both are true. Another is a circumstance that could not have been foreseen when Blair first took office: the election of Nicolas Sarkozy as French President and Angela Merkel as German Chancellor. The installation of a basically Atlanticist leadership at the heart of 'old Europe', with its own bilateral relation-ships with the United States – underlined by Barack Obama's choice of Berlin in July 2008 to make a keynote speech about transatlantic relations – has made a mockery of the idea of a 'bridge' across which Britain, basking in its 'special' status in Washington, bears instructions to the less favoured Continentals.

For Britain, this should be a liberation, allowing it to recognise more maturely other changes, in its approach to which Britain more naturally identifies with Europe than the United States. To take one example, there are latent differences, at least of emphasis, between the perceptions on the two sides of the Atlantic of international terrorism. For the United States, terrorism is fundamentally an external threat; it is more inclined to see the solution in terms of military force which can be exerted abroad without undue turbulence at home. Because for Europe – including Britain – the threat is also internal, it has a natural tendency to see part of the solution as tackling some of the underlying causes, or excuses, which help terrorism to flourish. This may not militate against continued, or even expanded, deployment of forces in Afghanistan. But it also means maintaining diplomatic engagement with Iran, adopting a more positive stance towards democracy in Pakistan, seeking a lasting solution to the Israel–Palestine conflict. The key question is how in this rapidly changing context Britain is best placed to persuade the United States to take its views and interests into account, to reinforce the multilateralist tendency in Washington and to restore the bond of 'shared values' which has helped to sustain the western alliance for so long.

Late in his premiership, in his Mansion House speech in November 2006, Blair implicitly defended his decision to stand by the United States in Iraq by reference to American indispensability:

> Take any problem Britain wants solving: global terrorism . . . climate change; Israel/Palestine; Iran and North Korea's nuclear programme; world trade; Africa in general, right now Sudan in particular; global poverty. We may agree or disagree with the US position on some or all of these issues. But none of these vital British concerns can be addressed, let alone solved, without America. Without America, Kosovo could not have been attempted. Without Kosovo, Milošević might still be running Serbia; and the Balkans, rather than stabilising with a potential future in Europe, would have remained the destabilising force it was for most of the twentieth century. We need America. That is a fact.

He concluded: 'Post 9/11, there were no half-hearted allies of America. There were allies and others. We were allies then and that's how we should stay; and the test of any alliance, I'm afraid, is not when it's easy but when it's tough.'

Embedded in the link between these two propositions, however, is a logical fallacy, one which comes perilously close to saying that because of the United States' undoubted global centrality, there is no alternative to sub-contracting large tracts of foreign and security policy to Washington. Blair's entirely correct account of the United States as the sine qua non of solving world problems naturally makes the case for maintaining a close US alliance; but it also speaks for the

fundamental importance for its allies of maximising their influence
over it. The history of the last decade does not lend much weight to
the argument that Britain is well placed to do this, alone, by means
of the 'special relationship'; rather the reverse. Over Kosovo, which
Blair is entitled to regard as a foreign policy success that arguably
helped to make the case for liberal interventionism that was to be so
disastrously undermined in Iraq, Britain had the support of France
and Germany. Over Iran – and allowing for the fact that at the time
of writing it has not so far succeeded in its primary objectives – it
has been the agreement between the same troika that has helped to
persuade the United States to accept the diplomatic route towards
curbing Tehran's nuclear ambitions. Obama's refusal to rule out talks
with the Iranian regime, and the signs that in its final months the
Bush administration was prepared to engage more actively with it,
go some way to vindicating Europe's steadfast pursuit of diplomacy.
On climate change, a subject which Blair can claim considerable
credit for pushing up the international agenda, Merkel's support in
shifting the American position in 2007, however modestly, was pivotal.
By contrast, one of the most decisive lessons of the Iraq episode has
been Britain's failure, acting alone as the key military ally to have
consistently backed the United States, to secure a tangible return for
the sacrifices, military, political and economic, it has made. It is
difficult to disagree with Geoffrey Howe's observation, post Iraq, that
'it is hard now to identify any decision of substance, as opposed to
process, on which Britain's Prime Minister secured any real change
in American plans. By contrast . . . [we] have seen serious damage to
the effectiveness and credibility of NATO, the United Nations and
the European Union.'

Two closely related consequences flow from all this. One is that
a retreat into British exceptionalism is not a serious agenda. Given
the collapse of the 'bridge' theory of British international diplomacy,
it no doubt has superficial attractions. For some on the left, it has the
benefit of allowing the UK to adopt morally unimpeachable positions
without looking over its shoulder at its allies on either side of the
Atlantic, to become a kind of Norway with an army. But inwardly
comforting as this may be, it conflicts directly with a core progressive
or social democratic belief, that governments should act, as well as
speak and think. Even from a position of domestic self-interest that

means acting abroad as well as at home, in an era when today's poppy grown in Afghanistan is tomorrow's drug problem in Manchester, or today's genocide in Darfur is tomorrow's Sudanese refugee crisis in east London. For the left the imperative of trying to influence a rapidly changing world for the better is also underpinned by principled ambitions which extend well beyond narrow national self-interest. But in any case, for the British government to exert such influence, it has to do it, as a medium-sized post-imperial power, albeit with substantial military and diplomatic assets, in conjunction with others.

And that in turn can only mean a constructive re-engagement with Europe. The consequences of Iraq are at least as profound as those which followed the lesser catastrophe of Suez. Much of the British political class – Harold Macmillan and Harold Wilson among them – saw that Britain's destiny lay in Europe, but repeatedly came up against the overriding proviso that the United States must never be crossed on an issue of strategic importance. For them, the 'bridge' was, as I have tried to show, a difficult strategy to put into practice, but at least a rational one. For a modern British leader it is at once impossible and purposeless. To exercise influence, not least on the United States, Britain needs to be part of something bigger than itself and that means a level of engagement with the EU that can only follow an end to half a century of ambivalence. As for the US alliance, it needs to be fully sustained, but in a spirit of candid friendship rather than blind loyalty, and from the heart of Europe.

Paradoxically, a post-Blair government is in some ways remarkably well placed to carry out this re-engagement – and without unduly risking in the long term a close, if significantly less subservient, relationship with the United States. For all his failure to resolve the existential debate over Britain's future, and for all the ground lost because of Iraq, Blair left Britain's relations with the EU in significantly better condition that he found them after the increasingly fractious Major years. The decision not to join the Eurozone has caused significantly less visible damage than predicted by many pro-Europeans at the time. Enlargement to the east – embracing former communist countries, many of them friendly to the United States – has helped to shape a less monolithic and distinctively less federalist EU. As importantly, from Britain's point of view, Gordon Brown, unlike Blair, has enjoyed counterparts in Germany and France, and in the presidency of the European Commission, who broadly share his attitudes. Much more than their predecessors they subscribe – within admittedly strict limits in the case of France – to liberal economic values and a pronounced if not always uncritical Atlanticism. In particular it may be an auspicious time to repair Britain's relationship with France, the one that has proved the most difficult of all those with its European partners since the post-Suez breach. Just as Britain needs to contemplate the possibility that the EU can act independently of the United States at times – a realisation that should be underpinned by the findings in that same Pew poll which showed a rise from 47 to 56 per cent between May 2002 and May 2004, a year after the fall of Saddam Hussein, in Britons supporting an independent EU foreign policy – so France has to come to terms with its failure to mobilise the EU as a bloc – the 'new Europe' as well as Britain – against the United States. Nicolas Sarkozy is a promising partner with whom to embark on that process. If a French President markedly friendlier to the United States than his predecessor and a British Prime Minister under pressure to be less uncritical than his predecessor were finally to converge, it would create a formidable alliance in shaping EU foreign policy.

The Middle East is a case in point. Precisely because France's position is likelier to be more appreciative of Israeli security concerns than in the past, a Franco-British axis might be easier to achieve, forming the basis of a coherent – and at times independent – EU stance and in turn exercising more influence on the United States, easily Israel's dominant ally. When in July 2006 Blair declined, like President Bush, to call for a ceasefire in the Second Lebanon War, or to argue that Israel, while wholly within its rights to react to the kidnap of two of its soldiers, was doing so disproportionately, it had the same effect. Yet while Germany, the Netherlands and Poland supported the British–US position, it is unlikely that they would have resisted a joint Franco-British call for a ceasefire.

The refusal to call a halt to the war in Lebanon contains yet another lesson in the dangers of adhering unquestioningly to US policy in the Middle East. It has since emerged, not least in the first report of the Winograd commission, set up by the then Israeli Prime Minister, Ehud Olmert, in response to widespread domestic criticism of his handling of the war, that there were serious doubts within the Israeli Cabinet almost from day one about the course it was taking. In particular, the then foreign minister, Tzipi Livni, was urging early recourse to the diplomatic solution which she correctly predicted would be needed to end the war. A senior British official has since said that Livni did not confide her doubts to the UK government. But even with the benefit of hindsight Livni's concerns – not to mention the subsequent scathing criticism in Winograd – underline the need for Britain, and other EU member states, to reach their own independent assessments of crucial global events such as the Lebanon War.

Ironically, international pressure was the one factor, given the massive public support the war commanded in Israeli public opinion from the outset, that would have allowed Olmert to abandon it without it looking like a military defeat. But whether or not the United States, as some commentators, both Israeli and American, have suggested, had its own motives in seeing the war prolonged, it is hard to escape the conclusion that what looks now like a serious foreign policy error – and one that was questioned at the time, to his credit, by David Miliband, who subsequently became Gordon Brown's first foreign minister – arose from a misplaced determination not to diverge from Washington.

The Israeli–Palestinian conflict is a crucial issue, correctly seen by many European leaders, including Blair during his premiership, as a critical obstacle to progress in the west's relationship with the wider Muslim world. But because the EU has always been subordinate to the United States as a diplomatic actor in the Middle East, it is sometimes forgotten to what extent it has a presence in the region, not least as a principal financial supporter of the Palestinian Authority (PA). Between 1994 and 2007 the EU contributed €2.3 billion and it remains a major participant in the $7.5 billion of funding pledged at the donors' conference co-chaired by Blair in the wake of the 2007 Annapolis summit. This is broadly welcome to Israel because it has staved off the risk of the PA's collapse, which at its most extreme would restore responsibility for service provision in the West Bank to Israel as the occupying authority. At the time of writing it is impossible to be certain – but also difficult to be optimistic – about the outcome of the negotiations between Israel and the Palestinians' moderate Ramallah-based leadership. The main chance of success for the strategy agreed at Annapolis was that the Israeli–Palestinian talks which the summit kick-started would show such rapid advances towards an agreement on the outlines of a two-state solution and, even before that, in improving the daily lives of Palestinians in the West Bank that Palestinians, even in Hamas-controlled Gaza, would have their belief restored in the path of negotiations. Towards the end of the Bush presidency – which chose not to lay down the parameters of an agreement as Bill Clinton had done at the abortive Camp David talks in 2000 – the omens were not encouraging. Although a majority of voters in the March 2006 Israeli elections supported parties committed to serious withdrawals from the occupied West Bank, the government appeared unwilling, if not unable, to deliver an agreement in the face of a right wing given disproportionate power by Israel's electoral system. But in any case, what is clear is that while the EU had a key role in bankrolling the Annapolis strategy it had little or no influence on its outcome.

This is nothing new about this, of course. Israel's disengagement from Gaza in August 2005 was a genuinely historic step, setting a huge potential precedent for further withdrawals. But the international community failed to bring pressure on Israel to let the Palestinian President, Mahmoud Abbas, show some benefits and take some credit for this, which was one – admittedly only one – of several reasons for the election of Hamas in January 2006. If, for example, the agreement on movement and access brokered by Condoleezza Rice in November 2005 had been reached earlier and implemented in full, it might have alleviated some of the economic misery for Palestinians that subsequently intensified and which the World Bank has in successive reports blamed on Israeli closures. Blair's predecessor as Middle East envoy, James Wolfensohn, became increasingly frustrated at what he saw as Israel's failure to subordinate short-term security interests to the longer-term – Israeli – interest of a viable Palestinian economy. But whatever private concerns there were in Europe, the EU was either unwilling or unable to support him when he realised his concerns were creating less and less interest in Washington.

A more coherent approach by the EU might also have led – and could still lead – to a deeper debate on the wisdom of an international boycott of Hamas, and on the US-led distaste for the coalition between Fatah and Hamas earnestly desired by most non-aligned Palestinians. The issue of how to handle Hamas is very complex. But there is a strong argument – privately subscribed to in varying degrees by some European, including British, diplomats closest to the issue – that, first, the boycott has had a much more adverse impact on the Palestinian public than on Hamas as an organisation; second, while under-estimating Hamas's role as a national movement and over-estimating it as a proxy for Iran, the architects of the blockade have actually tended to increase Hamas's dependence on Iran for support; third, the boycott tended to strengthen extreme elements in Hamas rather than the reverse; and fourth, it may have been better to impose, at least in the first instance, more realisable preconditions for continued economic support and contact – including a total and immediate halt to violence against Israel and adherence to the Saudi-brokered Arab peace initiative offering recognition in return for a Palestinian state based on 1967 borders – to test Hamas's ability to govern without affording it a ready-made excuse for its failures, and to strengthen its more pragmatic elements. Yet British policy remained tied to the US's with a minimum of internal debate.

The point of this is not to rehearse well-worn arguments about past policy for the sake of it, let alone suggest that the EU should engage in some destructive confrontation with the US or, more implausibly still, that it can replace it as an actor. But it is to suggest that an EU led by a troika of leaders from France, Britain and, for all its special problems in handling Israeli sensibilities, Germany, all highly credible in their desire to see a secure Israel flourish within agreed borders, would be in a much stronger position jointly to influence the United States towards engaging as an honest broker in negotiations than a UK Prime Minister acting on his own, and in private, as Blair did during the Bush presidency, pursuing what Timothy Garton Ash memorably describes as the 'Jeeves' school of diplomacy.

This need not mean that the EU should seek to establish itself as a 'pro-Palestinian' counter-weight to a 'pro-Israel' US. At times, the EU may need to use some public as well as private diplomacy; for arguments to have any traction, including in US politics, they have to be aired from time to time. This should no doubt be sparing and measured, particularly on the Middle East, a region already over-burdened with declarations. Yet the issue of how that public diplomacy should be cast goes to the heart of the wider role the EU can and should play. One of the biggest problems of the domestic US debate – or lack of it – is precisely the success of the 'pro-Israel' lobby – not always as representative of US Jewish opinion as it claims – in projecting international discussion of the conflict as a 'zero sum' game. This means that any US politician criticising a specific Israeli policy, or drawing the mildest attention to the sufferings inflicted by the occupation as well as by Israelis under terrorist attack, feels himself to be at risk by being depicted as anti-Israel. (One of the incidental results is a vastly less vigorous and unfettered debate on the conflict in the United States than in Israel itself.) With the more coherent foreign policy mechanisms embedded in its new treaty – including bringing funding for the Palestinians and diplomacy under the same figure instead of separating them between the European Commission and the high representative for the Common Foreign and Security Policy as at present, the EU might be better placed to start countering this phenomenon. That means not so much by striking a 'pro-Palestinian' stance calculated to inflame Israeli sensitivities but by arguing from a position of friendship with Israel that it is in Israel's own interests to see an early two-state solution to the conflict, indeed that the long-term future of a Jewish democratic state will be increasingly under threat the longer a solution is delayed, and that it is, finally, possible to be at once both pro-Israeli and pro-Palestinian. This is important externally, but even more so to the EU's self-confidence as an actor, above all as a persuader of the United States.

In this respect President Sarkozy's carefully crafted speech to the Knesset in June 2008, and a closely similar one by Gordon Brown to the same audience a month later in which he used his credentials as a 'constant friend' to Israel to stress the importance of Israel halting settlement construction in breach of international law and making the concessions vital to a two-state solution, contained the promising, if modest, beginnings of a joint approach. The question is whether this can be taken further than mere rhetoric. The EU's burden as a provider of last resort in the face of continued conflict and stalemate will not, and should not, be removed by a solution to the conflict;

rather it is a commitment that would be much more productively exercised in helping to assist a fledgling Palestinian state than in merely alleviating the worst consequences of the failure to achieve one. There continues to be considerable debate in the aid and development community about funding which can be held to subsidise the occupation. But while it may be unrealistic to expect the EU to apply pressure on Israel by conditioning such aid on diplomatic progress, the EU does have other levers. It could, for example, exclude imports from Jewish West Bank settlements, or even tie its favourable free trade agreement with Israel to its ability to implement the parallel – and, because of the huge Israeli-imposed obstacles obstructing Palestinian exports, effectively moribund – one with the PA. But in any case Britain, or any other European country, cannot hope to bring influence to bear in the Middle East without a common approach.

In a very different way, Turkish pursuit of EU accession, arguably the defining European issue in the coming years, presents another opportunity for a centre-left British government which is more unequivocally European in its approach. The changes currently taking place in Turkey are profound in their implications even if their outcome is not wholly predictable. The current success of the AKP, a party which is overtly Muslim in character but at the same time pro-European, democratic and professedly committed to respecting modern Turkey's deeply secular founding principles, presents a challenge which Europe will fumble at its peril. Turkish membership can help to guarantee energy supplies in ways which are not dependent on Russia. It can provide a new source of often skilled labour to contribute to the growing costs of supporting western Europe's ageing population. It could even contribute not only to the EU's 'soft power' – as a bridge to the Muslim world – but also, because it has a serious army, to its 'hard power' at a time when its claim to global influence is undermined by the reluctance of many of its member states to increase and better focus its military spending. And it would demonstrate to Europe's own Muslim populations that the EU does not see itself as some predominantly 'Christian' and excluding bloc. But rejection of the application will encourage the most nationalist, and in fact most anti-western, tendencies in the country. It will set back the determination of pro-Europeans in Turkey to make the reforms in politics, economics and human rights which are a condition of entry. But much more widely it will arrest an experiment with wide and positive implications for the rest of the Muslim world, especially in Arab countries but also perhaps even in Iran. At a time when more and more Arab intellectuals are beginning to question what their own largely authoritarian regimes have done wrong, and what Turkey has done right to achieve democracy in a predominantly Muslim country and to be well on the way to EU membership, rejection will set back Turkey's chances of becoming a model of success in the region.

After the religious Muslim Abdullah Gül's resounding popular victory in his bid for the Turkish presidency in August 2007, David Miliband sensibly and firmly reaffirmed the strong support of the UK government for Turkey's application. As a champion of Turkish accession, however, Britain will face strong opposition from France and, to a slightly lesser extent, Germany. It therefore needs to build strong alliances on the issue with countries such as Sweden and Italy, which have strongly supported the application. Turkish EU entry was also a frequently stated goal of the Bush administration (even if the United States unwisely remained silent in April 2007, when the EU rightly condemned the Turkish army for issuing a thinly veiled, but in the event unfulfilled, threat to intervene if Gül went ahead with his candidacy). But past history suggests that the UK has a better chance of convincing the more hostile opponents of Turkish accession with an essentially European argument – with all the trade-offs and alliances that such an argument entails – than as a messenger for a US administration which seeks Turkish EU entry for strategic reasons. Assuming that the United States maintains its present stance towards Turkish EU membership, this is a case in which a mild distancing by the UK from the US paradoxically serves the latter's stated interests.

But to secure the leadership role in the EU on these and many other issues, which Tony Blair envisaged but never quite managed to achieve, will require Britain to resolve the ambivalence which has characterised its approach to Europe for half a century. And this is no easy task, not least because of an inherently sceptical public opinion. Blair continued to pay the price for Labour's failure in his first two general elections to withstand the tide of Euroscepticism and use them to make the case for Britain in Europe. (By 2005 it was too late, given the spectacularly high-profile fissure with France and Germany over Iraq two years earlier.) That decision cannot be separated from – or wholly excused by – the relentless campaign of EU denigration by much of Britain's tabloid and parts of its broadsheet press. In particular Rupert Murdoch appears to have exercised an unhealthily strong influence on British foreign policy under Labour, not least through a direct contact with both Blair and Brown which both men have seemed to take with the utmost seriousness. The admission in 2007 in response to a Freedom of Information Act application by the Liberal Democrat peer Lord Avebury that Blair held four meetings with Murdoch around the time of the crucial decisions on Iraq four years earlier is no doubt fuel for the more extreme conspiracy theories; but it will leave, unless or until the content of the conversations are revealed, a strong suspicion that the invasion was the main topic under discussion. There is a remarkable insight into Murdoch's approach to the Middle East in Alastair Campbell's diaries, in which the newspaper owner remarks during a visit to Downing Street that he cannot 'understand what the Palestinians' problem is' – only to be berated by one of his own sons for his uncritical support for the Israeli government of the day. These may be mere incidentals; but on Europe, at least, it is well attested that Murdoch and his British papers frequently constrained Labour policy and argument on Europe – against Blair's instincts and better judgement, as indeed they sought to do in the debate over the Lisbon treaty, urging a referendum, which Brown commendably resisted. This is not the place to lament the exaggerated awe in which the Labour leadership has held the tabloid press – which in the case of the *Sun* has actually more often followed than shaped the party preferences of its readers. But it is hard to see how a British Prime Minister can fully liberate European policy from the grip of the proprietors without some kind of 'Stanley Baldwin moment' – the ringing assertion of authority by the elected over the unelected in Baldwin's castigation of Northcliffe and Beaverbrook in 1931.

While continuing to defend British EU membership, Brown has not created such a moment. Indeed the fracas over the signing of the Lisbon treaty in December 2007 – first he planned not to attend it, but then he compromised by arriving after the ceremony was over

– was seen, even if unfairly, as evidence of a residual ambivalence towards the EU. And as an undoubted and long-standing internationalist he has from time to time shown, for example as one of the few heads of government to attend the Jeddah summit on fuel prices in the summer of 2008, a preference for non-European forums at which to pursue his goals. On the other hand, he was steadfast in pushing through ratification of Lisbon, winning admiration in Europe for unflinchingly continuing to do so despite the 'no' vote in the Irish referendum. This was surely correct, and not only because not to do so would have been to undermine Britain's still under-exploited leadership opportunities in Europe, but also because of some provisions of the treaty itself. The appointment of a single high representative for foreign and security policy will surely – if the major parts of the treaty can survive the Irish vote – strengthen the EU's voice in world affairs. But even more fundamentally, the appointment of a full-time president will not only furnish the long-awaited answer to Henry Kissinger's impatient question: 'Who do I call if I want to speak to Europe?' It will also provide the EU with much greater coherence, both internal and external, and without further threatening national sovereignties. Less fundamentally perhaps, but despite considerable internal debate, Brown had also at the time of writing shown little sign of backing away from the extremely ambitious renewable energy targets signed up to by Blair at his last European summit as Prime Minister. And he has supported greater resort to the EU for the coordination of overseas aid, an issue close to his heart.

A crucial test for Brown's ability to stand up to pressures from the right, and the right-wing press especially, looked in the second half of 2008 to be the issue of European defence. Nicolas Sarkozy's willingness to bring France back into the military structures of NATO more than forty years after President de Gaulle pulled it out provides a historic opportunity. Whatever its successes, the European Security and Defence Policy launched by Blair and Jacques Chirac a decade ago has failed to halt a decline in European military capabilities. Sarkozy's desire to strengthen EU defence – and establish a joint European military planning mechanism of the sort Britain has traditionally resisted – as a quid pro quo for a full French return to NATO is an idea whose time has come. After decades of oscillating between deep suspicion of any European alternative to NATO on the one hand, and equally deep irritation at Europe's failure to share more of the burden of its own security on the other, the US political and military establishment now shows every sign of coming down in favour of a larger European military capability. A Labour government will have to confront the illusory spectre raised by the British right of a 'European army'. But the prize would be a tangibly greater degree of European security cooperation at a time when perceptions of what is needed in London, Paris and Washington have probably never been closer.

By no means all Eurosceptic public opinion can be attributed to the tabloid press. Without clear reforms – for example in increased investment in research and development, further dismantling of barriers to the free movement of goods, services and capital, and aggressive application of competition policy – it may be difficult to dissipate the sense, whether fair or not, that European institutions do not share – and may even act as a brake on – Anglo Saxon adherence to free market, free trade values in the private sector. The Common Agricultural Policy is widely – and largely correctly – seen as benefiting Continental farmers much more than Britain's while also acting as the 'dark corner' in Europe's credibility as a free trade negotiator. The dramatic rise in food prices during 2008 may have threatened the already slow progress in CAP reform, fuelling arguments that European production should not be reduced at a time of such instability. But if it is to come back on course, a Labour government will, sooner or later, have to accept, as an entirely logical price for such reform, the sacrifice of the totemic rebate negotiated by Margaret Thatcher in Fontainebleau in 1984 on the grounds that Britain did not benefit on anything like the scale of other European countries from the CAP. But beyond the details of individual headings, there is an overall question of how Britain approaches the issue of economic reform. It can overtly and publicly support, encourage, form an alliance with and, where necessary, stiffen the sinews of a European Commission whose sympathies, under its president, José Manuel Barroso, are with those of a British Labour government. Or it can revert to the default British position of berating 'Europe' for its failings as it has somehow consistently refrained from berating the United States, say, for its own agricultural protectionism. If the former, the government has a real chance of beginning to make the case for Britain's place in Europe. If the latter, then its chances of increasing either British public confidence in EU membership or the UK's leverage in Europe itself will be correspondingly diminished.

Partly because of a hostile press, and partly because the EU remained too long preoccupied with internal institutional questions, which have tended to eclipse the many advances in the single market that are directly to the UK's advantage, it has been difficult to focus the British public's mind on the union's capacity to deliver tangible benefits. Climate change, a major 21st-century transnational challenge, presents a centre-left government with a significant opportunity to do just that. While Britain's own record on some environmental issues lags behind some other European countries, it has already led the way in the cap it imposed on carbon emissions. Britain accounts for only 2 per cent of global emissions; its only chance of making a real difference to realising Kyoto commitments is by influencing Europe to take more drastic action and, by doing so, making it a correspondingly more formidable negotiator with the United States, China and India on measures needed to reduce climate change. This is a classic example of an issue of rapidly mounting importance to its own electorate in which Britain can, by leading in Europe, help Europe to lead the world. David Miliband, environment secretary before he became Foreign Secretary, was quick to declare, as he put it, that climate change 'can best reconnect Europe with its citizens and rebuild trust in European institutions'. But as he also pointed out, this is potentially an agenda specific, at least in British politics, to the centre-left. For while the Conservatives have sought to raise the salience of climate change as a domestic political issue, they are caught between their stated pursuit of a cleaner environment and their ideological reservations about – and in some cases outright hostility to – the EU.

None of this is easy. Ministers of both parties are frequently as irritated by the tedium of negotiating in Brussels as they are exhilarated by dealing with Washington. The lure of power, however refracted, that a Prime Minister senses at Camp David or the White House, or a Foreign Secretary at Foggy Bottom, should not be under-estimated. One senior official who worked closely for both

Tony Blair and John Major has explained the historic addiction of British Prime Ministers to the Washington inner circle by saying that 'if you are not an imperial power any more, the next best thing is to be close to a country that is'.

A less mystical obstacle to rebalancing Britain's relationships with the EU and the United States is frequently said to be the benefits of shared intelligence between the US and Britain. Neo-conservatives such as the former US ambassador to the UN, John Bolton, have even argued that the US would withhold intelligence from Britain if it became more integrated in the European foreign policy-making process. The intelligence professionals, however, are likely to have a more pragmatic approach to their counterparts, judging the relationship on its merits, and mindful that if Britain was inclined to share US secrets with its European allies, it has already had plenty of opportunity to do so. In a sharp attack in 2003 on Blair's uncritical adherence to the 'special relationship' with President Bush, Sir Rodric Braithwaite, an eminent former chairman of the Joint Intelligence Committee, was scornful of the argument that intelligence cooperation was a reason for uncritical adherence to Washington. He was dismissive of the notion that the relationship gave Britain significant influence on US policy, arguing that while MI6 and MI5 were of 'substantial importance to the Americans in the war against terrorism' GCHQ would be of 'little value' without US input. More generally, he asserted that 'the Americans are unlikely to respond to a show of British independence by withdrawing all cooperation; if they did, it would be a sign that they did not place much store by that cooperation in the first place'.

But Braithwaite also went on to touch on a more fundamental contradiction in residual British fears about closer engagement in Europe – one which is not only, but especially, prevalent in the thinking of Conservative Eurosceptics. The same people, he argued, who fear the erosion of sovereignty inside the EU 'fail to point out' that 'an even more intimate relationship with America' would 'constrain British sovereignty at least as much'. Indeed, he added: 'Our voice in Brussels is more decisive than it could ever be in Washington.' This is surely correct. Just as it is clear that an EU foreign policy in which Britain wholeheartedly participated as an independent partner would carry more external influence than one in which it didn't, so it is clear that Britain, with its military capability and diplomatic reach and experience, would play a leading role in formulating that policy.

A vastly greater catastrophe than Suez, Iraq demands at least as fundamental a reappraisal of Britain's foreign policy and its role in the world as Suez did. For this, ironically, the multilateralist and Europe-centred Clause IV, almost casually written fourteen years ago by Blair's staunchest ally, is a text worth taking a great deal more seriously – and literally – than it has been in the last decade. One of the greatest lessons from Iraq is precisely that Britain, acting alone and projecting itself as a privileged and private interlocutor, is much more likely to be taken for granted than it is to persuade the US to use its hegemony multilaterally and for the common international good. The message of the last six years is not that Britain should lapse into a dangerous anti-Americanism that can only increase US unilateralism. It should instead mean a hard-headed understanding that British influence, not least on the US, is best served by a pragmatic but wholehearted engagement with the EU – a grouping big enough to address the economic challenges from China, India and south-east Asia and the political one of a re-emerging Russian hegemony, to forge a common approach to the crisis posed by Islamic fundamentalism and the conflict in the Middle East, and to be a close but candid friend to the United States. Britain's mid-Atlantic project, formulated for another era, has had its day.

Conclusion

The challenge of renewal

Patrick Diamond and Roger Liddle

This book has sought to recast the debate about the future of social democracy in order that proper account might be taken of the structural transformations that are sweeping across the advanced capitalist economies in the early part of the twenty-first century. This concluding chapter addresses the present situation confronting the Labour Party as the leading exponent of social democracy in British politics. It reflects on the current crisis that has afflicted the global economic system, and assesses where on that basis the party should go next. That is not just an ideological or policy-orientated challenge: it means renewing a broad-based coalition of support that will enable Labour not only to win power but to govern in pursuit of radical social democratic ends.

This is not the place to review the institutional role of Labour as a democratic political party, though we are aware of the need to breathe new life into the party's structures and procedures locally and nationally. The record of governing aside, the central theme emerging from this book is that Labour since 1997 has not yet risen to the challenge of successfully renewing itself in office.

Labour's programme has of course helped to shift the axis of British politics to the left, creating a new ideological 'common sense' over the course of the last fifteen years. It set out to correct many fundamental problems inherited from previous administrations, in particular the anachronistic British constitution, under-investment in public services and the persistence of geographical inequalities where the shape and character of poorer areas has changed little since Charles Booth's surveys of poverty in the 1880s.

The historian Brian Brivati has argued that under Labour, Britain left behind it the shadow of post-war decline that dominated political debate from the 1950s to the 1980s.[1] A new 'Anglo-social' model has been developed in which Britain is able to compete with the rest of the world, while ensuring a more equal and fair society through a dynamic 'social investment' state.[2] Britain's relative stability has provided an effective platform to project British culture as the UK is increasingly seen as a hub of scientific, technological and creative excellence. This is a substantial legacy to bequeath the country. Arguably, Britain is now better placed to weather the storms ahead given the global financial crisis, investing in supply-side reforms and the modernisation of infrastructure that were neglected by previous governments.

Yet while this transformation has been genuine, its positive impact may well be dwarfed by the City of London's exposure to the global banking crisis. The consequences may prove deeper-seated and longer-lasting than the recession itself, which in its immediate effects is having its most devastating impact on the world's major exporting nations such as China, Germany and Japan. The scale of support required by the British banks, in terms of recapitalisation and public guarantees of so-called toxic assets, is very significant indeed. As the economy recovers, many of these toxic assets may prove to have real economic value and it may be possible at some distant point in the future to return the banks to the private sector at a profit to the Exchequer. But the public finances will in the meantime have to bear the burden of capital injections and public spending will inevitably be severely constrained. The political argument about how it happened and why will continue for a generation.

Against this pessimistic background, it is important to define what a genuinely radical social democratic project might entail, encapsulated by the 'forward offer' to Britain. There has been a lot of focus over the last five years on the reform of public services. Arguably, the government has got a lot of its policy programme for public services broadly right, though there are concerns as to whether reforms in areas such as the National Health Service are firmly entrenched.[3] For example, by 2007 health and education had slipped down the list of public concerns, in stark contrast to the early Blair years. Voters did not, of course, necessarily credit the government.

But objectively, the NHS and state schools are considerably stronger than in 1997, where performance is now comparable with the northern European countries such as the Netherlands and Sweden.[4]

In our view there are four major intellectual challenges that a period of social democratic renewal needs to address and consequently develop:

- a sufficiently sophisticated critique of the market
- a more coherent response to the rise of individualism in our societies
- greater clarity about Labour's approach to equality
- a redefinition of the role of the state.

We shall examine each of these challenges in turn from the perspective of post-war social democratic experience, before suggesting themes for forward development.

The need for a coherent critique of the market and capitalism

The 1945 government came into office with an ill-formed but passionate faith in democratic socialist planning. But Labour's view of how to tame capitalism changed in post-war conditions. For Stafford Cripps and his successor as Labour Chancellor, Hugh Gaitskell, democratic planning evolved into activist Keynesian demand management. In the 1950s Labour's arch-revisionist, Anthony Crosland, argued that the nature of capitalism had been transformed. Managerial capitalism, with the separation of ownership from control,[5] meant that profit-maximising shareholders had been marginalised. Companies were now mainly in the hands of technocrats who were motivated by growing their business in a socially acceptable way. Profit remained important – but its pursuit did not override everything else. This was the intellectual foundation of the idea of the 'mixed economy', where interventionist policies were assumed desirable and industrial relations difficulties could hopefully be resolved by compromise and, if necessary, by 'beer and sandwiches' at 10 Downing Street.

To New Labour's credit it recognised that this world had vanished completely by 1997. Big companies had become global, not national; company chief executives now spent most of their time appeasing international investor pressure for improved profit performance, not negotiating with trade unions; and investment decisions were taken not out of sentiment or patriotism but on the basis of where returns were highest. The modern business style does its best to be polished, accommodating and civilised, but its decision making is often as single minded in its consequences as with nineteenth-century capitalism. So New Labour accepted what it saw as an inevitable reality and designed its policies to make Britain an attractive environment in which modern capitalism could thrive.

There is a compelling 'growth and jobs' logic in this approach. Open markets are the best available means of stimulating innovation and efficiency. Shareholder capitalism has a better record of forcing rapid productivity growth than family-owned companies.[6] Globalisation has allowed far greater efficiencies to be achieved in the supply chain than in the days of relatively closed national economies. And markets do not inevitably deter risky long-term investments, as is shown in the pharmaceutical sector. New technology and new consumer demands, however, constantly create new patterns of 'winners' and 'losers'. Those with the right technical and personal skills stand to succeed, while there is a continued loss of 'good working-class jobs' in manufacturing as companies invest in new markets, outsource and delocalise. The confidence that economic growth automatically leads to a broad-based prosperity has been eroded.

Also, as the autumn 2008 financial crisis reminded many of what they had forgotten: markets can fail – and, when they do, wreak havoc.

Social democrats have long recognised that markets are a good servant but a bad master: but in the benign period created by the wave of globalisation that has gathered force since the mid-1990s, our beliefs seemed out of synch with economically exuberant times and many of us lost the rigour and courage to argue the case. Social democrats did foresee earlier than many that the fatal weakness of globalisation was not the economic dynamism it unleashed, but the fact that increased economic interdependence was not matched by new forms of global governance that recognised the shifting economic power balances in the world. But given neo-liberalism's intellectual hegemony, especially in Washington and New York, there was no willingness to act before it proved too late.

The global financial crisis has dramatically resurrected the social democratic case for an 'active state' just as the Conservatives were making headway in positioning themselves as the party of 'society' as against the state: the 'little platoons', as Burke envisaged them,[7] are no answer to the problems of a financial system on the brink of collapse. There are of course dangers here. We should not be dusting down Labour's 1945 manifesto, still less that of February 1974. This is not the time to return to a protectionist, anti-European, anti-global, 'socialism in one country' model. The need is not for social democracy to turn its back on the dynamic strengths of economic openness but, liberated from past neo-liberal constraints, to recognise explicitly that the market's limits, potential for failure and resulting inequalities need to be better managed in the public interest. The new paradigm should be a state with the necessary strategic capacity to act in order to shape the positive forces of globalisation at local, national, European and international level, not one that glorifies an all-powerful state and a return to old-fashioned corporatism.

Social democracy has yet to find a confident voice in dealing with these phenomena. It has consistently advocated some forms of market intervention. The New Labour government has been vigorous in curbing monopoly abuses and anti-competitive practices. It has also advocated active labour market policies to assist workers through transitions. In a recession it is the responsibility of government to promote new forms of labour market intervention that promote skills and labour market flexibility. Active labour market policies need to become still more 'active' in order to prevent job losses turning into long-term unemployment, and long-term unemployment turning into unemployability. Britain is still far from matching the successful Danish model of 'flexicurity', where the legal restraints on firms sacking employees are limited but the unemployed have clear 'rights and responsibilities'. They receive generous benefits, but in return accept obligations to retrain for new types of work, which are managed by localised job search and retraining agencies.

New Labour has also acknowledged the persistence of market failures in fields such as research, training and regional policy. Partly as a result of sensible government intervention, the last decade has seen the growth of specialised manufacturing that identifies and serves the needs of niche markets and research-based industrial clusters; the success of higher education as a large overseas earner; the rapid expansion of the creative sector and the increased economic importance of design, culture, broadcasting and sport, where the UK has key competitive strengths; and the success of devolution and regional policy in creating vibrant national capitals in Belfast, Cardiff and Edinburgh and transforming Leeds, Manchester, Merseyside and Tyneside.

A modern industrial policy now needs to build on these strengths. Britain has made significant progress in developing a modern 'knowledge economy' in the last decade: the question is what steps the government can now take to speed that progress, given the contraction in financial services, retail, commercial property and construction now taking place. Policy until 2008 concentrated on supporting the right framework conditions for growth such as skills, competition, infrastructure and research. But, arguably, this is no longer sufficient, given the huge problems of economic opportunity in the UK: the 'long tail' of under-performance in our education system and continued neglect of skills; stubbornly high levels of worklessness and poor labour market integration of certain ethnic minorities; regional problems of economic decline in old industrial areas, which are too often overdependent on a low-wage service economy and from which young talented people drift away.

The government now needs to move from a focus simply on framework conditions to the creation of deeper public–private partnerships across the whole economy. This means a new impetus for the development of sectoral policies, regional specialisation and lead technologies. A focus on sectors enables the government to think through how the many different aspects of public policy impact on a particular sector – for example, regulation at national and EU level, different public expenditure programmes, education and training priorities, public purchasing decisions – and how a more coherent approach for the successful development of a sector can be put in place. The focus on regional specialisation enables public policy to focus on what a region's strengths are and how they can be built upon for the future. A focus on lead technologies recognises that in research policy it is essential to 'pick winners' to the extent that decisions need to be made on where to concentrate resources. But more than that, the government has an essential role in the development of lead technologies that will not become commercially viable without its initial support – for example carbon capture and storage and other low-carbon technologies.

Climate change is, according to the government adviser Lord Stern of Brentford, 'the biggest market failure in human history'.[8] So far, however, there has been a timid and inconsistent approach to the need for long-term government planning in transport and energy. This is the only way to provide the certainty that will enable the necessary private long-term investment to be secured. Market mechanisms along the lines of the European Emissions Trading Scheme have a key role to play but on their own seem unlikely to provide the necessary conditions for certainty to facilitate the massive programme of carbon-reducing investments we need, given the exceptional volatility of the price of oil. The new economic opportunities now presented by energy and climate change policy, in civil nuclear power, renewables and energy efficiency and the new jobs flowing from them, depend on a stronger clarity of vision.

The new era of industrial activism must avoid the 'lame duck' bail-outs of the 1970s. Essentially, the effect of these was to freeze the old industrial structures of the time, in the vain hope that restructuring could be agreed that would raise performance. The impact was to slow national productivity growth and make the eventual shake-out, when it came in the early 1980s recession, extremely painful. Public policy today must not repeat that mistake. Instead we need to move from supply-side policies that enable to industrial policies that are developmental – recognising the vital role that only government can play.

More profoundly the task for modern social democracy is to design a new model of welfare capitalism. There is a moral revulsion against the excesses of financial capitalism: its dislike of any form of public accountability; its grossness of reward, unrelated to any concept of long-term wealth creation. One way or another, this shock can be seen in most western democracies. These resentments will only grow if financiers refuse to accept that their world has irreversibly changed. The task for politicians is to prevent a backlash against financiers turning into a backlash against capitalism and business itself. Hence the need to devise and promote a new model of 'responsible capitalism'.

This last phase of global super-capitalism led to unprecedented prosperity for the UK, but also some obvious downsides. The logic of providing a 'light touch' regime for financial regulation was that economic openness would advance the position of the City of London. Public policy regarded the City as a strategic sector where Britain had global competitive advantage vis-à-vis New York and other financial centres. On this basis foreign investment was attracted to the City from all over the world. Loose lending practices, however, facilitated by complex financial instruments containing risks that were imperfectly understood and regulated, fuelled an unprecedented, and in the end destabilising, house price and consumer boom. This was coupled with gross rewards at the top that incentivised excesses of risk and were unrelated to long-term profitability. Irresponsible, destabilising and inadequately regulated behaviour in financial markets led to the collapse of once prudent retail savings institutions. Of course in this crisis Britain was not alone: indeed the origins lay clearly in the sub-prime mortgage market in the United States. But UK regulatory policy was designed to enable the City of London to outdo the US financial markets at their own game. Some may still regard the renewal of this policy as a sensible long-term goal. But it is at least arguable that in circumstances where trust will take a long time to rebuild, and Asia will increasingly think it can manage its own money at less risk to itself, the City would be better to see itself as the financial centre of a properly regulated EU single market.

More widely, if more regulation is accepted as necessary, what is the new model of regulated capitalism that social democracy should favour? 'Models of capitalism' theories should be back in vogue.[9] But does British social democracy now have the appetite for remedies that could potentially constrain unacceptable business behaviour? And to prevent 'race to the bottom' regulatory competition, at least in Europe, does this imply greater rule making at European level: better scrutiny of top pay, competition rules that discourage merger and takeover fever, the inclusion of 'stakeholder' obligations in company law reforms, a Europe-wide authority to regulate financial markets and coordination of tax policy? When governments seek to bring back order to their public finances, but realise the vulnerability of their depleted corporate tax base to competition from their neighbours and partners, what will the social democratic response be? These are among the most fundamental questions to be confronted.

There is also a significant lacuna in developing a modern social democratic theory of industrial relations. The old arguments for trade unions remain valid: the basic inequality in the individual employment relationship and the prevention of arbitrary management behaviour. The social partnership model has survived more or less intact in Germany, despite steady falls in membership, because unionisation remains strong in big manufacturing firms and market pressures have forced the unions to adjust in order to survive. In Britain trade union membership outside the public sector has continued to decline, especially among younger workers. Within the public sector, collective bargaining is highly centralised, which thwarts the development of effective social partnership where local managers and trade unionists would have an incentive to work together to promote the interests of the local public service institutions they serve, particularly where contestability between public service providers is established. Like much of the rest of Europe, the strong growth in employment in private sector services is often in low-paid, casualised jobs with few prospects of advancement, where union organisation is chronically weak. How might British social democracy revitalise reformed trade unions as a means of democratic engagement and a strengthened civil society? It should no longer be acceptable to avoid serious examination of these issues in order to retain business support.

The global crisis could create a once-in-a-generation social democratic moment if only we define it correctly.

The need for a coherent response to the rise of individualism in our societies

Social democrats have tended to be sceptical of individualism because they equate it with materialism and what many on the left regard as the free market's chimera of 'choice'. But the trend to individualism is also about the new personal freedoms people enjoy in living their lives as they choose, which some on the left have tended to support uncritically without analysing their deeper impact on society.

Post-war social democrats believed with a passion that the claims of society should take precedence over those of the individual. During the Attlee government, Conservative-inspired campaigns against the exigencies of rationing were denounced as selfish individualism. By the end of the 1950s reformist social democrats recognised that Labour had to come to terms with working-class consumer aspirations and the affluent society: social democracy should be as much about defence of consumers' rights as of workers'. Yet Galbraith's critique of 'public squalor' and 'private affluence'[10] made a lasting impression on where social democrats thought the priorities of society should lie.

In the 1960s and 1970s, when real wages were being squeezed by higher taxes and prices, the social democrat argument that trade unionists should think of the value of the 'social wage' fell on largely deaf ears. In this period of the rise of the affluent worker, the instrumentalism of this new class, as John Goldthorpe described it,[11] was directed at achieving new possibilities of consumption. It was through the new ability to consume cars, clothes, toys for the children, holidays and hobbies that most people first exercised real choice in their lives. For them it was through wider access to these consumption opportunities that individual self-fulfilment in a classless marketplace was achieved. Those who rail against modern society's obsession with 'shopping' fail to understand the role that material consumption has played in bringing nearer the 1950s ideal of classlessness.

Conservatives have traditionally had a more acute sense of the changing nature of individual aspiration in British society. For example, in the 1950s they first promised to build more council houses than the Attlee government had and then delivered on it, shrewdly recognising that having a home was fundamental to individual aspirations for family life. In the 1980s they changed tack in response to social trends. Margaret Thatcher sold council houses to meet tenants' aspirations to become homeowners. But housing is a perfect illustration of how real choice can be attained only through society's recognition of its responsibility to enable that choice rather than through individual choice exercised through the market.

Social democrats have been less successful in thinking through the economic and social implications of these trends to individualism. The rise of individualism is a complex phenomenon and cannot simply be dismissed as a rise in Hobbesian atomistic selfishness. There has been a major change since the 1970s in the values of the affluent and 'post-material' society. Whereas before then, in a male-breadwinner world, the basic parameters of people's lives were determined by their job, their social class, the community in which they lived and married, and possibly their religion, individuals increasingly see their own lives as an autobiography they write for themselves.[12] There is far greater mobility and fewer jobs for life. Women have made great strides to gender equality. There is far greater fluidity in social relations as fewer couples are prepared to remain together in unsatisfactory situations. There is a wider acceptance of same-sex relationships and much greater openness about unconventional ways of living. The left tends to welcome these developments: indeed the Labour governments of the 1960s and 1970s as well as New Labour since 1997 have played a notable role in transforming public attitudes.

At the same time, however, the decline of community has heightened public fears of crime, even when the statistics indicate that crime rates are falling. The collapse of the male-breadwinner model of the welfare state and the rise in one-parent households have triggered debates about 'family' which social democrats find uncomfortable: the determination to tackle child poverty is a badge social democrats wear with pride, but discussion of the family is at best muted. The negative consequences of individualism, including the growth of social problems such as drug and alcohol abuse, obesity and mental illness, raise difficult issues of rights and responsibilities: New Labour liked the phrase, but was inconsistent as to where the state should intervene directly to change private behaviour. It has been egalitarian about sex and gender, but has appeared authoritarian in other spheres.

There are profound disagreements about the role that the pursuit of consumer choice plays in our societies. There is a rich intellectual critique of the market society to which social democrats need to pay attention, for example in the work of Robert E. Lane and Avner Offer.[13] Consumers are confronted with information overload, which makes it difficult for them to navigate modern markets. They can become locked into a 'hedonistic treadmill', attempting to keep up with the consumption patterns that they regard as societal norms but which in reality deny them genuine choice. In turn failure to keep up, or the perception of such failure, contributes to low self-esteem and a multitude of socio-psychological problems that go with it such as poor health, often fuelled by obesity, drink and drugs, and relationship problems.

For these reasons choice cannot in itself be a social democratic core value. It can be an important means to liberty and self-fulfilment. But choice cannot be elevated to the status of a goal, as it has sometimes come across in New Labour's advocacy of public service reform. It would be a great mistake, though, to dismiss choice in public services as a purely middle-class aspiration: research on public attitudes to New Labour's public service reforms suggests this presumption is quite false.[14] Complaints of 'lack of choice' may of course represent a legitimate reaction against supposedly universal public services that in practice vary greatly in both the quality and equality of their outcomes. In the real world of inequities in the way in which public services distribute opportunity, as against some non-existent universalist ideal, creating more choice exposes issues that should be top priorities for social democrats. Choice has the potential to be a powerful weapon that identifies and, in a well-designed regime, remedies these social injustices. But to make it a fundamental goal, not a potentially useful tool, would be to repeat the mistake for which Anthony Crosland berated the left in the 1950s on public ownership: to confuse means and ends.

At the same time we need to think more expansively about the role of the individual as an employee. In contrast to the 'affluent worker thesis' of the 1960s, the experience of work is now seen by many as crucial to their life satisfaction. Work is not just about the economic welfare and consumption that it facilitates, but is an opportunity to exercise individual skill and judgement and widen social relationships. Yet the operation of markets ignores these considerations of human well-being. This suggests that social democracy should shift its emphasis from a politics of more equal material consumption to a more sophisticated view of human contentment.

Gross domestic product is not an accurate measure of welfare, which perhaps accounts for the well-known phenomenon in affluent societies whereby subjective measures of happiness remain static even as living standards rise. Economists now recognise that a significant proportion of the GDP gap between Europe and the United States can be accounted for by factors that do not add to human well-being:[15] US extremes of weather, which result in increased energy consumption; the relative absence of good public transport, which increases car use and dependency; the well-known inefficiency of the US health system in terms of cost; and the criminal justice policy of the wholesale incarceration of (largely black) youth, which neither improves the welfare of criminals and their chances of not reoffending, nor reduces crime and the fear of crime in US society. But these comparisons could equally be made between different European countries, in all likelihood to Britain's disadvantage, except perhaps for the relative efficiency of the NHS. The shift in emphasis to well-being offers the potential for a more sophisticated critique of material affluence and consumer choice.

The need for greater clarity about Labour's approach to equality

This approach has varied through time. When earlier twentieth-century socialists and social democrats conceived of equality, they thought of it within the context of the nation state. This is not to diminish their noble attachment to ideas such as fraternity, based as often they were in Britain on the ideals of Gladstonian liberalism.[16] Today, by contrast, the debate among intellectuals and policy makers that rages most strongly is about global equality and the impact that the processes of globalisation are having on it. Clearly modern social democrats have to develop a concept for what they mean by social justice in the world as well as what they mean by greater equality at home.

The Attlee government's conception was a combination of 'fair shares' for the working classes and more equal opportunity for their children. The Beveridge reforms established a universal welfare state and abolished the inequities of the means test, not least the differences in treatment that had existed under the old Poor Law between the 'deserving' and the 'undeserving' and the discretion in applying the rules exercised by different authorities. At the same time fees for grammar schools and universities were abolished and student maintenance universalised, facilitating greater social mobility, though the eleven-plus exam proved an arbitrary, class-biased and objectively irrational means of selection. But Clement Attlee had no wider mission to transform the structures of class in Britain, delighting in the number of old Haileyburians he managed to appoint to his government. His many middle-class Labour ministers felt no obvious embarrassment in educating their children privately.

The conception of the 1950s revisionists was more radical. With a belief in 'social equality', they had a mission to break down class divisions. For Anthony Crosland comprehensive schools were the key to realise this vision, much more than redistributive taxation.[17] He wanted ordinary people to get a fair share of the good life. In the 1960s and 1970s social mobility rose. The power of the 'old school tie', particularly in business, the City and the professions, wilted under the pressures of meritocracy with the expansion and social opening up of the universities. The spread of comprehensive schools may initially have assisted these trends, though changing occupational structure and the steady decline in the size of the manual working class also played a part. The spread of broad-based affluence gradually broke down old divisions in dress, housing and consumption patterns.

At the same time as this progress towards 'classlessness' was being made, the consciousness grew that Beveridge had not in fact abolished poverty. While pensioner poverty was much reduced in the 1970s through large real-terms increases in universal benefits, the spread of family and child poverty proved more intractable.[18] Earnings-related unemployment benefits were attacked from the right as encouraging 'scroungers' and the concentration of poverty in one-parent and large families reignited debate about the ethics of entitlement and the social risks of dependency. By the beginning of the 1980s the welfare consensus was so undermined that the Thatcher government was able to reduce some benefits and freeze others, without apparent electoral disadvantage. The increase in unemployment to over three million as well as its geographic concentration and persistence, together with significant tax reductions at the top, contributed to an unprecedented increase in inequality in the UK. In 1997 one in five households of working age had no one with a job. The concentration of social disadvantage sometimes meant three generations where no family member was in work.

Against this dismal background the New Labour conception of equality was developed. In a 30-40-30 society, the majority was judged to have no appetite for general redistribution, even though their average living standards had increased by a third since 1979: those on middle incomes (40 per cent) were more likely to side with the top (30 per cent) than empathise with the bottom (the other 30 per cent). Policies to fight poverty were therefore carefully designed to win maximum public support. Benefits were targeted rather than universal, and focused on the politically most appealing groups – the reduction of child and pensioner poverty, not poverty per se. Higher benefits were in turn linked to 'welfare to work' policies designed to 'make work pay' and raise employment participation rates for the young employed and one-parent families, and latterly for those on long-term invalidity benefits.

These policies have made significant strides in reducing poverty. However, legitimate criticisms can be made of their impact. The needs of minority groups such as those who suffer from mental illness or other chronic health conditions, who don't attract wider sympathy, are unjustifiably neglected. Labour policies make controversial value judgements that for the able bodied, paid work is the only route out of poverty, even if that restricts individual choice and people's ability to be a good parent or committed carer.[19] More fundamentally, work has proved an unreliable route out of poverty because the minimum wage (with tax credits) is not a living wage in a two-adult household where only one adult works.[20]

The familiar criticism, however, that the New Labour conception is flawed because it focuses exclusively on poverty rather than inequality is only half true. The extent of poverty is assessed as a moving target set relative to median incomes. If the target is met, the poor will share in the general rise in prosperity. The key philosophical principle, that the less well off should have the resources commensurate with general living standards in order to participate properly as citizens in society, should be satisfied. Incomes may well have raced ahead for the top 1 per cent – but for the poor, how they relate to the median family is more important to their self-esteem, and their capacities for human development, than the issue of 'social exclusion' at the top.

Labour has also recognised that poverty is not simply a question of lack of material resources. It has accepted much of Amartya Sen's 'capabilities' approach.[21] Many of its public service reforms and social investments such as its SureStart and childcare programmes have been motivated by the desire to extend life chances for the most disadvantaged. These objectives, however, which require a concentration of resources on deprived groups, have had to compete with the understandable electoral imperative of extending 'choice' and quality for middle Britain. It can reasonably be argued that in a democratic society satisfying the latter is a necessary condition of holding out hope to the former.

There has been ambitious talk of increasing social mobility – but what are the criteria by which to judge success? It would certainly be egalitarian to raise the shockingly low proportion of manual workers' children who go to university. But there needs to be a credible parallel ambition to improve the life prospects of the growing numbers of young people who leave school at sixteen without entering further education, employment or training, whose economic prospects are worse than dismal in our increasingly sophisticated knowledge economy.

The truth is that New Labour under-estimated the profundity and complexity of the inequalities challenge in modern British society. That is why its ambitious targets have proved so difficult to meet. A much more profound examination of the modern drivers of economic inequality is required. What can be done about the declining position of the unskilled and the poor labour market prospects for those with minimal qualifications? What drives the new generational inequalities between the baby-boomer generation, the majority of whom can look forward to a long and comfortable retirement, and the insecurities and pressures younger cohorts face? What can be done to avert the new social risks that transmit inequalities from one generation of deprived children to another?

Social democrats see themselves, rightly, as the custodians of 'fairness'. But the social justice rationale for many policies is rarely set out in an explicit way. As a result alternative perceptions of 'fairness' or, more accurately, unfairness have taken hold: for example that new arrivals in this country worsen social conditions for the native population, and that asylum seekers benefit from unfairly favourable treatment. The question of who deserves what in a socially diverse society has not been addressed. Some argue that the Nordic social democracies are the most successful precisely because they are, or were until two decades ago, the most homogeneous countries in western Europe and the least diverse in terms of race, ethnicity and religion. Do modern social democrats have to accept the argument of sociologists such as Robert Putnam that diversity inevitably undermines feelings of social solidarity[22] and therefore the possibilities for a more social democratic society? Or is it possible to develop a concept of integration on the basis of shared citizenship that provides a solid foundation for a modern conception of social justice? In the 1960s Roy Jenkins, as Britain's most liberal ever Home Secretary, said that unlike the United States Britain would never be a 'melting pot'. Integration was not a 'flattening process' but based on the three principles of equal opportunity, cultural diversity and mutual tolerance. Such principles must continue to provide the basis for an egalitarian citizenship in modern Britain.

The need for a redefinition of the role of the state

There are two issues here. One is universal to social democracy as an idea, one is particular to Britain. There has always been vigorous debate among social democrats about the role of the state. Think for example about the debates in Sweden about building the 'people's home', the German SPD's recognition of the role of the market at Bad Godesberg in 1960, and the differing views of the role of the state in the French republican tradition. In addition there is a British issue: the deep emotional attachment of British social democracy to the institutions and assumptions of the British state.

There is a view that the doctrine of 'modernised' nation state social democracy is proving an increasingly blunt instrument. Professor Vernon Bogdanor argues that social democracy has been steadily 'emasculated' by the twin forces of globalisation and devolution, both of which fragment the power of the centralised state.[23] We do not agree with Bogdanor's conclusion that the state can no longer promote social justice, but he is surely right to draw attention to the 'golden straitjacket' that has been placed on national governments and the dilemmas this presents for social democrats in a world of global markets, rapid migration, borderless terrorism and climate change. The increasing shift towards devolution and localism might imperil the delivery of more equal outcomes across the nation.

As we also noted in the Introduction to this book, there has always been a tension about the role of the state in social democratic thinking. Is the state's role to shape citizens or to give citizens equally the power to shape themselves? The origins of the Labour Party were strongly 'voluntarist': how else could the movement have grown in a hostile culture and in a society where the majority of working people did not have the vote? They relied on the 'self-help' of friendly societies and trade unions, cooperatives and chapels. These institutions represented the ideals of collectivism but without reliance on the state. Yet the massive growth of the state in two world wars, the uneasy but gradual incorporation of the trade unions as an essential pillar of the British polity in the middle decades of the twentieth century, and the intellectual dominance of the idea of planning after the massive failure of capitalism in the inter-war years increasingly identified collectivism with the state. The key question for today is whether and how that identity could be broken.

New Labour was never very clear about any of these questions. At some important points, it acted in David Marquand's terminology as a 'democratic republican':[24] in pushing through Scottish and Welsh devolution; in entrenching citizens' rights and up to a point challenging the sovereignty of Parliament through the Human Rights Act. But in most areas of policy, its approach was at best confusing. Foundation hospitals were supposed to gain significant independence, but ministers still took it upon themselves in 2007 to instruct every hospital to undertake a 'deep clean' in order to combat the MRSA infection, whether or not local circumstances required it. Schools were offered independence from local authorities, but were subjected to ever tighter regimes of inspection and centralised intervention to secure performance improvement. Local authorities were rewarded with extra central government grants if they met performance targets but, in direct contradiction, compensated if they fell further behind on certain measures of deprivation. At times New Labour appeared to pursue an almost Leninist policy of strengthening the state, only to enable it to wither away.

The fact is that there are trade-offs in local autonomy. There may be gains in efficiency at the expense of sacrifices in equity – or vice versa, depending on local political choice. New Labour could never bring itself to accept this. There was a lot of talk of the 'new localism',[25] the need for 'double devolution'[26] and community participation. But largely it remained at the level of rhetoric because no one was willing to resolve the underlying intellectual confusion.

Then there is the issue of British social democrats' peculiar attachment to the uniqueness of the British state. This can be seen in the left's attitude to both the constitution and foreign policy. On the constitution, the scale of New Labour's reforms was unprecedented in twentieth-century history – but the reforms were also limited. Both devolution and the Human Rights Act were dressed up in the language of a theoretically untrammelled parliamentary sovereignty, even though in practice they represented a significant shift away from it. The failure to agree democratic reforms of the second chamber demonstrates an inability to come to terms with a constitutional settlement where part of the legislature would by definition not be under executive control. Labour's willingness to accept different forms of proportional representation for every representative body other than the House of Commons reflects a continuing prejudice that all democracy is of little consequence but the achievement of absolute control at Westminster through a first-past-the-post system. Unlike Continental social democrats, Labour remains unable to conceive of the possibility that gradual consensual steps through a pluralistic democratic system might achieve more for social democratic values in the long run than the alternation of successive elective dictatorships at Westminster.

The belief in the uniqueness of Britain has also had a baleful influence on Britain's relations with other countries. For the first two decades after the Second World War this contributed to massive over-reach, which greatly contributed to the balance of payments difficulties from which successive governments suffered. Then Harold Wilson and Edward Heath led a troubled period of adjustment in which Britain began to shed its illusions about its special status in the world. Margaret Thatcher's triumph in the Falklands reasserted that British sense of specialness and New Labour felt determined not to be outdone. So although Tony Blair fully recognised the damage to Britain's interests that its semi-detachedness from the European Union had caused over a quarter-century of membership, the mind-set of no contradiction between full engagement in Europe and the continuation of Britain's close relationship with the United States meant that when the two came in conflict, the US relationship without hesitation prevailed. As a result over Iraq, Britain ended up with less influence over US policy than if it had given first priority to the construction of a common European position.

The argument of this book is that the structural challenges facing Britain will only be met through the construction of a reformed 'developmental' state with far stronger, more focused strategic capabilities. That implies a very different approach to governing. Some will argue that this is the wrong argument to make when globalisation is in crisis and markets have conspicuously failed to provide stability. But in fact there are three credible views of the role of the state, not just two. One is the laissez-faire, minimalist view. Another is to support unequivocally the idea of the big state as a guarantor of equity. But the third view is of a state with a strong strategic capacity that doesn't try to run everything itself. New Labour might have described this 'third way' as an 'enabling state'. However, this may come across as more minimalist than the situation requires: to caricature, the answer to the global crisis must be more than a training scheme. A strategic capacity demands market ordering, not just market accepting.

So modern social democrats should certainly reject traditional neo-liberal hostility towards the state. They should also embrace Albert Hirschman's view that the best way for progressives to secure support for collective action in the public interest is to acknowledge that state intervention can have unintended consequences, and that there are limits to the scope of state power, as John Maynard Keynes argued in the 1920s.[27] Labour does not exist to promote and protect the state, but to ensure that the state advances the collective interest rather than the vested interests of an elite.

What social democrats need to fashion is not larger government but a more capable strategic state that can steer and intervene in the increasingly complex networks and institutions of a globalised economy and society. That means shaping new methods, capacities and instruments at different levels of governance from local areas to the European Union and the regulation of global financial institutions. An important theme running through the essays in this volume is whether social democracy can be liberalised and become more pluralist – that is, properly attuned to the need for bottom-up, localised democratic institutions; sensitive to the politics of personal behaviour and the variety and complexity of social values and norms; and capable of recognising the desire of people to experience greater choice and control in their lives.

The contributors to this book envisage six roles or functions of the state:

- First, **the state as regulator**: promoting competitive markets and upholding the public interest, as well as shaping quality of life and protecting ethical values from excessive interference by the market. Regulation is more consistent with a pluralistic approach to governing, setting national standards but allowing institutions to control themselves instead of mandating outcomes from the centre.
- Second, **the state as guarantor**: ensuring minimum standards and equity so that everyone is able to enjoy a decent and dignified life through universal public provision. As the delivery of public services becomes more devolved and often involves a diversity of institutions and providers, it is vital to uphold minimum standards of treatment and access for every citizen.
- Third, **the state as catalyst**: bringing together public, private and third sectors to forge new partnerships that deliver social change, particularly in the most disadvantaged communities. The state needs to incentivise and support local efforts rather than leaving vulnerable communities to 'go it alone' without adequate resources and infrastructure, as well as helping to foster active citizenship.
- Fourth, **the state as enabler**: ensuring people are able to develop their capabilities, increasing social mobility by breaking the insidious link between parental origins and destinations, and giving people new opportunities throughout their lives. This

includes public goods, from education to assets: it is up to individuals to seize new opportunities, but they can be helped or hindered by the presence of an active state.

- Fifth, **the state as shield**: protecting citizens from organised violence including robust policing and counter-terrorism measures, as well as being prepared to challenge despotic regimes that import terrorism across the world. That means tackling the causes as well as the actual manifestations of terrorism, including the genuine grievances that may be held against the west.
- Finally, **the state as global actor**: ensuring that Britain remains a responsible 'world citizen', fulfilling global obligations from international development to climate change. There is a moral duty to tackle social injustice across the world but it is also in the national interest, protecting the stability of 'weak' states and controlling flows of people to the west.

The reform of the state has to be underpinned by a revitalised notion of active citizenship to give the state legitimacy and credibility, strengthening the 'horizontal bonds' that exist between citizens and the 'vertical bonds' that exist between citizen and state. Indeed, support for active government is dependent on sustaining the continuing sense of 'we' and the collective ethic of belonging, shared identity and mutual respect.

The concept of 'Britishness' and the effort to frame a modern form of British identity is enriching, but it needs to be developed in the context of devolution, mass migration and the potential for conflict between multiple religious identities and secularism. It is closely related to the task of building a stable, cohesive society that reduces mistrust across ethnic and religious lines, as well as promoting more equitable social and economic outcomes for minority communities.[28]

The challenge for the future social democratic project after New Labour will be to resolve an enduring dilemma in a new form: ensuring that the plight of the worst off resonates with the middle-class majority, and securing a fairer distribution of income and wealth, as well as equitable access to institutions and public services. Social democrats must do this in a world that is more diverse and atomised, where the ties that bind individuals and communities together are no longer taken for granted, and where governments are viewed with scepticism rather than trust.

Labour's challenge is to continue to project itself as a vibrant, dynamic change agent. The party exists to transform society, far more than simply tidying up the worst excesses of globalisation and tinkering at the edges. The next generation of Labour politicians also have a great advantage: they can draw on the success of the New Labour project, confident that the centre-left is able to win the battle of ideas and govern competently in the name of a more equal and just society.

It is our belief that a 'next generation' social democratic project for Britain is needed: not a reversion to traditionalism, nor a further revisionist project on the Crosland model that argues for changed means to realise a constant, unchanging set of ends. We need an openness to the radical overhaul of both ends and means to produce a more liberal and pluralist social democracy. This nevertheless takes seriously the need for an active citizenship based on reciprocity and an ethic of mutual obligation. We have to refresh the goals of 'democratic equality' and 'individual self-fulfilment' for modern times and recognise and accept the tensions within the more liberal, pluralist model we favour.

Notes

Introduction

1. David Marquand, *The Progressive Dilemma: From Lloyd George to Blair* (London: Weidenfeld & Nicolson, 1999).
2. Peter Clarke, *Liberals and Social Democrats* (Cambridge: Cambridge University Press, 1978).
3. However, the term 'progressive' does provide a convenient platform for mutual dialogue between European social democrats and other centre-left forces in the world, notably the US Democrats, who run away from any identification with socialism or social democracy and where the alternative term 'liberal' places people controversially on the left of the Democrats, whereas in continental Europe 'liberals' tend to be right-wing supporters of free markets.
4. See Isaiah Berlin, 'Two Concepts of Liberty', in *Four Essays on Liberty* (Oxford: Oxford University Press, 1969).
5. R. H. Tawney, 'Social Democracy in Britain', in *The Radical Tradition* (London: George Allen & Unwin, 1964). First published 1949.
6. Ibid.
7. *New Statesman and Nation*, 22 June 1935.
8. See David Marquand, *Britain since 1918: The Strange Career of British Democracy* (London: Weidenfeld & Nicolson, 2008).
9. Ibid., p. 64, quoting Beatrice Webb.
10. Quoted in Elizabeth Durbin, *New Jerusalems: The Labour Party and the Economics of Democratic Socialism* (London: Routledge & Kegan Paul, 1985), p. 185.
11. Quoted in Alfred L. Malabre Jr, *Lost Prophets: An Insider's History of the Modern Economists* (Cambridge, MA: Harvard Business School Press, 1994), p. 220.
12. See Peter Clarke, *A Question of Leadership: Gladstone to Blair* (London: Penguin, 1999).
13. Andrew Gamble, Policy Network seminar on the future of social democracy, September 2008.

14. See for example Roger Liddle and Frédéric Lerais, *Europe's Social Reality* (European Commission, 2007).

15. Will Hutton, Policy Network seminar on the future of social democracy, September 2008.

16. See Roger Liddle, *Social Pessimism: The New Social Reality of Europe* (London: Policy Network, 2008).

17. *Standard Eurobarometer 69: Values of Europeans* (European Commission, 2008). The UK fieldwork was undertaken between 1 and 24 April 2008. Polling shows that only 36 per cent of Britons think positively of the benefits of EU membership, while 50 per cent think that Britain has not benefited from EU membership.

18. Gamble, Policy Network seminar.

19. René Cuperus, *From Polder Model to Postmodern Populism: Five Explanations for the 'Fortuyn Revolt' in the Netherlands* (Vienna: Renner Institut, 2003).

20. See for example Ross McKibbin, 'Mondeo Man in the Driving Seat', *London Review of Books*, 30 September 1999.

21. Patrick Diamond (ed.), *New Labour's Old Roots: Revisionist Thinkers in Labour's History 1931–1997* (Exeter: Imprint Academic, 2004).

22. These tensions were first elaborated by Peter Hyman, former head of strategic communications in 10 Downing Street, in his excellent book on New Labour, *1 out of 10: From Downing Street Vision to Classroom Reality* (London: Vintage, 2005).

23. See *Growing Unequal? Income Distribution and Poverty in OECD Countries* (Paris: Organisation for Economic Co-operation and Development, 2008).

Chapter 1: After progress

1. See David Marquand, *The Progressive Dilemma: From Lloyd George to Blair*, 2nd edn (London: Phoenix, 1999).

2. See John Gray, *Black Mass: Apocalyptic Religion and the Death of Utopia* (London: Allen Lane, 2007).

3. Norman Angell, *The Great Illusion: A Study of the Relation of Military Power to National Advantage* (London: William Heinemann, 1909).

4. Albert Hirschman, *The Rhetoric of Reaction: Perversity, Futility, Jeopardy* (Cambridge, MA and London: Belknap Press, 1991).

5. Evan Durbin, *The Politics of Democratic Socialism: An Essay on Social Policy* (London: Pickering & Chatto, [1940] 1994), p. 361.

6. C. A. R. Crosland, *The Future of Socialism* (London: Pickering & Chatto, [1956] 1994), p. 524.

7. J. A. Hobson, *The Crisis of Liberalism: New Issues of Democracy* (Brighton: Harvester Press, [1909] 1974), pp. 76–7.

8. J. Ramsay MacDonald, *Socialism and Government* (London: Independent Labour Party, 1909), vol. 1, pp. 3, 17.

9. Sir Isaiah Berlin, *Against the Current: Essays in the History of Ideas* (Oxford: Oxford University Press, 1981), p. 211.

Chapter 2: 'Broken Britain'?

1. See Gøsta Esping-Andersen, Duncan Gallie, Anton Hemerijck and John Myles (eds), *Why We Need a New Welfare State* (Oxford: Oxford University Press, 2002).

2. We draw in large part on the original empirical research undertaken in Roger Liddle and Frédéric Lerais, *Europe's Social Reality* (European Commission, 2007), unless otherwise stated.

3. See Ben Page, 'Is "broken Britain" piffle?', *Prospect*, October 2008.

4. *Standard Eurobarometer 69: Values of Europeans* (European Commission, 2008). The UK fieldwork was undertaken between 1 and 24 April 2008.

5. See Roger Liddle, *Social Pessimism: The New Social Reality of Europe* (London: Policy Network, 2008).

6. The scale of the manufacturing rundown may be somewhat exaggerated by the sub-contracting of activities that manufacturing companies once undertook themselves to service companies.

7. Office for National Statistics, *Social Trends No. 38* (Basingstoke: Palgrave Macmillan, 2008), p. 52.

8. See Maarten Goos and Alan Manning, *Lousy and Lovely Jobs: The Rising Polarization of Work in Britain* (London: Centre for Economic Performance, London School of Economics and Political Science, 2003).

9. Office for National Statistics, *Social Trends No. 38*, p. 59.

10. Ibid., p. 50.

11. See *Quarterly EU Labour Market Review*, Spring 2008 (European Commission).

12. Office for National Statistics, *Social Trends No. 38*, pp. 50–51.

13. See *Quarterly EU Labour Market Review*, Spring 2008.

14. Richard Dickens and Abigail McKnight, *The Impact of Policy Change on Job Retention and Advancement* (London: Centre for Economic

Performance, London School of Economics and Political Science, 2008).

15. Ibid.
16. Office for National Statistics, Labour Force Survey 2008.
17. See Steve Tombs and David Whyte, *A Crisis of Enforcement: The Decriminalisation of Death and Injury at Work* (London: Centre for Crime and Justice Studies, King's College London, 2008).
18. See *Work and Health in the EU: A Statistical Portrait*, 2003 edn (Luxembourg: Office for Official Publications of the European Communities, 2004).
19. See Marianne Barriaux, '21m suspect sickies cost UK economy £1.6bn', *Guardian*, 10 April 2007.
20. See *Report on Equality between Women and Men 2008* (European Communities, 2008).
21. See Ricardo Hausmann, Laura D. Tyson and Saadia Zahidi, *The Global Gender Gap Report 2008* (Geneva: World Economic Forum, 2008).
22. See *Report on Equality between Women and Men 2008*.
23. Ibid.
24. See *Sex and Power 2008* (London: Equality and Human Rights Commission, 2008).
25. See *Report on Equality between Women and Men 2008*.
26. See 'Rise in fertility continues', National Statistics website, 21 August 2008.
27. See Page, 'Is "broken Britain" piffle?'.
28. See *A Shared Responsibility: Annual Report and Accounts 2008* (London: Help the Aged, 2008), p. 5.
29. Ibid., p. 7.
30. Help the Aged, 'One is the saddest number' campaign, 2008.
31. See 'Million elderly people are lonely', BBC News online, 31 October 2008.
32. See Esping-Andersen et al., *Why We Need a New Welfare State*.
33. See Maurizio Ferrara, *The Boundaries of Welfare: European Integration and the New Spatial Politics of Social Protection* (Oxford: Oxford University Press, 2005).
34. Office of National Statistics, *Social Trends No. 38*.
35. A. H. Maslow, 'A Theory of Human Motivation', *Psychological Review* (1943), vol. 50, pp. 370–96.
36. See 'Sex Uncovered: The Poll', *Observer*, 26 October 2008. ICM research performed in September 2008.
37. See *The Family Law Review: An Interim Report* (London: Centre for Social Justice, 2008).

38. See Donald Hirsch, *What Is Needed to End Child Poverty in 2020?* (York: Joseph Rowntree Foundation, 2008).

39. See Donald Hirsch, *Estimating the Costs of Child Poverty* (York: Joseph Rowntree Foundation, 2008).

40. Esping-Andersen et al., *Why We Need a New Welfare State.*

41. See Anastasia de Waal, *Second Thoughts on the Family* (London: Civitas, 2008).

42. See *Meeting the Aspirations of the British People: 2007 Pre-Budget Report and Comprehensive Spending Review* (HM Treasury, 2007).

43. See Stephen Machin, *Social Disadvantage and Educational Experiences* (Paris: Organisation for Economic Co-operation and Development, 2006), p. 12, fig. 2.

44. See *Equality between Women and Men* (European Commission, 2008).

45. See Machin, *Social Disadvantage and Educational Experiences.*

46. See Jo Blanden and Stephen Machin, 'Recent Trends in Inter-generational Mobility: Will the Downward Trend Continue?', *Centre-Piece*, Autumn 2008.

47. See National Child Development Study, Sweep 7, 2004.

48. See Louis Chauvel, *Le Destin des générations: structure sociale et cohortes en France au XXe siècle*, 2nd edn (Paris: Presses Universitaires de France, 2002).

49. Sue Heath, *Housing Choices and Issues for Young People in the UK* (York: Joseph Rowntree Foundation, 2008).

50. Ibid.

51. Office for National Statistics, *Social Trends No. 38*, p. 49.

52. See *European Employment and Social Policy*, Special Eurobarometer 261 (2006).

53. Ibid.

54. Esping-Andersen et al., *Why We Need a New Welfare State.*

55. See *European Employment and Social Policy.*

56. 'Labour market and retirement: Chapter 3', National Statistics website, 22 October 2008.

57. A. C. Grayling, *Social Evils and Social Good* (York: Joseph Rowntree Foundation, 2008).

58. See Page, 'Is "broken Britain" piffle?'.

59. Grayling, *Social Evils and Social Good.*

60. See Brian Brivati, *The End of Decline: Blair and Brown in Power* (London: Politico's, 2007).

Chapter 3: The electoral map

1. Quoted in David Butler and Anthony King, *The British General Election of 1964* (London: Macmillan, 1965), p. 196.
2. Anthony King, 'The Implications of One Party Government', in Anthony King, Ivor Crewe, David Denver, Kenneth Newton and Philip Norton, *Britain at the Polls 1992* (Chatham, NJ: Chatham House Publishers, 1993), pp. 245–6.
3. David Butler and Dennis Kavanagh, *The British General Election of 1992* (London: St Martin's Press, 1992), p. 283.
4. See Ivor Crewe, 'The Electorate: Partisan Dealignment Ten Years On', in Hugh Berrington (ed.), *Change in British Politics* (London: Frank Cass, 1984).
5. See Harold D. Clarke, David Sanders, Marianne C. Stewart and Paul Whiteley, *Political Choice in Britain* (Oxford: Oxford University Press, 2004).
6. John Curtice, 'Elections and Public Opinion', in Anthony Seldon (ed.), *Blair's Britain 1997–2007* (Cambridge: Cambridge University Press, 2007), p. 41.
7. Ibid.
8. Ibid., p. 51.
9. Pippa Norris, 'Elections and Public Opinion', in Dennis Kavanagh and Anthony Seldon (eds), *The Blair Effect 2001–5* (Cambridge: Cambridge University Press, 2005), pp. 65–6.
10. Peter Taylor-Gooby, *A Taxing Dilemma* (London: Policy Network, 2008).
11. Robert Johns and Stephen Padgett, 'The Role of Government: Public Values and Party Politics', in Alison Park, John Curtice, Katarina Thomson, Miranda Phillips, Mark C. Johnson and Elizabeth Clery (eds), *British Social Attitudes: The 24th Report* (London: Sage, 2008).

Chapter 4: Progressive economics

1. Ian Brinkley, *The Knowledge Economy: How Knowledge Is Reshaping the Economic Life of Nations* (London: The Work Foundation, 2008).
2. Alexandra Jones, Neil Lee, Laura Williams, Naomi Clayton and Katy Morris, *How Can Cities Thrive in the Changing Economy?* (London: The Work Foundation, 2008).

Chapter 7: Family, gender and generation

1. See Elisabeth Beck-Gernsheim, *Reinventing the Family: In Search of New Lifestyles*, tr. Patrick Camiller (Cambridge: Polity, 2002); Anthony Giddens, 'Family', *Reith Lectures*, BBC Radio 4, 28 April 1999.
2. See Jane Lewis and Mary Campbell, 'Work/Family Balance Policies in the UK since 1997: A New Departure?', *Journal of Social Policy* (2007), vol. 36, p. 374.
3. See *Building on Progress: Families* (Cabinet Office, 2007).
4. Comparative data expenditure on family benefits and services finds the UK in the middle of the international league table on expenditure as a proportion of GDP, slightly above the average. See the OECD database PF1, 'Public Spending on Family Benefits', at http://www.oecd.org.
5. See *Aiming High for Children: Supporting Families* (HM Treasury/Department for Education and Skills, 2007), p. 2.
6. See Franz-Xaver Kaufmann, 'Politics and Policies towards the Family in Europe: A Framework and an Enquiry into Their Differences and Convergences', in Franz-Xaver Kaufmann, Anton Kuijsten, Hans-Joachim Schulze and Klaus Peter Strohmeier (eds), *Family Life and Family Policies in Europe, vol. 2: Problems and Issues in Comparative Perspective* (Oxford: Oxford University Press, 2002), pp. 426–8; Thomas Bahle, 'Family Policies in the Enlarged European Union: Persistent Diversity in "Old" and Transition to the Periphery in the "New Europe"?', Social Conditions in the Enlarged Europe conference, Wissenschaftszentrum, Berlin, 8–9 December 2005.
7. See for example Gøsta Esping-Andersen, 'Untying the Gordian Knot of Social Inheritance', *Research in Social Stratification and Mobility* (2004), vol. 21, pp. 115–38.
8. Ruth Lister, 'Investing in the Citizen-workers of the Future: Transformations in Citizenship and the State under New Labour', *Social Policy and Administration* (2003), vol. 37, pp. 433, 434.
9. Julia Brannen, Peter Moss and Ann Mooney, *Working and Caring over the Twentieth Century: Change and Continuity in Four-generation Families* (Basingstoke: Palgrave Macmillan, 2004), p. 216.
10. See E. Kay M. Tisdall, 'Antisocial Behaviour Legislation Meets Children's Services: Challenging Perspectives on Children, Parents and the State', *Critical Social Policy* (2006), vol. 26, pp. 101–20.
11. See Gillian Pascall and Jane Lewis, 'Emerging Gender Regimes and Policies for Gender Equality in a Wider Europe', *Journal of Social Policy* (2004), vol. 33, p. 389.

12. See Trudie Knijn, 'Private Responsibility and Some Support: Family Policies in the Netherlands', in Ilona Ostner and Christoph Schmitt (eds), *Family Policies in the Context of Family Change: The Nordic Countries in Comparative Perspective* (Wiesbaden: VS, 2008), pp. 155–73.

13. Ibid.

14. See Anália Torres, Rui Brites, Barbara Haas and Nadia Steiber, *First European Quality of Life Survey: Time Use and Work–Life Options over the Life Course* (Luxembourg: Office for Official Publications of the European Communities, 2007).

15. Ibid.

16. See Anne Barlow, Simon Duncan and Grace James, 'New Labour, the Rationality Mistake and Family Policy in Britain', in Alan Carling, Simon Duncan and Rosalind Edwards (eds), *Analysing Families: Morality and Rationality in Policy and Practice* (London: Routledge, 2002).

17. See Brannen et al., *Working and Caring over the Twentieth Century*.

18. See Mary Daly, 'A Fine Balance: Women's Labor Market Participation Patterns in International Comparison', in Fritz W. Scharpf and Vivien A. Schmidt (eds), *Welfare and Work in the Open Economy, vol. 2: Diverse Responses to Common Challenges* (Oxford: Oxford University Press, 2000).

19. See Nabanita Datta Gupta, Nina Smith and Mette Verner, *Child Care and Parental Leave in the Nordic Countries: A Model to Aspire To?* (Bonn: IZA, 2006).

20. Ibid.

21. See Nancy Fraser, 'After the Family Wage: Gender Equality and the Welfare State', *Political Theory* (1994), vol. 22, pp. 591–618.

22. See Jonathan Gershuny, *Changing Times: Work and Leisure in Postindustrial Society* (New York: Oxford University Press, 2000).

23. See Kaufmann, 'Politics and Policies towards the Family in Europe'.

24. See Pascall and Lewis, 'Emerging Gender Regimes and Policies for Gender Equality in a Wider Europe', p. 280.

25. See Miriam Glucksmann, 'Shifting Boundaries and Interconnections: Extending the "Total Social Organisation of Labour"', in Lynne Pettinger, Jane Perry, Rebecca Taylor and Miriam Glucksmann (eds), *A New Sociology of Work?* (Oxford: Wiley-Blackwell, 2006).

26. See Tisdall, 'Antisocial Behaviour Legislation Meets Children's Services', p. 105.

27. See Ruth Lister, 'Investing in Children and Childhood: A New Welfare Paradigm and Its Implications', *Comparative Social Research* (2008), vol. 25, pp. 383–408.

28. See Ruth Lister, 'Why Citizenship: Where, When and How Children?', *Theoretical Inquires in Law* (2007), vol. 8, pp. 693–718.

29. See James J. Heckman, 'Policies to Foster Human Capital', *Research in Economics* (2000), vol. 54, pp. 3–56; Esping-Andersen, 'Untying the Gordian Knot of Social Inheritance'.

30. See Jo Blanden, Paul Gregg and Stephen Machin, *Intergenerational Mobility in Europe and North America* (London: Centre for Economic Performance, London School of Economics and Political Science, 2005).

31. See Jens Alber and Tony Fahey, *Perceptions of Living Conditions in an Enlarged Europe* (Luxembourg: Office for Official Publications of the European Communities, 2004).

32. See Hans-Peter Blossfeld, Erik Klijzing, Melinda Mills and Karin Kurz (eds), *Globalization, Uncertainty and Youth in Society: The Losers in a Globalizing World* (London: Routledge, 2005).

33. See Peter Squires, 'New Labour and the Politics of Antisocial Behaviour', *Critical Social Policy* (2006), vol. 26, pp. 144–68.

34. Ibid.

35. See Günther Schmid, *Transitional Labour Markets: A New European Employment Strategy* (Berlin: Wissenschaftszentrum Berlin für Sozialforschung, 1998).

Chapter 8: Social justice in a changing world

1. See John Hills, *Inequality and the State* (Oxford: Oxford University Press, 2004).

2. See *Growing Unequal: Income Distribution and Poverty in OECD Countries* (Paris: Organisation for Economic Co-operation and Development, 2008).

3. See Mike Brewer, Alissa Goodman, Jonathan Shaw and Luke Sibieta, *Poverty and Inequality in Britain 2006* (London: Institute for Fiscal Studies, 2006).

4. See Geoff Mulgan, 'Living in the wrong postcode can shorten your life', *Independent*, 16 December 2004.

5. See Hills, *Inequality and the State*; Richard Sennett, *Respect: The Formation of Character in a World of Inequality* (London: Allen Lane, 2003).

6. See 'Inequality and the American dream', *Economist*, 17 June 2006; William Keegan, 'Of bankers and Goldman Sachs', *Observer*, 18 June 2006.

7. See Jo Blanden, Paul Gregg and Stephen Machin, *Intergenerational*

Mobility in Europe and North America (London: Centre for Economic Performance, London School of Economics and Political Science, 2005).

8. David Miller, *Principles of Social Justice* (Cambridge, MA: Harvard University Press).

9. See John Rawls, *A Theory of Justice* (Cambridge, MA: Belknap Press, 1971).

10. See Amartya Sen, 'Equality of What?', in Sterling M. McMurrin (ed.), *Tanner Lectures on Human Values, vol. 1* (Cambridge: Cambridge University Press, 1980).

11. See Jon Elster, *Solomonic Judgements: Studies in the Limitation of Rationality* (Cambridge: Cambridge University Press, 1989).

12. See Gøsta Esping-Andersen, 'Inequality of Incomes and Opportunities', in Anthony Giddens and Patrick Diamond, *The New Egalitarianism* (Cambridge: Polity, 2005); Gøsta Esping-Andersen, *Social Foundations of Postindustrial Economies* (Oxford: Oxford University Press, 1999).

13. Michael Sherraden, 'Stakeholding: Notes on a Theory Based on Assets', *Social Service Review* (1990), vol. 64, pp. 580–601.

14. Mickey Kaus, *The End of Equality* (New York: Basic, 1992).

15. Richard Layard, *Happiness: Lessons from a New Science* (London: Allen Lane, 2004).

16. Ibid.

Chapter 9: Identity in Britain

1. See Maria O'Beirne, *Religion in England and Wales: Findings from the 2001 Home Office Citizenship Survey* (Home Office, 2004), p. 20.

2. See Tufyal Choudhury, *The Role of Muslim Identity Politics in Radicalisation* (Department for Communities and Local Government, 2007), p. 10.

3. Paul Statham, 'New Conflicts about Integration and Cultural Diversity in Britain', in René Cuperus, Karl A. Duffeck and Johannes Kandel (eds), *The Challenge of Diversity: European Social Democracy Facing Migration, Integration, and Multiculturalism* (Innsbruck: Studienverlag, 2003), cited ibid.

4. See Lucy Stone and Rick Muir, *Who Are We? Identities in Britain 2007* (London: Institute for Public Policy Research, 2007), p. 8.

5. See MORI/Commission for Racial Equality, 'The voice of Britain', April 2002.

6. Ibid.

7. See Anthony Heath, Bridget Taylor, Lindsay Brook and Alison Park, 'British National Sentiment', *British Journal of Political Science* (1999), vol. 29, pp. 155–75.

8. Ibid., p. 157.

9. See Paula Surridge, 'Class Belonging: A Quantitative Exploration of Identity and Consciousness', *British Journal of Sociology* (2007), vol. 58, p. 216.

10. See Peter Clarke, *A Question of Leadership: Gladstone to Thatcher* (London: Penguin, 1992), p. 17.

11. See K. Fisher, A. McCulloch and J. Gershuny, *British Fathers and Children* (Colchester: Institute for Social and Economic Research, University of Essex, 1999).

12. See Surridge, 'Class Belonging', p. 216.

13. Peter Clarke, *Liberals and Social Democrats* (Aldershot: Gregg Revivals, [1978] 1993), p. 110.

14. Michael Ignatieff, 'There's No Place like Home', in Sarah Dunant and Roy Porter (eds), *The Age of Anxiety* (London: Virago, 1997).

15. See William Davies, 'The Governmentality of New Labour', *Public Policy Research* (2006), vol. 13, p. 253.

16. Beginning with the Race Relations (Amendment) Act (2000).

17. See Nick O'Brien, 'Equality and Human Rights: Foundations of a Common Culture?', *Political Quarterly* (2008), vol. 79, p. 30.

18. See for example Linda Colley, Prime Minister's Millennium Lecture, 10 Downing Street, 1999.

19. Ibid.

Chapter 10: Constitutional reform

1. On the 'England question', see Iain McLean, *The Fiscal Crisis of the United Kingdom* (Basingstoke: Palgrave Macmillan, 2005); Robert Hazell (ed.), *The English Question* (Manchester: Manchester University Press, 2006).

2. 'I have always said I am an Orangeman first and a politician and Member of this parliament afterwards . . . The Hon. Member must remember that in the South they boasted of a Catholic state. They still boast of Southern Ireland being a Catholic state. All I boast is that we are a Protestant parliament and Protestant state.' Sir James Craig, Unionist Party, then Prime Minister of Northern Ireland, 24 April 1934. *Reported in Parliamentary Debates, Northern Ireland House of Commons*, vol. 16, col. 1095.

3. See Iain McLean and Benjamin Linsley, *The Church of England and the State: Reforming Establishment for a Multi-faith Britain* (London: New Politics Network, 2004), Table 2.

4. *The House of Lords: Reform* (Cm 7027, 2007); *An Elected Second Chamber: Further Reform of the House of Lords* (Cm 7438, 2008).

5. Except Northern Ireland, which uses the single transferable vote. In a closed list system, each party submits a ranked list of candidates. Parties are awarded as many seats (rounded off to the nearest whole number) as their share of the regional vote. Voters simply vote for a party and have no say in the composition of the list. Therefore a party can punish its rebels by ranking them low on its list for the next election. A partially open list, as proposed for the upper house, enables voters to rank candidates within parties if they wish.

6. For more on the 2003 votes see Iain McLean, Arthur Spirling and Meg Russell, 'None of the Above: The UK House of Commons Votes on Reforming the House of Lords, February 2003,' *Political Quarterly* (2003), vol. 74, pp. 298–310. For more on the 2007 votes see Arthur Spirling and Iain McLean, *Dimensions of House of Lords Reform, March 2007: Roll Calls, Cycling and the 'Iowa School' Research Tradition in British Political Science* (Oxford: Nuffield College, 2007).

7. For the attack from the left, see for example almost any weekly column in the *Observer* by Henry Porter. For the attack from the right, see for example 'Time to liberate the country from human rights laws', Conservative Party news release, 18 March 2005. The prisoner was actually *refused* consent to import pornography.

8. In fact, the immigration tribunal ruled that EU law forbade it, before any question of Chindamo's rights under ECHR Article 8 became engaged. The government announced its intention to appeal against the ruling.

9. The list can be found at http://www.dca.gov.uk/peoples-rights/human-rights/pdf/decl-incompat-tabl.pdf.

10. The interaction between the HRA and the devolution statutes is particularly tangled. It seems that the courts can strike down acts of the Scottish Parliament and the National Assembly of Wales.

11. A.V. Dicey, *Introduction to the Study of the Law of the Constitution*, 8th edn (London: Macmillan, 1915), p. 141.

12. A search using the Westlaw engine discloses nine UK cases since 2000 that cite Dicey's *Introduction to the Study of the Law of the Constitution*, including the fundamental constitutional case *R. (Jackson and others)* v. *Attorney General* (2005) 3 WLR 733 ('A.V. Dicey, our greatest constitutional lawyer' [95]). This compares with three cases

citing (among other foundational works in jurisprudence) H. L. A. Hart's *The Concept of Law* (again including *Jackson*), two citations of Lon Fuller's *The Morality of Law* and none for Hans Kelsen's *Pure Theory of Law*.

13. 'Parliament means, in the mouth of a lawyer, . . . the King, the house of Lords, and the house of Commons.' (Dicey, *Introduction to the Study of the Law of the Constitution*, p. 37.)

14. A Condorcet system chooses the candidate, if any exists, who wins a majority against each of the others. A tie-break is needed because this Condorcet winner does not always exist.

15. Iain McLean and Alistair McMillan, 'Professor Dicey's Contradictions', *Public Law*, Autumn 2007.

16. Lord Cooper, in *MacCormick* v. *Lord Advocate* [1953] SC 396, at 411.

17. *The Governance of Britain* (Cm 7170, 2007), Box 1.

18. *Review of the Implementation of the Human Rights Act* (Department for Constitutional Affairs, 2006), pp. 29, 32.

19. *R.* v. *Secretary of State for Transport ex parte Factortame Ltd and others* (No. 2) [1991] 1 AC 603, per Lord Bridge at pp. 658–9.

20. See *A Bill of Rights for Britain?* (London: Justice, 2007).

21. *R. (Jackson and others)* v. *Attorney General* [2006] 1 AC 262.

Conclusion

1. See Brian Brivati, *The End of Decline: Blair and Brown in Power* (London: Politico's, 2007).

2. See Nick Pearce and Mike Dixon, 'New model welfare', *Prospect*, May 2005.

3. See for example Colin Brown, 'Patricia Hewitt: "The stakes are high"', *Independent*, 24 April 2006.

4. See Ben Lucas, 'The Context for Reform and Why Progressives Need a New Narrative on Public Services', in Patrick Diamond (ed.), *Public Matters: The Renewal of the Public Realm* (London: Politico's, 2007), p. 20.

5. One of the best expositions of this view is in Robin Marris, *The Economic Theory of 'Managerial' Capitalism* (London: Macmillan, 1964).

6. See for example John Plender, 'A stake of one's own', *Prospect*, February 1997.

7. Edmund Burke, *Reflections on the Revolution in France* (1790).

8. Nicholas Stern, *Stern Review on the Economics of Climate Change* (HM Treasury, 2006).

9. See for example Peter A. Hall and David Soskice (eds), *Varieties of Capitalism: The Institutional Foundations of Comparative Advantage* (Oxford: Oxford University Press, 2001); David Coates, *Models of Capitalism: Growth and Stagnation in the Modern Era* (Cambridge: Polity, 2000).

10. John Kenneth Galbraith, *The Affluent Society* (London: Hamish Hamilton, 1958).

11. See John H. Goldthorpe, David Lockwood, Frank Bechhofer and Jennifer Platt, *The Affluent Worker in the Class Structure* (Cambridge: Cambridge University Press, 1969).

12. See for example Fred Block, *Postindustrial Possibilities: A Critique of Economic Discourse* (Berkeley: University of California Press, 1990); Roger Liddle, *Social Pessimism: The New Social Reality of Europe* (London: Policy Network, 2008).

13. See for example Robert E. Lane, *The Market Experience* (Cambridge: Cambridge University Press, 1991); Avner Offer, *The Challenge of Affluence: Self-control and Well-being in the United States and Britain since 1950* (Oxford: Oxford University Press, 2007).

14. The best exposition of this is in Julian Le Grand, *The Other Invisible Hand: Delivering Public Services through Choice and Competition* (Princeton, NJ: Princeton University Press, 2007).

15. The persistence of long working hours, for instance. See Robert J. Gordon, 'Issues in the Comparison of Welfare between Europe and the United States', paper presented to the Bureau of European Policy Advisers, Brussels, 4 December 2007.

16. The classic exposition of this was made by James Keir Hardie. See Kenneth O. Morgan, *Keir Hardie: Radical and Socialist* (London: Phoenix, 1997).

17. Anthony Crosland, *The Future of Socialism*, 50th anniversary edn (London: Constable Robinson, 2006).

18. See Brian Abel-Smith and Peter Townsend, *The Poor and the Poorest* (London: G. Bell, 1965); Paul Dornan, 'The Welfare State at 60', *Poverty*, Summer 2008.

19. See Joan Smith, 'There is only one route out of poverty', *Independent*, 12 June 2008.

20. See Graeme Cooke and Kayte Lawton, *Working out of Poverty: A Study of the Low-paid and the 'Working Poor'* (London: Institute for Public Policy Research, 2008).

21. See for example Amartya Sen, *Resources, Values and Development* (Oxford: Blackwell, 1984); Amartya Sen, *The Standard of Living: The Tanner Lectures* (Cambridge: Cambridge University Press, 1987);

22. Amartya Sen, *Inequality Re-examined* (Oxford: Clarendon Press, 1992); Amartya Sen, *Development as Freedom* (Oxford: Oxford University Press, 1999).

23. See Robert D. Putnam (ed.), *Democracies in Flux: The Evolution of Social Capital in Contemporary Society* (Oxford: Oxford University Press, 2002).

24. See Vernon Bogdanor, 'Social Democracy', in Anthony Seldon (ed.), *Blair's Britain 1997–2007* (Cambridge: Cambridge University Press,

25. 2007).
    David Marquand, *Britain since 1918: The Strange Career of British Democracy* (London: Weidenfeld and Nicolson, 2008).

26. See Dermot Finch, 'Governance of Place: Shaping a New Localism', in Patrick Diamond (ed.), *Public Matters: The Renewal of the Public*

27. *Realm* (London: Politico's, 2007).
    David Miliband, speech to the National Council for Voluntary

28. Organisations annual conference, 21 February 2006.
    See Albert O. Hirschman, *Shifting Involvements: Private Interest and Public Action* (Princeton, NJ: Princeton University Press, 1982).
    See Shamit Saggar, *Pariah Politics: Understanding Western Radical Islam and What Should Be Done* (Oxford: Oxford University Press, 2008).

Index